ALABAMA
FOO
HU

Christopher Walsh

"I ain't never been nothing but a winner."
—PAUL W. "BEAR" BRYANT

TRIUMPH
BOOKS

Table of Contents

Introduction

When Nick Saban arrived on the Capstone—after making his way through the throng of fans waiting for him at the airport—and was announced as the University of Alabama's 27th head football coach, he didn't wait to send a clear and distinctive message to the program's players, fans, and boosters.

"Be a champion in everything that we do," he proclaimed. "Every choice, every decision, everything that we do every day, we want to be a champion."

It was a new beginning for Crimson Tide football, which had struggled for a decade or so, having endured a recruiting scandal that resulted in NCAA sanctions, numerous coaching changes, and a perception that the program's glory days were well behind it.

Alabama had won 12 "recognized" national championships, with the *Official NCAA Football Records Book* crediting it with five more. The 21 Southeastern Conference titles were far and away the most, and no program in the nation could rival their postseason appearances (now numbering 56).

Re-establishing that legacy was why school officials hardly even blinked at giving Saban, who hoped to become the first coach ever to win national championships at two different schools, an eight-year contact averaging $4 million plus additional incentives.

"We want to be a big, physical, aggressive football team that is relentless in the competitive spirit that we go out and play with week-in and week-out," Saban said. "What I would like is for every football team that we play to sit there and say, 'I hate playing against these guys. I hate playing them, their effort, their toughness, their relentless resiliency on every play, focus on the next play, and competing for 60 minutes. I can't handle it.'

So how long did it take for Alabama to establish that kind of mentality? Just over a year.

For the first game of the 2008 season, the Crimson Tide was considered an underdog in a neutral-site game against Clemson at Atlanta. The game wasn't close, with Alabama posting a crushing 34–10 victory.

"Alabama played with an attitude and viciousness that we did not," Clemson Coach Tommy Bowden admitted.

"I just saw a team that had a mentality," said Georgia Coach Mark Richt, who was at the game to support his son, a backup quarterback for the Tigers. "They were going to be physical, they were going to play physical, and they did. Clemson didn't have any answers on that day."

The Tide didn't make more big plays. It didn't throw all over the field. It was were anything but flashy. All Alabama did was attack and crush No. 9 Clemson nearly every way imaginable. A few weeks later, they were equally impressive at Georgia, which was No. 1 in the preseason Associated Press poll.

"I think it's the identity that we've always tried to create," Saban said. "Be aggressive, physical, play with a lot of toughness. Strike them, knock them back. Be aggressive and relentless in your style of how you play and how you compete.

Despite having just nine scholarship seniors on the roster, Alabama, which played 16 true freshmen in 2008, spent five weeks at No. 1, reached the SEC Championship Game, and was just a handful of minutes away from playing for the national title.

Now that's a message. ∎

SEASON PREVIEW

After the University of Alabama football team lost four games during the stretch run of the 2007 season, Nick Saban's first on the Capstone, the coach tried to motivate his players throughout the subsequent year with posters of the Louisiana-Monroe and Mississippi State losses serving as a daily reminder.

Everywhere the players looked—in the football building, on the walls, in the locker room, even in their lockers—there it was, impossible to ignore.

Apparently, it worked. The Crimson Tide had a successful 12-win season that exceeded everyone's expectations by not only including an SEC Championship Game appearance but five weeks at No. 1.

Yet after the Crimson Tide fell short at the Sugar Bowl, a 31–17 loss to Utah, one has to wonder if the printer was again busy cranking out copies of the Utes' logo.

"It's big motivation because we want to get back here," junior linebacker Cory Reamer said. "We don't want this to be our only chance at a BCS or national championship."

Although the finish was disappointing, with Alabama losing twice after a perfect 12-0 regular season, and being just minutes away from playing for the national championship, a lot was still accomplished.

ALABAMA FOOTBALL

Alabama had five players named an All-American by at least one organization—Andre Smith, Antoine Caldwell, Terrence Cody, Rashad Johnson, and Mike Johnson—which was more than twice as many as the Crimson Tide totaled the rest of the decade.

The coaching staff scored a recruiting class that many thought was the nation's best in 2008 and then went out and did it again.

"I think we changed the attitude, the mentality of the team, that we can go out there and play with anybody," quarterback John Parker Wilson said. "You know, it was a lot different my freshman and sophomore year than it is now."

However, it begs the age-old question in football of which is harder, getting to the top or staying there? Alabama is about to find out.

"We need to continue to improve as a program for the future," Saban said. "We need more good players, more depth in the program. We need quality big people. We need quality skill guys. We need a lot of things for us to continue to improve to be the kind of program that is recognized as kind of a dominant program on a national level."

Considering the Tide had only nine scholarship seniors and saw 16 true freshmen play this past season, the program appears to be in a good position numbers-wise. Nine defensive starters are expected to return along with many of the offensive playmakers, and with those strong recruiting classes Alabama is expected to have something it's been lacking for years: depth.

Which only makes the 2008 accomplishments that much more impressive.

"They've gone out and smash-mouth kicked fanny on everybody they've played, basically," Kentucky Coach Rich Brooks said just before his Wildcats lost to the Tide. "They've not only beaten people, but destroyed them." ∎

Offense

Offense

Though the University of Alabama football team will need to replace three starting offensive linemen, including Outland Trophy winner Andre Smith who left a year early for the NFL, and running back Glen Coffee, the biggest offensive concern is at a completely different position.

It's at quarterback, where John Parker Wilson had started every game for three seasons en route to breaking nearly every school career-passing record.

Fortunately, after a couple of years serving as Wilson's understudy, junior Greg McElroy may know the offense better than anyone. Also on the depth chart are duel-threat quarterback Star Jackson, a redshirt freshman, and incoming recruit A.J. McCarron.

"Each one of them, we've got to find out what they do best and then how it's going to fit with the rest of our offense," offensive coordinator Jim McElwain said. "We're going to do what it takes to win, and so if that means we adapt our offense differently to take advantage of our personnel, we'll do it. I've got nothing against the spread nor am I solely an old-school type of guy, but we're going to look at what we have and make the decision based on the players. We're not just replacing a quarterback; we're replacing some great offensive linemen. So this spring we'll have a lot of things to see."

On the line, the 2008 standout signing trio of Barrett Jones, John Michael Boswell, and Tyler Love will be in the mix, along with early signee James Carpenter, a junior college product.

For any starting job not nailed down entering fall camp, expect other members of the Class of 2009 to get a chance to immediately step in when they arrive, especially massive D.J. Fluker, who stands at 6-foot-7, 340 pounds and could be the left tackle of the future. Overall though, the goal will be to have established starters and backups at all five spots to avoid situations like the Sugar Bowl—where Alabama was without left tackle Smith and left guard Mike Johnson and wound up yielding eight sacks—from happening again.

As for the skill positions, Alabama appears to have some depth at tight end, wide receiver, and running back, but can always use more.

At tight end Colin Peek will finally be able to suit up after having to sit out a season due to his transfer from Georgia Tech. Brad Smelley, brother of former South Carolina quarterback Chris Smelley, who has returned to his hometown Tuscaloosa to concentrate on baseball, emerged as a legitimate receiving threat as a true freshman.

The goal at wide receiver will be to find a viable and consistent threat opposite Julio Jones, who as a true freshman posted the fourth-best single season in Crimson Tide receiving history with 924 yards. Among those who might challenge for playing time are incoming freshmen Kenny Bell, Michael Bowman, Kendall Kelly, and Kevin Norwood.

Depending on how things play out during camps, the Tide may not have a primary running back like Coffee was in 2008, when his 1,383 rushing yards tied Shaun Alexander (1999) for the second-best season in program history. Sophomore Mark Ingram figures to be better prepared for the rigorous collegiate season and Roy Upchurch is coming back from neck surgery. The real name to watch may be Trent Richardson, who was easily one of the nation's top recruits.

Two things working in favor of the incoming freshmen are that Nick Saban isn't afraid to play rookies, and the offense isn't as complicated as some systems. Last year the Tide thrived on long, sustained, backbreaking drives and ran only a couple of trick plays. ∎

Defense

Defense

Heading into the 2008 season, the biggest question the Crimson Tide had was at linebacker, where Alabama was tabbed to start the season with only one starter out of the four positions, and he was a sophomore.

Meanwhile, there was a glaring need for a big-time pass-rusher, defensive tackle was a question mark, and the starting secondary consisted of a former walk-on running back, a former star baseball pitcher, an athlete who otherwise probably would be at Florida Atlantic, and a cornerback who first needed some time at a military prep school.

Somehow, everything either worked out, or the Tide found an answer, except for the pass rusher.

At linebacker the returning starter, Rolando McClain, led the team in tackles. The emergence of Dont'a Hightower allowed coaches to slide Cory Reamer into another spot he was better suited for. Safety Rashad Johnson became an All-American, and punt-returner Javier Arenas developed into Alabama's best cornerback.

The key, though, to making it almost impossible to run on the Tide was junior college transfer Terrence Cody, nicknamed "Mt. Cody," at nose guard. Unveiling him at Clemson, the Tigers tallied zero yards on the ground, and after Georgia managed only 50 yards, just about every opponent started considering other options.

With Cody back for his senior season, in hopes of becoming a potential top NFL Draft pick, the strength of the unit figures to be again up the middle.

The Tide will need to replace only two starters, with junior Lorenzo Washington a natural replacement for Bobby Greenwood at end. That makes the chief defensive concern for 2009 the departure of unit leader Johnson.

"Rashad, in particular, probably has more pressure than anyone on the defense, every single play, to make a decision, to make a call, get people right, get people in the right places," defensive coordinator Kirby Smart said. "We're not going to be able to replace that. We're just going to have to do the best we can with what we have and keep trying to get better."

While the other starters in the secondary will all have another year's experience, junior Ali Sharrief had the most playing time among the reserves and at numerous positions. Considering his size and ability to hit, look for coaches to find more playing time for true freshman Mark Barron.

Cornerback is another spot to closely watch even though Arenas, Kareem Jackson, and Marquis Johnson should all be back. True freshman Robby Green was in place to immediately step in had the Tide sustained an injury, and Smart singled out Robert Lester as someone who has greatly improved. Freshman Chris Jackson has already made the switch from wide receiver and was followed by B.J. Scott.

It may be only a matter of time before incoming true freshman Dre Kirkpatrick wins a starting job at cornerback, and hard-hitting Rod Woodson could be a safety of the future.

Meanwhile, Alabama will look for new options for pass rushing, possibly moving Hightower into an outside linebacker spot.

"We didn't get any pressure early in the game," Saban said after the Sugar Bowl, signaling the obvious priority. ∎

Player to Watch: Julio Jones

You know a player is good when, after only his freshman year, fans argue about which of his moments is their favorite.

For some it's the over-the-shoulder touchdown catch against Georgia. Former Tennessee Coach Phillip Fulmer made it clear he thought Jones' key catch in Knoxville was the turning point of that game. Maybe it's at LSU, Wilson only looking to Jones in overtime, when his catch and drag-the-defender play to the 1-yard line set up the winning score. Or maybe it's his outstanding play in the SEC Championship Game, where Jones probably would have been the game MVP had Alabama won.

"It speaks for itself," junior cornerback Javier Arenas said of Jones' performance against Florida. "Exciting to watch. He's a physical receiver. I love going against him in practice. You all see it, watch it. He's great."

By finishing with 124 receiving yards on five catches, Jones recorded his third of four 100-yard performances of the season and joined junior running back Glen Coffee to become just the third teammates in SEC Championship Game history to have simultaneous 100-yard rushing and receiving games (joining Alabama's Derrick Lassic and David Palmer, 1992).

Overall, Jones' 924 receiving yards was the fourth-best season in Tide history.

"He's probably going to be the best ever at Alabama at wide receiver," left tackle Andre Smith said.

Two plays by Jones stood out in particular in Atlanta.

Some fans say this was the definitive Julio Jones catch. Georgia's Bryan Evans had good coverage, but Jones was able to get just enough separation to make this over-the-shoulder grab in the end zone for six.

After No. 2 Florida (12–1, 8–1) scored a touchdown on its opening possession, Jones' 64-yard reception—when sophomore cornerback Joe Haden missed a tackle and the receiver faked his way by another defensive back—swung the momentum Alabama's way. Coffee scored on the following play to tie the game.

Not only was it Alabama's longest offensive play of the game but longest of the season.

"It was a routine catch," Jones said. "I do it all the time in practice."

His other key reception came on an outstanding adjustment to reach up and snare the ball for an 18-yard sideline reception and prevented UA from having to punt from its own end zone. Instead, the offense went 91 yards on 15 plays to tie the game at 17.

Incidentally, all of his receptions came on scoring drives.

"I think I did okay," Jones said. "I can get better."

A number of other freshmen made key contributions in 2008 as well.

Running back Mark Ingram scored 12 touchdowns to set a UA freshman record and the eighth most in program history. Although his production decreased during the stretch run, which can be common for players enduring their first collegiate season, Ingram still finished among the conference rushing leaders with 728 yards on 143 carries.

"We just came in with the attitude that we were going to turn the program around," Ingram said. "A lot of us played major roles. A lot of us played minor roles."

Linebacker Dont'a Hightower finished with 64 tackles to finish among the team leaders.

"It was one of the greatest years I've had since I started playing football," he said. "The time with the guys I played with, Terrence Cody, Antoine Caldwell, Andre Smith, it's been great. I learned a lot from Coach (Kevin) Steele and Coach (Nick) Saban.

"Hopefully we can take it to the next level." ■

Florida's defense had no answer for Jones in the SEC Championship. Had the Crimson Tide been able to pull out the win, Jones would certainly have been named the MVP of the game.

Julio Jones was not the only stellar freshman in 2008. Players like running back Mark Ingram made a difference in the Crimson Tide's season, and the question for the incoming freshmen is: who will be there to make an impact in 2009?

2009 National Signing Day Class

Jonathan Atchison	LB	6-2	220	Atlanta, GA/Douglass HS
Kenny Bell	WR	6-1	170	Rayville, AL/Rayville HS
Chris Bonds	DL	6-4	280	Columbia, SC/Richland Northeast HS
Michael Bowman	WR	6-4	210	Rossville, GA/Ridgeland HS
James Carpenter	OL	6-5	305	Augusta, GA/Coffeyville (Kan.) CC /Hephzibah HS
Quinton Dial	DL	6-5	310	Pinson, AL/Clay-Chalkville HS
D.L. Fluker	OL	6-8	340	Foley, AL/Foley HS
Nico Johnson	LB	6-3	225	Andalusia, AL/Andalusia HS
Kendall Kelly	WR	6-3	215	Gadsden, AL/Gadsden City HS
Dre Kirkpatrick	DB	6-3	185	Gadsden, AL/Gadsden City HS
Eddie Lacy	RB	5-11	210	Geismar, LA/Dutchtown HS
Mike Marrow	FB	6-2	240	Holland, OH/Central Catholic HS
A.J. McCarron	QB	6-4	190	Mobile, AL/Saint Paul's Episcopal School
Darius McKeller	OL,	6-5	280	Jonesboro, GA/Jonesboro HS
William Ming	DL,	6-3	260	Athens, AL/Athens HS
Brandon Moore	DL	6-5	320	Montgomery, AL/Carver HS
Kerry Murphy	DL	6-5	315	Hoover, AL/Hoover HS
Kevin Norwood	WR	6-2	180	D'Iberville, MS/D'Iberville HS
Anthony Orr	DL	6-5	260	Madison, AL/Sparkman HS
Tana Patrick	LB	6-3	215	Stevenson, AL/North Jackson HS
Trent Richardson	RB	5-11	220	Pensacola, FL/Escambia HS
Darrington Sentimore	DL	6-3	280	Norco, LA/Destrahan HS
Petey Smith	LB	6-1	245	Tampa, FL/Armwood HS
Anthony Steen	OL/DL	6-3	305	Lambert, MS/Lee Academy
Ed Stinson	DL/LB	6-4	240	Homestead, FL/South Dade HS
Chance Warmack	OL	6-3	325	Atlanta, GA/Westlake HS
Kellen Williams	OL	6-3	290	Lawrenceville, GA/Brookwood HS
Rod Woodson	DB	5-11	200	Olive Branch, MS/Olive Branch HS

The University of Alabama

Location: Tuscaloosa, Alabama

Founded: 1831

Enrollment: 27,052

Nickname: Crimson Tide

Colors: Crimson and White

Mascot: Big Al (The Elephant)

Stadium: Bryant-Denny Stadium (92,138, but being expanded to bring capacity near 101,000)

Website: www.rolltide.com

Ticket Office: (205) 348-BAMA (2262), 1-877-TIDETIX or ticketoffice@ia.ua.edu.

National Championships (12): 1925, 1926, 1930, 1934, 1941, 1961, 1964, 1965, 1973, 1978, 1979, 1992

The "Other" Five: *The Official NCAA Football Records Book* also recognizes Alabama as producing national champions in 1945, 1962, 1966, 1975, and 1977

SEC Championships (21): 1933, 1934, 1937, 1945, 1953, 1961, 1964, 1965, 1966, 1971, 1972, 1973, 1974, 1975, 1977, 1978, 1979, 1981, 1989, 1992, 1999

Bowl appearances: 56 (31–22–3)

First season: 1892

2008
SEASON
REVIEW

Clemson's Aaron Kelly (80) is corralled by Brandon Fanney, back, Rolando McClain (25), and Rashad Johnson (bottom) in the their game at the Georgia Dome in Atlanta on August 30, 2008.

Game 1: No. 24 Alabama 34,
No. 9 Clemson 10

ATLANTA | Although Clemson was considered by many to be the team to beat in the Atlantic Coast Conference, Alabama dominated from the start and outgained the Tigers 239 rushing yards to zero, the worst Tigers showing since having minus-1 yard against Boston College in 1947.

Clemson's impressive "Thunder and Lightning" backfield of James Davis and C.J. Spiller combined for just 20 rushing yards in the neutral-site game.

"We were whipped pretty bad," said Coach Tommy Bowden, who did not survive the season and was replaced by former Alabama player and assistant coach Dabo Swinney.

Senior quarterback John Parker Wilson completed 22 of 30 passes for 180 yards and surpassed Brodie Croyle's school career completions record of 488 with 500.

"I think we got something special here," Wilson said.

	1st Qtr	2nd Qtr	3rd Qtr	4th Qtr	Final
ALABAMA (24)	13	10	8	3	34
CLEMSON (9)	0	3	7	0	10

SCORING PLAYS

ALABAMA–FG, L Tiffin 54 YD 5:17 1st Qtr

ALABAMA–FG, L Tiffin 21 YD 7:59 1st Qtr

ALABAMA–TD, J Parker Wilson 1 YD RUN (L Tiffin KICK) 12:09 1st Qtr

CLEMSON–FG, M Buchholz 33 YD 0:43 2nd Qtr

ALABAMA–TD, N Walker 4 YD PASS FROM J Parker Wilson (L Tiffin KICK) 8:59 2nd Qtr

ALABAMA–FG, L Tiffin 34 YD 15:00 2nd Qtr

CLEMSON–TD, C Spiller 96 YD KICKOFF RETURN (M Buchholz KICK) 0:12 3rd Qtr

ALABAMA–TD, J Jones 4 YD PASS FROM J Parker Wilson (M Ingram RUN FOR TWO-POINT CONVERSION) 10:52 3rd Qtr

ALABAMA–FG, L Tiffin 26 YD 11:21 4th Qtr

GAME STATISTICS

	ALABAMA (24)	CLEMSON (9)
First Downs	25	11
Yards Rushing	50–239	14–0
Yards Passing	180	188
Sacks-Yards Lost	0–0	3–28
Passing Efficiency	22–30–0	20–34–1
Punts	2–36.5	4–40
Fumbles-Lost	0–0	1–1
Penalties-Yards	6–40	6–43
Time of Possession	41:13	18:47

INDIVIDUAL STATISTICS – RUSHING
ALABAMA–Mark Ingram 17–96, Glen Coffee 17–90, Roy Upchurch 8–37, John Parker Wilson 4–19, Terry Grant 4–MINUS 3. CLEMSON–James Davis 6–13, C.J. Spiller 2–7, Jacoby Ford 1–5, Tyler Grisham 1–3, Cullen Harper 1–0, Jamie Harper 3–MINUS 28.

INDIVIDUAL STATISTICS – PASSING
ALABAMA–John Parker Wilson 22–30–180–0. CLEMSON–Cullen Harper 20–34–188–1.

INDIVIDUAL STATISTICS – RECEIVING
ALABAMA–Nick Walker 7–67, Mike McCoy 2–33, Roy Upchurch 4–30, Julio Jones 4–28, Glen Coffee 1–9, Travis McCall 1–8, Mark Ingram 2–5, B.J. Scott 1–0. CLEMSON–Jacoby Ford 2–53, Tyler Grisham 6–42, Aaron Kelly 5–28, C.J. Spiller 2–27, Terrance Ashe 3–18, James Davis 1–11, Durrell Barry 1–9.

ATTENDANCE: 70,097

Game 2: No. 13 Alabama 20, Tulane 6

TUSCALOOSA | Javier Arenas set a school record with 212 return yards, and his 87-yard punt return for a touchdown sparked the win for flat Alabama, which was missing injured offensive linemen Andre Smith and Marlon Davis.

The Crimson Tide scored one offensive touchdown, totaled just 172 yards, allowed four sacks, and missed two field goals. Its other touchdown came on Roy Upchurch's punt block that Chris Rogers returned for a touchdown.

"It's a little disappointing," said Coach Nick Saban, who notched career win No. 100 at the collegiate level. "It's our goal to play with consistency, but we were unable to do that. We did not make progress as a team."

Tulane spent the previous week in Birmingham and trained at Samford Stadium after evacuating the New Orleans campus due to Hurricane Gustov. The team headed home wondering if it would soon be on the road again with Hurricane Ike looming.

2008 Review

	1st Qtr	2nd Qtr	3rd Qtr	4th Qtr	Final
TULANE	0	3	0	3	**6**
ALABAMA (13)	13	0	7	0	**20**

SCORING PLAYS

ALABAMA–TD, J Arenas 87 YD PUNT RETURN (L Tiffin KICK) 4:15 1st Qtr

ALABAMA–TD, C Rogers 17 YD BLOCKED PUNT RETURN (PAT FAILED) 11:45 1st Qtr

TULANE–FG, R Thevenot 35 YD 1:53 2nd Qtr

ALABAMA–TD, M Ingram 15 YD RUN (C Smith KICK) 15:00 3rd Qtr

TULANE–FG, R Thevenot 21 YD 3:13 4th Qtr

GAME STATISTICS

	TULANE	ALABAMA (13)
First Downs	18	11
Yards Rushing	32–86	26–99
Yards Passing	232	73
Sacks-Yards Lost	1–8	4–29
Passing Efficiency	29–50–0	11–23–0
Punts	7–32.3	7–40
Fumbles-Lost	2–0	1–1
Penalties-Yards	4–29	6–43
Time of Possession	36:35	23:25

INDIVIDUAL STATISTICS – RUSHING
TULANE–Andre Anderson 13–32, Nathan Austin 5–24, Albert Williams 5–18, Jeremy Williams 4–11, Kevin Moore 4–1, Cody Blackwelder 1–0. ALABAMA–Mark Ingram 11–63, Glen Coffee 9–55, Team 1–MINUS 1, John Parker Wilson 5–MINUS 18.

INDIVIDUAL STATISTICS – PASSING
TULANE–Kevin Moore 28–49–225–0, Joe Kemp 1–1–7–0. ALABAMA–John Parker Wilson 11–23–73–0.

INDIVIDUAL STATISTICS – RECEIVING
TULANE–Brian King 6–51, Chris Dunn 1–45, Justin Kessler 1–26, Jeremy Williams 4–26, Andre Anderson 4–26, Cody Blackwelder 3–22, Michael Batiste 3–17, Cody Sparks 2–14, Troy Wainwright 1–7, Casey Robottom 1–3, Nathan Austin 3–MINUS 5. ALABAMA–Marquis Maze 4–22, Nick Walker 1–15, Julio Jones 1–13, Terry Grant 1–9, Roy Upchurch 1–7, Mark Ingram 1–7, Travis McCall 1–3, Glen Coffee 1–MINUS 3.

ATTENDANCE: 92,138

Game 3: No. 11 Alabama 41, Western Kentucky 7

TUSCALOOSA | Quarterback John Parker Wilson threw for 215 yards and two touchdowns, becoming the school's all-time leader in total offense with 6,321 yards and tying Brodie Croyle for most career passing touchdowns (41).

Freshman running back Mark Ingram also ran in two scores as the Crimson Tide tallied 557 total yards, its highest total since 644 against LSU in 1989.

"This just gets the kinks out," said junior running back Glen Coffee, who had a career-long 51-yard gain and finished with 97 yards on 11 carries before sitting out the second half.

Western Kentucky had just 42 rushing yards. With massive defensive tackle Terrence Cody clogging up the middle, Alabama gave up just 128 rushing yards in its first three games.

	1st Qtr	2nd Qtr	3rd Qtr	4th Qtr	Final
WKU	0	7	0	0	**7**
ALABAMA (11)	17	14	10	0	**41**

SCORING PLAYS

ALABAMA–TD, M Ingram 7 YD RUN (L Tiffin KICK) 6:18 1st Qtr

ALABAMA–FG, L Tiffin 22 YD 8:30 1st Qtr

ALABAMA–TD, M Ingram 5 YD RUN (L Tiffin KICK) 14:11 1st Qtr

ALABAMA–TD, T Grant 8 YD RUN (L Tiffin KICK) 5:09 2nd Qtr

WKU–TD, T Jones 30 YD PASS FROM D Wolke (T Siewert KICK) 10:39 2nd Qtr

ALABAMA–TD, N Walker 2 YD PASS FROM J Parker Wilson (L Tiffin KICK) 13:03 2nd Qtr

ALABAMA–FG, L Tiffin 25 YD 5:03 3rd Qtr

ALABAMA–TD, J Jones 13 YD PASS FROM J Parker Wilson (L Tiffin KICK) 10:03 3rd Qtr

GAME STATISTICS

	WKU	ALABAMA (11)
First Downs	9	30
Yards Rushing	22–42	49–281
Yards Passing	116	276
Sacks-Yards Lost	1–12	0–0
Passing Efficiency	14–26–1	21–33–1
Punts	7–36.4	0–0
Fumbles-Lost	2–1	1–1
Penalties-Yards	5–27	3–25
Time of Possession	22:39	37:21

INDIVIDUAL STATISTICS – RUSHING
WKU–Bobby Rainey 4–11, David Wolke 7–10, Tyrell Hayden 5–9, Derrius Brooks 1–7, Dexter Taylor 1–5, Marell Booker 4–0. ALABAMA–Glen Coffee 11–97, Roy Upchurch 11–53, Mark Ingram 9–51, Terry Grant 8–39, Demetrius Goode 7–21, John Parker Wilson 3–20.

INDIVIDUAL STATISTICS – PASSING
WKU–David Wolke 14–25–116–1, Brandon Smith 0–1–0–0. ALABAMA–John Parker Wilson 17–27–215–1, Greg McElroy 4–6–61–0.

INDIVIDUAL STATISTICS – RECEIVING
WKU–Derrius Brooks 6–40, Tristan Jones 1–30, Wenquel Graves 4–29, Jessie Quinn 1–11, Brad Savko 1–9, Tyrell Hayden 1–MINUS 3. ALABAMA–Julio Jones 5–66, Earl Alexander 3–50, Mike McCoy 3–42, Marquis Maze 2–25, Terry Grant 1–22, Nikita Stover 1–18, Darius Hanks 1–18, Nick Walker 3–14, Will Oakley 1–13, Preston Dial 1–8.

ATTENDANCE: 92,138

Game 4: No. 9 Alabama 49, Arkansas 14

FAYETTEVILLE | Junior running back Glen Coffee's 87-yard touchdown run started the rout, with defensive backs Javier Arenas and Justin Woodall both scoring touchdowns on long interception returns as Alabama crushed Arkansas in Bobby Petrino's SEC debut.

Coffee finished with 163 rushing yards, and senior quarterback John Parker Wilson set a school record with his 42nd career touchdown pass.

It was Alabama's most lopsided victory against Arkansas since 1993 and Petrino's most lopsided loss as a college coach.

"All week Coach was talking about coming out firing and hitting them in the mouth quick," Arenas said. "I think we did that. It seemed like they knew we were here to play a little football from the get-go."

	1st Qtr	2nd Qtr	3rd Qtr	4th Qtr	Final
ALABAMA (9)	21	14	7	7	**49**
ARKANSAS	0	7	0	7	**14**

SCORING PLAYS

ALABAMA–TD, M Ingram 1 YD RUN (L Tiffin KICK) 4:20 1st Qtr

ALABAMA–TD, G Coffee 87 YD RUN (L Tiffin KICK) 8:08 1st Qtr

ALABAMA–TD, J Arenas 63 YD INTERCEPTION RETURN (L Tiffin KICK) 14:07 1st Qtr

ARKANSAS–TD, A Davie 12 YD PASS FROM C Dick (A Tejada KICK) 4:30 2nd Qtr

ALABAMA–TD, J Jones 25 YD PASS FROM J Parker Wilson (L Tiffin KICK) 6:29 2nd Qtr

ALABAMA–TD, J Woodall 74 YD INTERCEPTION RE-

TURN (L Tiffin KICK) 8:45 2nd Qtr

ALABAMA–TD, G Coffee 31 YD RUN (L Tiffin KICK) 0:55 3rd Qtr

ARKANSAS–TD, M Smith 10 YD PASS FROM T Wilson (A Tejada KICK) 4:01 4th Qtr

ALABAMA–TD, R Upchurch 62 YD RUN (L Tiffin KICK) 4:24 4th Qtr

GAME STATISTICS

	ALABAMA (9)	ARKANSAS
First Downs	15	19
Yards Rushing	35–328	31–92
Yards Passing	74	217
Sacks–Yards Lost	1–12	2–15
Passing Efficiency	6–15–1	24–46–4
Punts	5–45.2	7–43.4
Fumbles–Lost	2–0	2–0
Penalties–Yards	1–10	5–30
Time of Possession	25:14	34:46

INDIVIDUAL STATISTICS – RUSHING
ALABAMA–Glen Coffee 10–162, Roy Upchurch 7–91, Mark Ingram 6–53, Terry Grant 10–32, John Parker Wilson 2–MINUS 10. ARKANSAS–Michael Smith 19–91, De'Anthony Curtis 3–10, Casey Dick 4–5, Dennis Johnson 1–1, Brandon Barnett 2–0, Tyler Wilson 2–MINUS 15.

INDIVIDUAL STATISTICS – PASSING
ALABAMA–John Parker Wilson 6–14–74–0, Greg McElroy 0–1–0–1. ARKANSAS–Casey Dick 20–39–190–3. Tyler Wilson 4–7–27– 1.

INDIVIDUAL STATISTICS – RECEIVING
ALABAMA–Earl Alexander 2–38, Julio Jones 1–25, Nick Walker 1–6, Terry Grant 2–5. ARKANSAS–Michael Smith 6–67, D.J. Williams 5–48, Jarius Wright 2–26, Lucas Miller 2–20, London Crawford 2–15, An-

drew Davie 1–12, Greg Childs 2–11, Joe Adams 1–7, De'Anthony Curtis 2–6, Dennis Johnson 1–5.

ATTENDANCE: 72,315

Game 5: No. 8 Alabama 41, No. 3 Georgia 30

ATHENS | Alabama scored on its first five possessions to ruin the blackout celebration at Georgia, which had been No. 1 in the preseason Associated Press poll.

"That was nice," said junior quarterback John Parker Wilson, who completed 13 of 16 passes for 205 yards and a touchdown. "That is what you practice for, that is what you strive to do on every drive."

The high-profile game was essentially a coming out party for freshman wide receiver Julio Jones, who caught five passes for 94 yards, including an impressive over-the-shoulder 22-yard touchdown with 1:25 remaining in the first half for a 31–0 lead.

However, even though Alabama held Knowshon Moreno to just 34 yards on nine carries, Coach Nick Saban wasn't pleased about the team's second-half performance and bristled when asked if the Crimson Tide was a nation championship contender.

"I'm happy," he said without smiling. "I know I don't look happy, but I am."

	1st Qtr	2nd Qtr	3rd Qtr	4th Qtr	Final
ALABAMA (8)	10	21	0	10	**41**
GEORGIA (3)	0	0	10	20	**30**

SCORING PLAYS

ALABAMA–TD, M Ingram 7 YD RUN (L Tiffin KICK) 6:28 1st Qtr

ALABAMA–FG, L Tiffin 23 YD 14:11 1st Qtr

ALABAMA–TD, G Coffee 3 YD RUN (L Tiffin KICK) 3:02 2nd Qtr

ALABAMA–TD, R Upchurch 4 YD RUN (L Tiffin KICK)
8:13 2nd Qtr

ALABAMA–TD, J Jones 22 YD PASS FROM J Parker
Wilson (L Tiffin KICK) 13:35 2nd Qtr

GEORGIA–FG, B Walsh 43 YD 3:53 3rd Qtr

GEORGIA–TD, K Moreno 2 YD RUN (B Walsh KICK)
13:44 3rd Qtr

GEORGIA–TD, P Miller 92 YD PUNT RETURN (B Walsh
KICK) 0:19 4th Qtr

ALABAMA–FG, L Tiffin 32 YD 5:15 4th Qtr

ALABAMA–TD, G Coffee 12 YD RUN (L Tiffin KICK)
10:47 4th Qtr

GEORGIA–TD, M Moore 24 YD PASS FROM M Stafford
12:00 4th Qtr

GEORGIA–TD, A Green 21 YD PASS FROM M Stafford (B
Walsh KICK) 13:25 4th Qtr

GAME STATISTICS

	ALABAMA (8)	GEORGIA (3)
First Downs	21	18
Yards Rushing	45–129	16–50
Yards Passing	205	274
Sacks-Yards Lost	1–5	2–18
Passing Efficiency	13–16–0	24–43–1
Punts	3–34	4–30.3
Fumbles-Lost	2–1	1–1
Penalties-Yards	2–9	10–81
Time of Possession	35:46	24:14

INDIVIDUAL STATISTICS – RUSHING

ALABAMA–Glen Coffee 23–86, Roy Upchurch 6–18,
Mark Ingram 7–17, John Parker Wilson 5–13, Team 4–
MINUS 5. GEORGIA–Knowshon Moreno 9–34, Matthew
Stafford 6–11, Caleb King 1–5.

INDIVIDUAL STATISTICS – PASSING

ALABAMA–John Parker Wilson 13–16–205–0. GEOR-
GIA–Matthew Stafford 24–42–274–1, Mohamed Massaquoi 0–1–0–0.

INDIVIDUAL STATISTICS – RECEIVING
ALABAMA–Julio Jones 5–94, Roy Upchurch 2–51, Mike
McCoy 2–22, Nikita Stover 1–14, Nick Walker 1–11, BJ
Scott 1–7, Glen Coffee 1–6. GEORGIA–A.J. Green 6–88,
Michael Moore 5–65, Kris Durham 2–44, Mohamed
Massaquoi 4–33, Kenneth Harris 2–28, Knowshon
Moreno 3–14, Caleb King 2–2.

ATTENDANCE: 92,746

Game 6: No. 2 Alabama 17, Kentucky 14

TUSCALOOSA | Junior Glen Coffee had a career-best
218 rushing yards, including a 78-yard touchdown run,
for the most rushing yards by an Alabama running
back since Shaun Alexander ran for a school-record 291
in 1996.

The Crimson Tide jumped out to an early 14–0
lead, but Leigh Tiffin's 24-yard field goal gave Alabama
a 17–7 lead with 2:12 remaining.

"We're certainly happy to win, but we also put on
a clinic today for how to keep the other team in the
game," Saban said.

Coming in, Kentucky was allowing just 73 rushing yards per game. Instead, the Tide outgained the
Wildcats on the ground, 282–35.

Kentucky has never beaten the Tide in the state of
Alabama (0–20–1), with just one overall victory in the
last 35 meetings.

	1st Qtr	2nd Qtr	3rd Qtr	4th Qtr	Final
KENTUCKY	0	0	7	7	**14**
ALABAMA (2)	14	0	0	3	**17**

SCORING PLAYS

ALABAMA–TD, G Coffee 78 YD RUN (L Tiffin KICK) 5:12 1st Qtr

ALABAMA–TD, R McClain 4 YD FUMBLE RETURN (L Tiffin KICK) 13:58 1st Qtr

KENTUCKY–TD, D Lyons Jr. 26 YD PASS FROM M Hartline (L Seiber KICK) 9:11 3rd Qtr

ALABAMA–FG, L Tiffin 24 YD 12:48 4th Qtr

KENTUCKY–TD, D Ford 48 YD PASS FROM M Hartline (L Seiber KICK) 14:20 4th Qtr

GAME STATISTICS

	KENTUCKY	ALABAMA (2)
First Downs	12	15
Yards Rushing	20–35	49–282
Yards Passing	241	106
Sacks-Yards Lost	1–6	3–20
Passing Efficiency	20–42–1	7–17–1
Punts	10–43.2	6–43.2
Fumbles-Lost	1–1	3–2
Penalties-Yards	9–58	10–92
Time of Possession	24:15	35:45

INDIVIDUAL STATISTICS – RUSHING

KENTUCKY–Derrick Locke 6–28, Alfonso Smith 7–18, Tony Dixon 3–10, Moncell Allen 1–MINUS 2, Mike Hartline 3–MINUS 19. ALABAMA–Glen Coffee 25–218, Mark Ingram 11–66, Roy Upchurch 5–19, Marquis Maze 1–1, – Team 1–MINUS 2, John Parker Wilson 6–MINUS 20.

INDIVIDUAL STATISTICS – PASSING
KENTUCKY–Mike Hartline 20-42-241-1. ALABAMA–
John Parker Wilson 7-17-106-1.

INDIVIDUAL STATISTICS – RECEIVING
KENTUCKY–Derrick Locke 8-81, Dicky Lyons Jr. 6-63,
DeMoreo Ford 1-48, Maurice Grinter 3-29, E.J. Adams
2-20. ALABAMA–Julio Jones 3-52, Nick Walker 2-30,
Glen Coffee 1-15, Nikita Stover 1-9.

ATTENDANCE: 92,138

2008 Review

Game 7: No. 2 Alabama 24, Ole Miss 20

TUSCALOOSA | After trailing for the first time all sea-
son, Alabama scored 24 unanswered points and then
managed to hold on despite being outgained 359-326
for the game.

"That hadn't happened to us yet this year," said
senior quarterback John Parker Wilson, who passed for
a season-high 219 yards and two touchdowns. "It was
good to see us respond."

The comeback attempt didn't end until Jevan
Snead's pass to Dexter McCluster on fourth-and-5 fell
incomplete with just more than a minute remaining.
Although it dropped the Rebels to 3-4, it was their last
loss of the season.

Junior nose guard Terrence Cody sustained a scary
right knee injury in the third quarter, but it did not
require surgery.

	1st Qtr	2nd Qtr	3rd Qtr	4th Qtr	Final
OLE MISS	3	0	7	10	**20**
ALABAMA (2)	7	17	0	0	**24**

SCORING PLAYS
OLE MISS–FG, J Shene 25 YD 9:35 1st Qtr

ALABAMA–TD, M Maze 26 YD PASS FROM J Parker Wilson (L Tiffin KICK) 10:50 1st Qtr

ALABAMA–TD, M Ingram 2 YD RUN (L Tiffin KICK) 8:26 2nd Qtr

ALABAMA–FG, L Tiffin 41 YD 10:15 2nd Qtr

ALABAMA–TD, M McCoy 30 YD PASS FROM J Parker Wilson (L Tiffin KICK) 12:09 2nd Qtr

OLE MISS–TD, J Cook 9 YD PASS FROM R Park (J Shene KICK) 4:23 3rd Qtr

OLE MISS–TD, S Hodge 17 YD PASS FROM J Snead (J Shene KICK) 5:33 4th Qtr

OLE MISS–FG, J Shene 35 YD 8:51 4th Qtr

GAME STATISTICS

	OLE MISS	ALABAMA (2)
First Downs	14	15
Yards Rushing	34–158	34–107
Yards Passing	201	219
Sacks-Yards Lost	2–13	2–16
Passing Efficiency	17–33–2	16–25–1
Punts	5–45.4	7–39.7
Fumbles-Lost	2–1	1–1
Penalties-Yards	4–27	6–55
Time of Possession	29:35	30:25

INDIVIDUAL STATISTICS – RUSHING

OLE MISS–Enrique Davis 11–70, Dexter McCluster 7–28, Brandon Bolden 7–25, Jevan Snead 5–23, Markeith Summers 1–6, Cordera Eason 3–6. ALABAMA–Mark Ingram 17–73, Glen Coffee 13–52, Team 2–MINUS 2, John Parker Wilson 2–MINUS 16.

INDIVIDUAL STATISTICS – PASSING

OLE MISS–Jevan Snead 16–31–192–1, Rob Park 1–1–9–0, Dexter McCluster 0–1–0–1. ALABAMA–John Parker Wilson 16–25–219–1.

ALABAMA FOOTBALL

INDIVIDUAL STATISTICS – RECEIVING
OLE MISS–Shay Hodge 4-64, Lionel Breaux 2-55, Mike Wallace 2-24, Dexter McCluster 3-21, Jason Cook 2-13, Brandon Bolden 2-10, Markeith Summers 1-9, Jevan Snead 1-5. ALABAMA–Nick Walker 5-65, Julio Jones 3-63, Mike McCoy 3-45, Marquis Maze 2-29, Brad Smelley 1-16, Glen Coffee 2-1.

ATTENDANCE: 92,138

Game 8: No. 2 Alabama 29, Tennessee 9

KNOXVILLE | Alabama ran for three touchdowns against a Tennessee defense that had given up just two all season and beat the Volunteers back-to-back for the first time since 1991-92.

Glen Coffee and Roy Upchurch combined for 164 rushing yards and two touchdowns. Alabama outgained Tennessee 366–173 and finished with 178 yards rushing. Freshman wide receiver Julio Jones caught six passes for a career-high 103 yards.

"It's just a special rivalry and a special game to all of us involved in it in different ways," Tennessee Coach Phillip Fulmer said. "I'll be back up tomorrow. I'm not down. I just got a lot on my mind right now."

After losing his following game to South Carolina, Fulmer agreed to step down as head coach effective the end of the season.

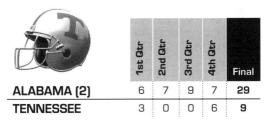

	1st Qtr	2nd Qtr	3rd Qtr	4th Qtr	Final
ALABAMA (2)	6	7	9	7	**29**
TENNESSEE	3	0	0	6	**9**

SCORING PLAYS
ALABAMA–FG, L Tiffin 39 YD 4:42 1st Qtr

TENNESSEE–FG, D Lincoln 31 YD 8:32 1st Qtr

ALABAMA–FG, L Tiffin 43 YD 13:23 1st Qtr

ALABAMA–TD, G Coffee 3 YD RUN (L Tiffin KICK) 12:19 2nd Qtr

ALABAMA–FG, L Tiffin 30 YD 4:32 3rd Qtr

ALABAMA–TD, J Parker Wilson 1 YD RUN 13:22 3rd Qtr

ALABAMA–TD, R Upchurch 4 YD RUN (L Tiffin KICK) 5:17 4th Qtr

TENNESSEE–TD, J Briscoe 10 YD PASS FROM N Stephens 7:34 4th Qtr

GAME STATISTICS

	ALABAMA (2)	TENNESSEE
First Downs	23	10
Yards Rushing	43–178	21–36
Yards Passing	188	137
Sacks-Yards Lost	0–0	2–16
Passing Efficiency	17–24–0	16–28–0
Punts	3–38	7–43.7
Fumbles-Lost	1–1	0–0
Penalties-Yards	3–35	7–60
Time of Possession	35:32	24:28

INDIVIDUAL STATISTICS – RUSHING

ALABAMA–Roy Upchurch 14–86, Glen Coffee 19–78, Terry Grant 4–11, John Parker Wilson 2–2, Mark Ingram 4–1. TENNESSEE–Arian Foster 6–21, Montario Hardesty 8–12, Lennon Creer 3–7, Nick Stephens 4–MINUS 4.

INDIVIDUAL STATISTICS – PASSING

ALABAMA–John Parker Wilson 17–24–188–0. TENNESSEE–Nick Stephens 16–28–137–0.

INDIVIDUAL STATISTICS – RECEIVING
ALABAMA–Julio Jones 6–103, Nick Walker 3–24, Will Oakley 1–14, Roy Upchurch 2–13, Mike McCoy 1–13, Brad Smelley 1–8, Nikita Stover 1–6, Glen Coffee 1–4, Marquis Maze 1–3. TENNESSEE–Josh Briscoe 4–46, Arian Foster 3–32, Luke Stocker 2–30, Austin Rogers 2–17, Brandon Warren 2–8, Lucas Taylor 1–4, Eric Berry 1–3, Denarius Moore 1–MINUS 3.

ATTENDANCE: 106,138

Game 9: No. 2 Alabama 35, Arkansas State 0

TUSCALOOSA | Alabama freshman running back Mark Ingram had his first 100-yard rushing game with 113 yards on just 12 carries, and Alabama had its fifth 200-yard rushing game of the season.

Senior quarterback John Parker Wilson's 12 consecutive completions, including the previous game at Tennessee, tied Andrew Zow's school record set in 2000.

Alabama recorded its first shutout since a 17–0 victory over Mississippi State on Nov. 5, 2005. The Crimson Tide had trailed just 1 minute, 15 seconds all season.

Senior safety Rashad Johnson had 13 tackles, including 2½ for a loss, and scored UA's fourth defensive touchdown of the season on a 32-yard interception return.

"It felt great," Johnson said. "I've never scored before. It was a big play. We needed some momentum, and it boosted the offense, too. I looked up, saw it, reeled it in, and then all I saw was the sideline."

	1st Qtr	2nd Qtr	3rd Qtr	4th Qtr	Final
ARKANSAS ST	0	0	0	0	**0**
ALABAMA (2)	7	7	14	7	**35**

2008 Review

SCORING PLAYS

ALABAMA–TD, G Coffee 9 YD RUN (L Tiffin KICK) 10:37 1st Qtr

ALABAMA–TD, R Johnson 32 YD INTERCEPTION RETURN (L Tiffin KICK) 6:06 2nd Qtr

ALABAMA–TD, R Upchurch 22 YD RUN (L Tiffin KICK) 1:23 3rd Qtr

ALABAMA–TD, M Ingram 5 YD RUN (L Tiffin KICK) 12:40 3rd Qtr

ALABAMA–TD, M Ingram 17 YD RUN (L Tiffin KICK) 10:23 4th Qtr

GAME STATISTICS

	ARKANSAS ST	ALABAMA (2)
First Downs	11	21
Yards Rushing	37–91	36–205
Yards Passing	67	152
Sacks-Yards Lost	4–26	2–19
Passing Efficiency	8–17–1	15–28–1
Punts	7–37	3–40.3
Fumbles-Lost	1–0	1–0
Penalties-Yards	7–73	3–33
Time of Possession	31:59	28:01

INDIVIDUAL STATISTICS – RUSHING

ARKANSAS ST–Reggie Arnold 15–72, Derek Lawson 6–24, Jermaine Robertson 3–14, Corey Leonard 13–MINUS 19. ALABAMA–Mark Ingram 12–113, Glen Coffee 9–56, Roy Upchurch 5–31, John Parker Wilson 8–7, Terry Grant 2–MINUS 2.

INDIVIDUAL STATISTICS – PASSING

ARKANSAS ST–Corey Leonard 8–17–67–1. ALABAMA–John Parker Wilson 15–28–152–1.

INDIVIDUAL STATISTICS – RECEIVING
ARKANSAS ST–Jahbari McLennan 1–26, Kevin Jones 3–16, Taylor Clements 1–9, Anthony Robinson 1–6, Jeff Blake 1–6, Trevor Gillott 1–4. ALABAMA–Julio Jones 5–62, Mike McCoy 3–26, Marquis Maze 1–24, Brad Smelley 1–11, Darius Hanks 1–10, Glen Coffee 1–9, Travis McCall 1–6, Earl Alexander 1–2, Mark Ingram 1–2.

ATTENDANCE: 92,138

Game 10: No. 1 Alabama 27, No. 15 LSU 21

BATON ROUGE | Coach Nick Saban's long-awaited return to LSU lived up to expectations as the Crimson Tide, playing as No. 1 for the first time since 1980, won in overtime to snap a five-game losing streak against the Tigers.

Alabama intercepted four Jarrett Lee passes, with Rashad Johnson tying a school record with three picks, the last of which was in the end zone to finish LSU's opening drive in overtime. On the next play, John Parker Wilson connected with freshman receiver Julio Jones, who reached the LSU 1, and the senior quarterback subsequently scored on a keeper.

The game went into overtime after defensive lineman Ricky-Jean Francois blocked Leigh Tiffin's 29-yard field-goal attempt at the end of regulation.

Jones finished with 126 receiving yards, and junior running back Glen Coffee matched that in rushing yards as Alabama clinched its first SEC West title since 1999.

"We are at about 19,000 feet," Saban said. "The mountain is at 26,000 feet, and the air is changing a little bit. The air is a little rarer."

	1st Qtr	2nd Qtr	3rd Qtr	4th Qtr	OT	Final
ALABAMA (1)	7	7	7	0	6	**27**
LSU (15)	14	0	0	7	0	**21**

SCORING PLAYS

ALABAMA–TD, J Wilson 1 YD RUN (L Tiffin KICK) 6:37 1st Qtr

LSU–TD, D Byrd 30 YD PASS FROM J Lee (C David KICK) 8:39 1st Qtr

LSU–TD, C Scott 30 YD RUN (C David KICK) 9:03 1st Qtr

ALABAMA–TD, R Johnson 54 YD INTERCEPTION RETURN (L Tiffin KICK) 10:27 2nd Qtr

ALABAMA–TD, G Coffee 3 YD RUN (L Tiffin KICK) 6:46 3rd Qtr

LSU–TD, C Scott 1 YD RUN (C David KICK) 8:48 4th Qtr

ALABAMA–TD, J Parker Wilson 1 YD RUN (PAT FAILED) 1st Ot

GAME STATISTICS

	ALABAMA (1)	LSU (15)
First Downs	16	17
Yards Rushing	37–138	46–201
Yards Passing	215	181
Sacks-Yards Lost	0–0	1–3
Passing Efficiency	15–31–1	13–34–4
Punts	7–42.1	8–40.1
Fumbles-Lost	3–2	0–0
Penalties-Yards	2–24	5–32
Time of Possession	26:40	33:20

INDIVIDUAL STATISTICS – RUSHING

ALABAMA–Glen Coffee 26–126, John Parker Wilson 5–7, Mark Ingram 5–6, Team 1–MINUS 1. LSU–Charles Scott 24–92, Keiland Williams 13–88, Trindon Holliday 2–9, Richard Murphy 2–8, Quinn Johnson 4–7, Jarrett Lee 1–MINUS 3.

INDIVIDUAL STATISTICS – PASSING

ALABAMA–John Parker Wilson 15–31–215–1. LSU–Jarrett Lee 13–34–181–4.

INDIVIDUAL STATISTICS – RECEIVING

ALABAMA–Julio Jones 7–128, Earl Alexander 1–26, Glen Coffee 2–19, Nick Walker 1–18, Travis McCall 2–14, Mike McCoy 2–10. LSU–Brandon LaFell 4–74, Demetrius Byrd 4–51, Terrance Toliver 3–34, Richard Dickson 1–22, Keiland Williams 1–0.

ATTENDANCE: 93,039

Game 11: No. 1 Alabama 32, Mississippi State 7

TUSCALOOSA | Javier Arenas returned a punt 80 yards for a touchdown to give Alabama a 19–7 lead early in the third quarter, en route to tallying a school-record 153 yards on six punt returns.

Coach Nick Saban called the touchdown a "picture-perfect return" by the whole unit. "We pretty much controlled the game after that," he added.

Kareem Jackson blocked a punt in the end zone for a safety and Leigh Tiffin kicked three field goals.

Alabama's defense held Mississippi State to just nine first downs, 35 rushing yards, and 167 yards of total offense. For the season, the Crimson Tide had outgained opponents in rushing yards, 2,184 to 826.

It was former Alabama All-American center Sylvester Croom's final time facing his alma mater as Mississippi State's coach.

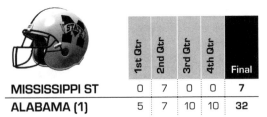

	1st Qtr	2nd Qtr	3rd Qtr	4th Qtr	Final
MISSISSIPPI ST	0	7	0	0	7
ALABAMA (1)	5	7	10	10	32

SCORING PLAYS

ALABAMA–SAFETY, 4:57 1st Qtr

ALABAMA–FG, L Tiffin 35 YD 13:17 1st Qtr

MISSISSIPPI ST–TD, J Smith 31 YD PASS FROM T Lee (A Carlson KICK) 4:41 2nd Qtr

ALABAMA–TD, J Parker Wilson 1 YD RUN (L Tiffin KICK) 10:13 2nd Qtr

ALABAMA–TD, J Arenas 80 YD PUNT RETURN (L Tiffin KICK) 2:46 3rd Qtr

ALABAMA–FG, L Tiffin 34 YD 11:09 3rd Qtr

ALABAMA–FG, L Tiffin 35 YD 3:46 4th Qtr

ALABAMA–TD, M Ingram 1 YD RUN (L Tiffin KICK) 7:02 4th Qtr

GAME STATISTICS

	MISSISSIPPI ST	ALABAMA (1)
First Downs	9	17
Yards Rushing	22–35	48–198
Yards Passing	132	166
Sacks-Yards Lost	2–12	2–10
Passing Efficiency	11–28–0	12–19–0
Punts	10–37.4	5–43
Fumbles-Lost	2–1	2–0
Penalties-Yards	5–25	5–52
Time of Possession	24:27	35:33

INDIVIDUAL STATISTICS – RUSHING
MISSISSIPPI ST–Anthony Dixon 11-26, Wesley Carroll 1-7, Tyson Lee 6-5, Christian Ducr 1-0, Arceto Clark 1-0, Arnil Stallworth 2–MINUS 3. ALABAMA–Mark Ingram 13-78, Glen Coffee 17-71, Jeramie Griffin 5-27, John Parker Wilson 11-19, Demetrius Goode 2-3.

INDIVIDUAL STATISTICS – PASSING
MISSISSIPPI ST–Tyson Lee 11-28-132-0. ALABAMA–John Parker Wilson 10-17-148-0, Greg McElroy 2-2-18-0.

INDIVIDUAL STATISTICS – RECEIVING
MISSISSIPPI ST–Jamayel Smith 2-46, Anthony Dixon 4-32, Arnil Stallworth 1-32, Brandon McRae 2-15, Aubrey Bell 1-7, Arceto Clark 1-0. ALABAMA–Julio Jones 3-53, Brad Smelley 2-46, Darius Hanks 2-24, Travis McCall 1-12, Glen Coffee 1-11, Jeramie Griffin 1-9, Nick Walker 1-6, Mark Ingram 1-5.

ATTENDANCE: 92,138

2008 Review

28

Years it had been since the Crimson Tide stood as the undisputed No. 1 team in the country during the regular season. They reached the top in Week 10, topping both human polls and the BCS standings.

Game 12: No. 1 Alabama 36, Auburn 0

TUSCALOOSA | Alabama crushed Auburn to end its six-game losing streak in the series in its most lopsided score since 1962.

Junior running back Glen Coffee scored the first touchdown on an impressive 41-yard carry around the right side and finished with 144 yards. Freshman running back Mark Ingram scored two touchdowns.

"I'm happy, I really am happy," Coach Nick Saban said after pulling most of the seniors one-by-one so they could be applauded during their last game at Bryant-Denny Stadium. "I was happy and dancing in the locker room. Miss Terry gave me a big kiss coming up here. I was real happy about that."

It was actually the first time the Crimson Tide ever beat the Tigers in Tuscaloosa (Alabama had been 0–6 because most of the series was played at Legion Field).

Auburn totaled just 170 yards in Tommy Tuberville's final game.

"Well, all good streaks come to an end, and it came to a screeching halt," he said days before meeting with university President Jay Gogue and leaving without a job. "It was a tough night for us."

	1st Qtr	2nd Qtr	3rd Qtr	4th Qtr	Final
AUBURN	0	0	0	0	**0**
ALABAMA (1)	3	7	19	7	**36**

SCORING PLAYS

ALABAMA–FG, L Tiffin 37 YD 15:00 1st Qtr

ALABAMA–TD, G Coffee 41 YD RUN (L Tiffin KICK) 4:32 2nd Qtr

ALABAMA–TD, N Stover 39 YD PASS FROM J Parker Wilson (PAT BLOCKED) 1:45 3rd Qtr

Mark Ingram and Nikita Stover leap to celebrate one of Ingram's two third-quarter touchdowns in the Iron Bowl. Stover had gotten in on the scoring with a touchdown reception earlier in the quarter.

ALABAMA–TD, M Ingram 1 YD RUN 7:25 3rd Qtr

ALABAMA–TD, M Ingram 14 YD RUN (L Tiffin KICK) 12:50 3rd Qtr

ALABAMA–TD, M Maze 34 YD PASS FROM G McElroy (L Tiffin KICK) 12:11 4th Qtr

GAME STATISTICS

	AUBURN	ALABAMA (1)
First Downs	8	21
Yards Rushing	30–57	50–234
Yards Passing	113	178
Sacks-Yards Lost	2–20	1–3
Passing Efficiency	9–23–0	10–18–0
Punts	9–42.6	5–33.4
Fumbles-Lost	3–3	1–0
Penalties-Yards	4–45	1–4
Time of Possession	24:23	35:37

INDIVIDUAL STATISTICS - RUSHING
AUBURN–Mario Fannin 8–28, Ben Tate 4–12, Brad Lester 6–11, Kodi Burns 12–6. ALABAMA–Glen Coffee 20–144, Mark Ingram 15–64, Roy Upchurch 2–15, Terry Grant 7–11, Jeramie Griffin 1–2, John Parker Wilson 4–0, – Team 1–MINUS 2.

INDIVIDUAL STATISTICS - PASSING
AUBURN–Kodi Burns 9–23–113–0. ALABAMA–John Parker Wilson 8–16–134–0, Greg McElroy 2–2–44–0.

INDIVIDUAL STATISTICS - RECEIVING
AUBURN–Mario Fannin 3–44, Rodgeriqus Smith 2–39, Robert Dunn 1–10, Montez Billings 1–9, Gabe McKenzie 1–6, Derek Winter 1–5. ALABAMA–Nikita Stover 1–39, Julio Jones 3–36, Marquis Maze 1–34, Mark Ingram 1–27, Darius Hanks 1–17, Brad Smelley 1–10, Travis McCall 1–9, Nick Walker 1–6.

ATTENDANCE: 92,138

SEC Championship: No. 2 Florida 31, No. 1 Alabama 20

ATLANTA | Defending Heisman Trophy winner Tim Tebow led Florida to two late touchdowns as the Gators came back from a 20–17 deficit entering the fourth quarter to win its second Southeastern Conference title in three seasons.

The decisive touchdown came with 2:50 remaining when Tebow found Riley Cooper on a 5-yard pass. He finished with 216 passing yards and three touchdowns.

"He's a great competitor," Coach Nick Saban said. "He takes his teammates on his shoulders a lot. They have a lot of confidence he's going to make plays, and they play that way. They scored two touchdowns where we had them covered about as well as we could cover them."

Alabama had never trailed in the second half this season, and the loss snapped a 13-game winning streak. Florida went on to defeat Oklahoma in the Bowl Championship Series title game.

	1st Qtr	2nd Qtr	3rd Qtr	4th Qtr	Final
ALABAMA (1)	10	0	10	0	**20**
FLORIDA (2)	7	10	0	14	**31**

SCORING PLAYS

FLORIDA–TD, C Moore 3 YD PASS FROM T Tebow (J Phillips KICK) 6:43 1st Qtr

ALABAMA–TD, G Coffee 18 YD RUN (L Tiffin KICK) 7:37 1st Qtr

ALABAMA–FG, L Tiffin 30 YD 11:32 1st Qtr

FLORIDA–FG, J Phillips 19 YD 6:01 2nd Qtr

FLORIDA–TD, D Nelson 5 YD PASS FROM T Tebow (J Phillips

KICK) 12:01 2nd Qtr

ALABAMA–TD, M Ingram 2 YD RUN (L Tiffin KICK) 8:40 3rd Qtr

ALABAMA–FG, L Tiffin 27 YD 14:52 3rd Qtr

FLORIDA–TD, J Demps 1 YD RUN (J Phillips KICK) 5:39 4th Qtr

FLORIDA–TD, R Cooper 5 YD PASS FROM T Tebow (J Phillips KICK) 12:10 4th Qtr

GAME STATISTICS

	ALABAMA (1)	FLORIDA (2)
First Downs	18	19
Yards Rushing	33–136	42–142
Yards Passing	187	216
Sacks-Yards Lost	1–11	1–2
Passing Efficiency	12–25–1	14–22–0
Punts	4–41	3–47.7
Fumbles-Lost	0–0	0–0
Penalties-Yards	2–31	6–45
Time of Possession	27:56	32:04

INDIVIDUAL STATISTICS – RUSHING
ALABAMA–Glen Coffee 21-112, Mark Ingram 8-21, John Parker Wilson 3-2, P.J. Fitzgerald 1-1. FLORIDA–Tim Tebow 17-57, Jeffery Demps 14-53, Emmanuel Moody 4-23, Brandon James 3-7, Louis Murphy 1-4, Chris Rainey 1-1, Team 2-MINUS 3.

INDIVIDUAL STATISTICS – PASSING
ALABAMA–John Parker Wilson 12-25-187-1.
FLORIDA–Tim Tebow 14-22-216-0.

INDIVIDUAL STATISTICS – RECEIVING
ALABAMA–Julio Jones 5-124, Nick Walker 3-37, Darius Hanks 3-19, Glen Coffee 1-7. FLORIDA–Louis Murphy 4-86, Riley Cooper 2-56, Aaron Hernandez 3-43, David Nelson 3-27, Carl Moore 1-3, Kestahn Moore 1-1.

ATTENDANCE: 75,892

Sugar Bowl: No. 7 Utah 31,
No. 4 Alabama 17

NEW ORLEANS | Playing without Outland Trophy winner Andre Smith, who was suspended by Coach Nick Saban after the team was already in New Orleans, and left guard Mike Johnson, who sustained an ankle injury early in the game, Alabama gave up a season-high eight sacks and averaged just 0.9 yards per carry.

When Utah scored its third touchdown with 4 minutes and 1 second remaining in the first quarter, it had outgained Alabama 150–10, with a 139–6 advantage in passing yards, while having the ball for only 4:53. The Tide had outscored opponents 133–27 in the first quarter.

"He played a phenomenal football game," Utah Coach Kyle Whittingham said about Brian Johnson, who completed 27 of 41 passes for 336 yards and three touchdowns.

Sparked by a 73-yard punt return for a touchdown by Javier Arenas, Alabama scored 17 unanswered points to make it 21–17, but Utah answered with a touchdown drive and kept going after Wilson, forcing a fumble with roughly five minutes remaining to begin the victory celebration.

"They jumped ahead of us early in the game. I don't think we gave them their due respect coming into the game," junior running back Glen Coffee said. "That's something we never should have allowed to happen."

	1st Qtr	2nd Qtr	3rd Qtr	4th Qtr	Final
UTAH (7)	21	0	7	3	**31**
ALABAMA (4)	0	10	7	0	**17**

SCORING PLAYS

UTAH–TD, B Casteel 7 YD PASS FROM B Johnson (L Sakoda KICK) 3:58 1st Qtr

UTAH–TD, M Asiata 2 YD RUN (L Sakoda KICK) 6:23 1st Qtr

UTAH–TD, B Godfrey 18 YD PASS FROM B Johnson (L Sakoda KICK) 10:59 1st Qtr

HUDDLEUP!

ALABAMA–FG, L Tiffin 52 YD 0:05 2nd Qtr

ALABAMA–TD, J Arenas 73 YD PUNT RETURN (L Tiffin KICK) 9:32 2nd Qtr

ALABAMA–TD, G Coffee 4 YD PASS FROM J Parker Wilson (L Tiffin KICK) 3:19 3rd Qtr

UTAH–TD, D Reed 28 YD PASS FROM B Johnson (L Sakoda KICK) 4:56 3rd Qtr

UTAH–FG, L Sakoda 28 YD 12:11 4th Qtr

GAME STATISTICS

	UTAH (7)	ALABAMA (4)
First Downs	22	15
Yards Rushing	24–13	33–31
Yards Passing	336	177
Sacks-Yards Lost	2–10	8–53
Passing Efficiency	27–41–0	18–30–2
Punts	6–45.2	4–41.5
Fumbles-Lost	3–1	1–1
Penalties-Yards	10–91	7–67
Time of Possession	28:42	31:18

INDIVIDUAL STATISTICS – RUSHING
UTAH–Matt Asiata 13–29, Darrell Mack 4–8, Team 3–MINUS 9, Brian Johnson 4–MINUS 15. ALABAMA–Glen Coffee 13–36, Mark Ingram 8–26, John Parker Wilson 12–MINUS 31.

INDIVIDUAL STATISTICS – PASSING
UTAH–Brian Johnson 27–41–336–0. ALABAMA–John Parker Wilson 18–30–177–2.

INDIVIDUAL STATISTICS – RECEIVING
UTAH–Freddie Brown 12–125, Bradon Godfrey 6–75, David Reed 2–58, Jereme Brooks 4–45, Brent Casteel 1–17, Darrell Mack 1–14, Colt Sampson 1–2. ALABAMA–Julio Jones 7–77, Glen Coffee 4–40, Nick Walker 3–25, Nikita Stover 1–15, Mark Ingram 1–8, Brad Smelley 1–7, Earl Alexander 1–5.

ATTENDANCE: 71,872

Nikita Stover was in prime position to haul in this John Parker Wilson pass, but Utah's Brice McCain managed to reach around Stover to deflect it away. Stover was held to just one catch for 15 yards.

Julio Jones, who led Alabama receivers with seven catches for 70 yards, makes sure he holds onto this John Parker Wilson pass against Utah in the 2009 Sugar Bowl.

FINAL STATISTICS

Team Statistics	UA	OPP
SCORING	422	200
Points Per Game	30.1	14.3
FIRST DOWNS	263	197
Rushing	133	60
Passing	112	120
Penalties	18	17
RUSHING YARDAGE	2,585	1,038
Yards gained rushing	2,867	1,374
Yards lost rushing	282	336
Rushing Attempts	568	391
Average Per Rush	4.6	2.7
Average Per Game	184.6	74.1
TDs Rushing	32	5
PASSING YARDAGE	2,396	2,651
Att-Comp-Int	334–195–9	467–246–15
Average Per Pass	7.2	5.7
Average Per Catch	12.3	10.8
Average Per Game	171.1	189.4
TDs Passing	11	18
TOTAL OFFENSE	4,981	3,689
Total Plays	902	858
Average Per Play	5.5	4.3
Average Per Game	355.8	263.5
KICK RETURNS: #-Yards	40–816	81–1,765
PUNT RETURNS: #-Yards	49–701	27–242
INT RETURNS: #-Yards	15–305	9–83
KICK RETURN AVERAGE	20.4	21.8
PUNT RETURN AVERAGE	14.3	9.0
INT RETURN AVERAGE	20.3	9.2
FUMBLES-LOST	19–10	20–10
PENALTIES-Yards	57–520	87–666
Average Per Game	37.1	47.6
PUNTS-Yards	61–2,460	94–3,782

2008 Review

Average Per Punt	40.3	40.2
Net Punt Average	35.0	31.5
TIME OF POSSESSION/Game	32:08	27:52
3rd-Down Conversions	76/183	56/199
3rd-Down Pct	42%	28%
4th-Down Conversions	8/10	10/20
4th-Down Pct	80%	50%
SACKS BY-Yards	26–189	25–178
MISC YARDS	0	–11
TOUCHDOWNS SCORED	52	25
FIELD GOALS-ATTEMPTS	20–30	9–16
ONSIDE KICKS	0–0	1–2
RED-ZONE SCORES	46–54 85%	22–26 85%
RED-ZONE TOUCHDOWNS	31–54 57%	14–26 54%
PAT-ATTEMPTS	46–48 96%	23–23 100%
ATTENDANCE	644,966	364,238
Games/Avg Per Game	7/92,138	4/91,060
Neutral Site Games	3/72,620	

SCORE BY QUARTERS

	1st	2nd	3rd	4th	OT	Total
Alabama	133	121	108	54	6	422
Opponents	48	37	38	77	0	200

6 Teams on Alabama's schedule in 2008 that were ranked in the AP Top 25. Five of those six were in the top 10.

INDIVIDUAL STATISTICS
Rushing

	Gp–Gs	Att	Gain	Loss	Net	Avg	TD	Lg	Avg/G
Glen Coffee									
	14–14	233	1,417	34	1383	5.9	10	87	98.8
Mark Ingram									
	14–0	143	743	15	728	5.1	12	40	52.0
Roy Upchurch									
	10–0	58	351	1	350	6.0	4	62	35.0
Terry Grant									
	14–0	35	119	31	88	2.5	1	18	6.3
Jeramie Griffin									
	2–0	6	29	0	29	4.8	0	8	14.5
Demetrius Goode									
	3–0	9	24	0	24	2.7	0	7	8.0
P J. Fitzgerald									
	14–0	1	1	0	1	1.0	0	1	0.1
Marquis Maze									
	14–4	1	1	0	1	1.0	0	1	0.1
John Parker Wilson									
	14–14	72	182	188	–6	–0.1	5	20	–0.4
Team									
	9–0	10	0	13	–13	–1.3	0	0	–1.4
Total									
	14	568	2,867	282	2,585	4.6	32	87	184.6
Opponents									
	14	391	1,374	336	1,038	2.7	5	62	74.1

Passing

	Gp–Gs	Effic	Comp–Att–Int	Pct	Yds	TD	Lg	Avg/G
John Parker Wilson								
	14–14	122.27	187–323–8	57.9	2273	10	64	162.4
Greg McElroy								
	6–0	178.47	8–11–1	72.7	123	1	34	20.5
Total								
	14	124.12	195–334–9	58.4	2396	11	64	171.1
Opponents								
	14	106.66	246–467–15	52.7	2651	18	51	189.4

Receiving

	Gp–Gs	No.	Yds	Avg	TD	Lg	Avg/G
Julio Jones							
	14–14	58	924	15.9	4	64	66.0
Nick Walker							
	14–11	32	324	10.1	2	40	23.1
Mike McCoy							
	13–9	16	191	11.9	1	30	14.7
Glen Coffee							
	14–14	16	118	7.4	1	15	8.4
Marquis Maze							
	14–4	11	137	12.5	2	34	9.8
Roy Upchurch							
	10–0	9	101	11.2	0	29	10.1
Earl Alexander							
	12–0	8	121	15.1	0	27	10.1
Darius Hanks							
	8–0	8	88	11.0	0	18	11.0
Brad Smelley							
	8–0	7	98	14.0	0	37	12.2
Mark Ingram							
	14–0	7	54	7.7	0	27	3.9
Travis McCall							
	14–12	7	52	7.4	0	12	3.7

Nikita Stover						
14–5	6	101	16.8	1	39	7.2
Terry Grant						
14–0	4	36	9.0	0	22	2.6
Will Oakley						
8–0	2	27	13.5	0	14	3.4
B.J. Scott						
9–0	2	7	3.5	0	7	0.8
Jeramie Griffin						
2–0	1	9	9.0	0	9	4.5
Preston Dial						
12–1	1	8	8.0	0	8	0.7
Total						
14	195	2,396	12.3	11	64	171.1
Opponents						
14	246	2,651	10.8	18	51	189.4

Punt Returns

	No.	Yds	Avg	TD	Lg
Javier Arenas					
	41	650	15.9	3	87
Marquis Maze					
	2	8	4.0	0	5
Julio Jones					
	2	11	5.5	0	10
Marquis Johnson					
	1	0	0.0	0	0
Mark Barron					
	1	1	1.0	0	1
Roy Upchurch					
	1	6	6.0	0	0
Kareem Jackson					
	1	8	8.0	0	0
Chris Rogers					
	0	17	0.0	1	17
Total					
	49	701	14.3	4	87
Opponents					
	27	242	9.0	1	92

Interceptions

	No.	Yds	Avg	TD	Lg
Rashad Johnson	5	125	25.0	2	54
Justin Woodall	4	99	24.8	1	74
Marquis Johnson	2	7	3.5	0	7
Kareem Jackson	1	5	5.0	0	5
Rolando McClain	1	12	12.0	0	12
Javier Arenas	1	63	63.0	1	63
Chris Rogers	1	-6	-6.0	0	0
Total	15	305	20.3	4	74
Opponents	9	83	9.2	0	24

Kick Returns

	No.	Yds	Avg	TD	Lg
Javier Arenas	26	614	23.6	0	41
Mike McCoy	5	60	12.0	0	23
Terry Grant	3	52 1	7.3	0	18
Baron Huber	1	15	15.0	0	15
Marquis Maze	1	19	19.0	0	19
Travis McCall	1	9	9.0	0	9
Team	1	0	0.0	0	0
Mark Ingram	1	26	26.0	0	26
Julio Jones	1	21	21.0	0	21
Total	40	816	20.4	0	41
Opponents	81	1,765	21.8	1	96

ALABAMA FOOTBALL

Fumble Returns

	No.	Yds	Avg	TD	Lg
Rolando McClain	1	4	4.0	1	4
Bobby Greenwood	1	5	5.0	0	5
Dont'a Hightower	1	8	8.0	0	8
Kareem Jackson	1	-9	-9.0	0	0
Total	4	8	2.0	1	8
Opponents	0	0	0.0	0	0

Scoring

TD	FG	PAT	Rush	Rcv	Pass	Saf	Pts
Leigh Tiffin							
–	20–29	46–47	–	–	–	–	106
Mark Ingram							
12	–	–	1–1	–	–	–	74
Glen Coffee							
11	–	–	–	–	–	–	66
John Parker Wilson							
5	–	–	–	–	0–2	–	30
Julio Jones							
4	–	–	–	–	–	–	24
Javier Arenas							
4	–	–	–	–	–	–	24
Roy Upchurch							
4	–	–	–	–	–	–	24
Nick Walker							
2	–	–	–	–	–	–	12
Marquis Maze							
2	–	–	–	–	–	–	12
Rashad Johnson							
2	–	–	–	–	–	–	12
Nikita Stover							
1	–	–	–	–	–	–	6
Chris Rogers							
1	–	–	–	–	–	–	6
Justin Woodall							
1	–	–	–	–	–	–	6
Terry Grant							
1	–	–	–	–	–	–	6
Mike McCoy							
1	–	–	–	–	–	–	6

Rolando McClain

1	–	–	–	–	–	–	6

Team

–	–	–	–	–	–	1	2

Corey Smith

–	0-1	0-1	–	–	–	–	0

Total

52	20-30	46-48	1-1	–	0-2	1	422

Opponents

25	9-16	23-23	–	–	0-2	–	200

Total Offense
Field Goals

Fg	Pct.	01-19	20-29	30-39	40-49	50-99	Lg	Blk
Leigh Tiffin
20-29	69.0	0-0	7-8	9-11	2-7	2-3	54	1
Corey Smith
0-1	0.0	0-0	0-0	0-1	0-0	0-0	0	0

Punting

	No.	Yds	Avg	Lg	TB	Fc	I20	50+	Blk
P J. Fitzgerald
	59	2,427	41.1	56	4	16	15	4	0
Team
	2	33	16.5	20	0	0	0	0	2
Total
	61	2,460	40.3	56	4	16	15	4	2
Opponents
	94	3,782	40.2	61	6	14	21	12	2

2 Kickers in Alabama history that have made a pair of 50-yard or longer field goals in a game. Muscle Shoals native Leigh Tiffin and his father Van are the only two to have accomplished the feat.

Leigh Tiffin follows his first-half field goal against Vanderbilt as P.J. Fitzgerald looks on. Tiffin had a fine season,
making 20 of 29 field goals and 46 of 47 points after
touchdown.

Kickoffs

	No.	Yds	Avg	TB	OB	Retn	Net	Ydln
Leigh Tiffin								
	75	4,805	64.1	2	0			
Andrew Friedman								
	5	291	58.2	0	0			
Corey Smith								
	2	116	58.0	0	1			
Heath Thomas								
	2	119	59.5	0	0			
Total								
	84	5,331	63.5	2	1	21.8	42.0	28
Opponents								
	47	2,905	61.8	5	1	20.4	42.3	27

All Purpose

	GP	Rush	Rcv	PR	KR	IR	Total	Avg/G
Glen Coffee								
	14	1,383	118	0	0	0	1,501	107.2
Javier Arenas								
	14	0	0	650	614	63	1,327	94.8
Julio Jones								
	14	0	924	11	21	0	956	68.3
Mark Ingram								
	14	728	54	0	26	0	808	57.7
Roy Upchurch								
	10	350	101	6	0	0	457	45.7
Nick Walker								
	14	0	324	0	0	0	324	23.1
Mike McCoy								
	13	0	191	0	60	0	251	19.3
Terry Grant								
	14	88	36	0	52	0	176	12.6
Marquis Maze								
	14	1	137	8	19	0	165	11.8
Rashad Johnson								
	14	0	0	0	0	125	125	8.9
Earl Alexander								
	12	0	121	0	0	0	121	10.1
Nikita Stover								
	14	0	101	0	0	0	101	7.2

Player	G	Rush	Rec	PR	KOR	IR/Fum	Total	Avg
Justin Woodall								
	14	0	0	0	0	99	99	7.1
Brad Smelley								
	8	0	98	0	0	0	98	12.2
Darius Hanks								
	8	0	88	0	0	0	88	11.0
Travis McCall								
	14	0	52	0	9	0	61	4.4
Jeramie Griffin								
	2	29	9	0	0	0	38	19.0
Will Oakley								
	8	0	27	0	0	0	27	3.4
Demetrius Good								
	3	24	0	0	0	0	24	8.0
Baron Huber								
	14	0	0	0	15	0	15	1.1
Kareem Jackson								
	14	0	0	8	0	5	13	0.9
Rolando McClai								
	14	0	0	0	0	12	12	0.9
Chris Rogers								
	14	0	0	17	0	-6	11	0.8
Preston Dial								
	12	0	8	0	0	0	8	0.7
B J. Scott								
	9	0	7	0	0	0	7	0.8
Marquis Johnson								
	14	0	0	0	0	7	7	0.5
P J. Fitzgerald								
	14	1	0	0	0	0	1	0.1
Mark Barron								
	14	0	0	1	0	0	1	0.1
John Parker Wilson								
	14	-6	0	0	0	0	-6	-0.4
Team								
	9	-13	0	0	0	0	-13	-1.4
Total								
	14	2,585	2,396	701	816	305	6,803	485.9
Opponents								
	14	1,038	2,651	242	1,765	83	5,779	412.8

Defensive Statistics

Player	GP-GS	Tackles			TFL	-Yds	Sacks	
		Solo	Ast	Total			No	-Yds
25 Rolando McClain	14-14	48	47	95	12.0	-45	3.0	-22
49 Rashad Johnson	14-14	60	29	89	5.0	-15	1.0	-7
98 Brandon Fanney	14-14	26	40	66	9.0	-19	1.0	-5
30 Dont'a Hightower	14-12	26	38	64	2.5	-6	0	0
28 Javier Arenas	14-14	44	19	63	3.5	-24	2.0	-21
24 Marquis Johnson	14-3	32	17	49	1.0	-4	0	0
27 Justin Woodall	14-14	33	14	47	1.5	-4	0	0
3 Kareem Jackson	14-14	28	16	44	1.0	-4	0	0
93 Bobby Greenwood	14-14	19	21	40	7.0	-30	5.0	-28
95 Brandon Deaderick	14-14	14	22	36	5.5	-25	4.0	-24
13 Cory Reamer	14-11	16	19	35	6.0	-16	1.0	-8
26 Ali Sharrief	14-2	20	11	31	2.5	-7	0	0
32 Eryk Anders	14-0	14	10	24	4.5	-26	2.5	-22
62 Terrence Cody	12-12	7	17	24	4.5	-14	0.5	-5
41 Courtney Upshaw	13-0	12	10	22	3.0	-3	0	0
4A Mark Barron	14-0	9	9	18	1.5	-11	1.5	-11
21 Prince Hall	12-0	7	10	17	2.0	-5	0.5	-4
1H Josh Chapman	13-2	9	7	16	4.0	-7	0	0
20 Tyrone King	14-0	11	4	15	0	0	0	0
1F Lorenzo Washington	14-0	3	10	13	2.5	-12	1.0	-10
8A Chris Rogers	14-0	10	3	13	0	0	0	0
96 Luther Davis	14-0	6	6	12	2.5	-4	0	0
19 Chris Jackson	12-0	1	5	6	0	0	0	0
23 Robby Green	12-0	4	2	6	0	0	0	0
99 Leigh Tiffin	14-0	3	3	6	0	0	0	0
45 Charlie Higgenbotham	14-0	2	2	4	1.0	-8	1.0	-8
57 Marcell Dareus	8-0	1	3	4	0	0	0	0
5 Roy Upchurch	10-0	0	3	3	0	0	0	0
97 P. J. Fitzgerald	14-0	2	1	3	0	0	0	0
29 Terry Grant	14-0	2	1	3	0	0	0	0
36 Chris Jordan	10-0	0	3	3	0	0	0	0
5A Jerrell Harris	10-0	1	2	3	0	0	0	0
38 Glen Coffee	14-14	1	1	2	0	0	0	0
90 Milton Talbert	4-0	1	1	2	0	0	0	0
83 Travis McCall	14-12	2	0	2	0	0	0	0
8 Julio Jones	14-14	2	0	2	0	0	0	0
88 Nick Walker	14-11	1	0	1	0	0	0	0
78 Mike Johnson	14-14	1	0	1	0	0	0	0
4 Marquis Maze	14-4	1	0	1	0	0	0	0
55 Chavis Williams	5-0	1	0	1	1.0	-9	1.0	-9
TM Team	9-0	0	0	0	0	-0		
58 Nick Gentry	9-0	0	0	0	0	-0		
Total	14-0	480	406	886	83	-298	26	-189
Opponents	14-0	508	538	1,046	58	-264	25	-178

ALABAMA FOOTBALL

Starting Lineups

First Game (Clemson)	Last Game (Utah)
Offense	
WR 8 Julio Jones	WR 8 Julio Jones
LT 71 Andre Smith	LT 78 Mike Johnson
LG 78 Mike Johnson	LG 74 David Ross
C 59 Antoine Caldwell	C 59 Antoine Caldwell
RG 76 Marlon Davis	RG 76 Marlon Davis
RT 79 Drew Davis	RT 79 Drew Davis
TE 83 Travis McCall	TE 83 Travis McCall
WR 4 Marquis Maze	TE 88 Nick Walker
WR 80 Mike McCoy	WR 8 Nikita Stover
RB 38 Glen Coffee	RB 38 Glen Coffee
QB 14 John Parker Wilson	QB 14 John Parker Wilson

Defense

First Game (Clemson)	Last Game (Utah)
DE 93 Bobby Greenwood	DE 93 Bobby Greenwood
NG 62 Terrence Cody	NG 62 Terrence Cody
DE 95 Brandon Deaderick	DE 95 Brandon Deaderick
JLB 98 Brandon Fanney	JLB 98 Brandon Fanney
MLB 25 Rolando McClain	MLB 25 Rolando McClain
LB 30 Dont'a Hightower	DB 24 Marquis Johnson
LB 13 Cory Reamer	DB 26 Ali Sharrief
SS 27 Justin Woodall	S 27 Justin Woodall
FS 49 Rashad Johnson	FS 49 Rashad Johnson
CB 3 Kareem Jackson	CB 3 Kareem Jackson
CB 28 Javier Arenas	CB 28 Javier Arenas

Javier Arenas comes from a very athletically gifted family. His cousin, Gilbert Arenas, plays for the NBA's Washington Wizards.

2008 SEC Standings

Eastern Division

	W-L	Pct.	PF	PA	W-L	Pct.	PF	PA
				SEC			**Overall**	
*^Florida								
	7-1	.875	359	100	13-1	.929	611	181
Georgia								
	6-2	.750	215	214	10-3	.769	409	319
Vanderbilt								
	4-4	.500	144	174	7-6	.538	249	255
South Carolina								
	4-4	.500	163	186	7-6	.538	270	274
Tennessee								
	3-5	.375	129	149	5-7	.417	208	201
Kentucky								
	2-6	.250	143	238	7-6	.538	294	279

Western Division

	W-L	Pct.	PF	PA	W-L	Pct.	PF	PA
#Alabama								
	8-0	1.000	255	115	12-2	.857	422	200
Ole Miss								
	5-3	.625	208	149	9-4	.692	417	247
LSU								
	3-5	.375	207	254	8-5	.615	402	314
Arkansas								
	2-6	.250	167	248	5-7	.417	263	374
Auburn								
	2-6	.250	93	149	5-7	.417	208	216
Mississippi State								
	2-6	.250	97	204	4-8	.333	183	296

* Eastern Division Champion; # Western Division Champion;
^ SEC Champion

SEC Championship: No. 2 Florida 31, No. 1 Alabama 20

ALABAMA FOOTBALL

Future Schedules

2009	Opponent	Location
Sept. 5	Virginia Tech	Atlanta
Sept. 12	Florida International	Tuscaloosa
Sept. 19	North Texas	Tuscaloosa
Sept. 26	Arkansas	Tuscaloosa
Oct. 3	Kentucky	Lexington
Oct. 10	Ole Miss	Oxford
Oct. 17	South Carolina	Tuscaloosa
Oct. 24	Tennessee	Tuscaloosa
Nov. 7	LSU	Tuscaloosa
Nov. 14	Mississippi State	Starkville
Nov. 21	Chattanooga	Tuscaloosa
Nov. 28	Auburn	Auburn

Tentative Schedules

Alabama will play each SEC Western Division opponent (Arkansas, Auburn, LSU, Ole Miss, and Mississippi State) and Tennessee every year, alternating between home and away sites. It will also play two SEC teams from the Eastern Division on a rotating basis:

2010: at South Carolina, Florida
2011: at Florida, Vanderbilt

Alabama is scheduled to play at Duke in 2010 and has upcoming home-and-away games scheduled with Penn State and Georgia State.

9 **Starters from the Alabama defense who returned in 2009. This number includes four linebackers and three members of the secondary. Additionally, the special teams will return both Leigh Tiffin and P.J. Fitzgerald.**

Through the Years

THROUGH THE YEARS

1892
2-2

Nov. 11	Birmingham H.S.	Birmingham	W	56-0
Nov. 12	Birmingham A.C.	Birmingham	L	5-4
Dec. 10	Birmingham A.C.	Birmingham	W	14-0
Feb. 22, 1893	Auburn	Birmingham	L	32-22
Coach: E.B. Beaumont				96-37
Captain: William G. Little				

William G. Little, originally from Livingston, Alabama, returned to his home state after the death of his brother and enrolled at the University of Alabama. He subsequently organized a group of students to play a game he learned at Phillips Exeter Academy in New England and served as captain. The day before facing the more-experienced Birmingham Athletic Club, Alabama played a group of high school players and won 56–0. It then lost to the club team but won the rematch a month later. Helping make up the roster were a future speaker of the United States House of Representatives, a governor, a state senator, a judge, a doctor, and other prominent businessmen and lawyers. ... The season also featured the first game against Auburn.

1893
0-4

Oct. 14	Birmingham A.C.	Tuscaloosa	L	4-0
Nov. 4	Birmingham A.C.	Birmingham	L	10-8
Nov. 11	Sewanee	Birmingham	L	20-0
Nov. 30	Auburn	Montgomery	L	40-16
Coach: Eli Abbott				24-74
Captains: G.H. Kyser, William Walker				

Eli Abbott, who played fullback and tackle, took over as coach. ... Alabama played its first out-of-state opponent, losing 20–0 to Sewanee in Birmingham. ... The first two women were allowed to enroll at Alabama.

1894
3–1

Oct. 27	Ole Miss	Jackson	L	6–0
Nov. 3	Tulane	New Orleans	W	18–6
Nov. 15	Sewanee	Birmingham	W	24–4
Nov. 29	Auburn	Montgomery	W	18–0
Coach: Eli Abbott				60–16
Captain: S.B. Slone				

Alabama picked up the nickname "The Thin Red Line," which was borrowed from the Rudyard Kipling poem "Tommy" about a British soldier. ... After losing its first game in another state, 6–0 to Ole Miss, Eli Abbott scored four touchdowns (worth four points each) for a 18–6 victory against Tulane in New Orleans. Abbott's 75-yard touchdown keyed the first victory against Auburn, 18–0. Abbott was also accused of being paid a salary, making him a professional, in the school's first coaching controversy.

1895
0–4

Nov. 2	Georgia	Columbus	L	30–6
Nov. 16	Tulane	New Orleans	L	22–0
Nov. 18	LSU	Baton Rouge	L	12–6
Nov. 23	Auburn	Tuscaloosa	L	48–0
Coach: Eli Abbott				12–112
Captain: H.M. Bankhead				

Alabama played Auburn in Tuscaloosa for the first time and lost 48–0. ... The first three games of the season were played on the road, including losses to Tulane and LSU just two days apart.

Through the Years

1896
2-1

Oct. 24	Birmingham A.C.	Tuscaloosa	W	30-0
Oct. 31	Sewanee	Tuscaloosa	L	10-6
Nov. 14	Mississippi State	Tuscaloosa	W	20-0
Coach: Otto Wagonhurst				56-10
Captain: S.B. Slone				

Otto Wagonhurst took over as coach, while Eli Abbott continued to play. ... Alabama won its first game against Mississippi A&M, now known as Mississippi State.

1897
1-0

Nov. 13	Tuscaloosa A.C.	Tuscaloosa	W	6-0
Coach: Allen McCants				6-0
Captain: Frank S. White Jr.				

Alabama's Board of Trustees ruled it was undignified to play games off campus, making scheduling all but impossible. Alabama didn't play any games in 1898, but T.G. Burk was still named team captain.

1899
3-1

Oct. 21	Tuscaloosa A.C.	Tuscaloosa	W	16-5
Nov. 11	Montgomery A.C.	Tuscaloosa	W	16-0
Nov. 24	Ole Miss	Jackson	W	7-5
Nov. 25	New Orleans A.C.	New Orleans	L	21-0
Coach: W.A. Martin				39-31
Captain: T.W. Wert				

After students protested, the trustees lifted the travel ban for athletics. ... Alabama defeated Tuscaloosa Athletics, Montgomery Athletics, and Ole Miss before losing to New Orleans Athletics. Alabama finished the decade 11-13.

1900
2-3

Oct. 21	Taylor School	Tuscaloosa	W	35-0
Oct. 26	Ole Miss	Tuscaloosa	W	12-5
Nov. 3	Tulane	Tuscaloosa	L	6-0
Nov. 17	Auburn	Montgomery	L	53-5
Nov. 29	Clemson	Birmingham	L	35-0
Coach: M. Griffin				52-99
Captain: W.E. Drennen				

Alabama lost its last two games by a combined score of 88–5. ... Against Auburn, an upset Alabama fan threw his hat into the air, only to see Auburn tackle Michael Harvey mockingly kick it for an imaginary field goal. It led to a dispute, but after the season-ending loss to Clemson, Harvey was hired to coach Alabama.

1901
2-1-2

Oct. 19	Ole Miss	Tuscaloosa	W	41-0
Nov. 9	Georgia	Montgomery	T	0-0
Nov. 15	Auburn	Tuscaloosa	L	17-0
Nov. 16	Mississippi State	Tuscaloosa	W	45-0
Nov. 28	Tennessee	Birmingham	T	6-6
Coach: M.S. Harvey				92-23
Captain: W.E. Drennen				

Alabama played its first tie game, 0–0 against Georgia. ... The first game against Tennessee was called due to darkness with the score tied 6–6. Many of the 2,000 fans on hand rushed the field in protest.

The Tide may have been embarrassed by Clemson and Auburn in 1900, but more than a century later that has changed dramatically. The 2008 edition of the Crimson Tide beat the two Tigers by a combined score of 70–10.

1902
4–4

Oct. 10	Birmingham H.S.	Tuscaloosa	W	57–0
Oct. 13	Marion Institute	Tuscaloosa	W	81–0
Oct. 18	Auburn	Birmingham	L	23–0
Nov. 1	Georgia	Birmingham	L	5–0
Nov. 8	Mississippi State	Tuscaloosa	W	27–0
Nov. 11	Texas	Tuscaloosa	L	10–0
Nov. 27	Georgia Tech	Birmingham	W	26–0
Nov. 29	LSU	Tuscaloosa	L	11–0
Coaches: Eli Abbott, James Heyworth				191–49
Captain: J.R. Forman				

Alabama was led on the field by Auxford Burks. ...
James Heyworth and Eli Abbott served as co-head
coaches on a volunteer basis. According to the
Corolla yearbook: "Both refused any compensation
for their services. Mr. Heyworth not only did this
because of his love for the game, but he paid the
expenses of the substitutes to the Georgia game
in Birmingham." ... Alabama failed to score in its
four losses.

1903
3–4

Oct. 10	Vanderbilt	Nashville	L	30–0
Oct. 16	Mississippi State	Columbus	L	11–0
Oct. 23	Auburn	Montgomery	W	18–6
Nov. 2	Sewanee	Birmingham	L	23–0
Nov. 9	LSU	Tuscaloosa	W	18–0
Nov. 14	Cumberland	Tuscaloosa	L	44–0
Nov. 26	Tennessee	Birmingham	W	24–0
Coach: W.B. Blount				60–114
Captains: W.S. Wyatt				

Alabama pulled off a surprising upset of Auburn,
but the rivalry kicked up a notch when an Alabama
player was kicked in the head, rendering him
unconscious. ... Alabama played in Nashville for
the first time, losing 30–0 to Vanderbilt, but
pulled off shutouts against LSU and Tennessee.

1904

7–3

Oct. 3	Florida	Tuscaloosa	W	29–0
Oct. 8	Clemson	Birmingham	L	18–0
Oct. 15	Mississippi State	Columbus	W	6–0
Oct. 24	Nashville U	Tuscaloosa	W	17–0
Nov. 5	Georgia	Tuscaloosa	W	16–5
Nov. 12	Auburn	Birmingham	L	29–5
Nov. 24	Tennessee	Birmingham	L	5–0
Dec. 2	LSU	Baton Rouge	W	11–0
Dec. 3	Tulane	New Orleans	W	6–0
Dec. 4	Pensacola A.C.	Pensacola	W	10–5
Coach: W.B. Blount				100–62
Captain: W.S. Wyatt				

Alabama's first 10-game season was highlighted by a stretch with wins on three successive days: LSU in Baton Rouge, Tulane in New Orleans, and Pensacola Athletic Club in Pensacola. ... Alabama played Florida for the first time and won 29–0. ... The team was led by Auxford Burks, who in 1942 would be selected to the school's first all-time team.

After 10 years, business was thriving in the Southern Intercollegiate Athletic Association. When the conference finally disbanded in 1942, 27 of the current Division I-A teams had been a member at one time, along with 19 other schools.

Today the Crimson Tide usually have plenty to celebrate when it visits Atlanta, such as 2008's whipping of Clemson. Alabama lost 12–5 in its Atlanta debut, a visit to Georgia Tech.

1905
6–4

Oct. 3	Maryville	Tuscaloosa	W	17–0
Oct. 7	Vanderbilt	Nashville	L	34–0
Oct. 14	Mississippi State	Tuscaloosa	W	34–0
Oct. 21	Georgia Tech	Atlanta	L	12–5
Oct. 25	Clemson	Columbia	L	25–0
Nov. 4	Georgia	Birmingham	W	36–0
Nov. 9	Centre	Tuscaloosa	W	21–0
Nov. 18	Auburn	Birmingham	W	30–0
Nov. 23	Sewanee	Birmingham	L	42–6
Nov. 30	Tennessee	Birmingham	W	29–0
Coach: Jack Leavenworth				178–113
Captain: Auxford Burks				

Auxford Burks scored the first touchdown with a 95-yard kickoff return vs. Maryville. It apparently was the first kickoff return for a score in Alabama history. ... Alabama also played before the largest crowd in its history when 5,000 fans turned out in Birmingham for the Auburn game. ... Alabama played in Atlanta for the first time, losing to Georgia Tech.

1906
5–1

Oct. 6	Maryville	Tuscaloosa	W	6–0
Oct. 13	Howard	Tuscaloosa	W	14–0
Oct. 20	Vanderbilt	Nashville	L	78–0
Nov. 3	Mississippi State	Starkville	W	16–4
Nov. 17	Auburn	Birmingham	W	10–0
Nov. 29	Tennessee	Birmingham	W	51–0
Coach: J.W.H. "Doc" Pollard				97–82
Captain: Washington Moody				

With 11 players out due to injuries, new coach J.W.H. "Doc" Pollard tried to postpone or cancel the Vanderbilt game. Instead the Commodores handed Alabama its worst-ever defeat, 78–0. ... Pollard unveiled his new offense, the "Military Shift," against Auburn. Tigers Coach Mike Donahue was so upset with the formation, which had never been seen in the South before (Pollard learned it at Dartmouth), that he threatened to cancel the series.

1907
5-1-2

Oct. 5	Maryville	Tuscaloosa	W	17-0
Oct. 12	Ole Miss	Columbus	W	20-0
Oct. 21	Sewanee	Tuscaloosa	L	54-4
Oct. 25	Georgia	Montgomery	T	0-0
Nov. 2	Centre	Birmingham	W	12-0
Nov. 16	Auburn	Birmingham	T	6-6
Nov. 23	LSU	Mobile	W	6-4
Nov. 28	Tennessee	Birmingham	W	5-0
Coach: J.W.H. "Doc" Pollard				70-64
Captain: Emile Hannon				

"Pollard's Pets" had another new formation for Auburn, further intensifying the rivalry. When other issues couldn't be resolved, the series took a 41-year hiatus. ... Hugh Robert of the *Birmingham Age-Herald* referred to Alabama as the "Crimson Tide" for the first time in his article about the Auburn game. ... A blocked field goal returned for a touchdown by Derrill Pratt led a 5-0 victory against Tennessee on a cold, rainy Thanksgiving.

1908
6-1-1

Oct. 3	Wetumpka	Tuscaloosa	W	27-0
Oct. 10	Howard	Birmingham	W	17-0
Oct. 17	Cincinnati	Birmingham	W	16-0
Oct. 24	Georgia Tech	Atlanta	L	11-6
Oct. 31	Chattanooga	Tuscaloosa	W	23-6
Nov. 14	Georgia	Birmingham	T	6-6
Nov. 20	Haskell Institute	Tuscaloosa	W	9-8
Nov. 26	Tennessee	Birmingham	W	4-0
Coach: J.W.H. "Doc" Pollard				108-31
Captain: Henry Burks				
All-Conference: C.C. Countess, center				

A 9–8 victory against the Heskell Indians high-lighted the season, with Bryant Edwards' 65-yard interception return for a touchdown the difference. ... More than 4,000 attended the victory against Tennessee. A 47-yard field goal by Derrill Pratt, who missed seven other attempts, was the only score.

1909
5-1-2

Oct. 2	Union	Tuscaloosa	W	16-0
Oct. 9	Howard	Tuscaloosa	W	14-0
Oct. 16	Clemson	Birmingham	W	3-0
Oct. 23	Ole Miss	Jackson	T	0-0
Oct. 30	Georgia	Atlanta	W	14-0
Nov. 13	Tennessee	Knoxville	W	10-0
Nov. 20	Tulane	New Orleans	T	5-5
Nov. 25	LSU	Birmingham	L	12-6
Coach: J.W.H. "Doc" Pollard				68-17
Captain: Derrill Pratt				

Alabama played in Knoxville for the first time, winning 10–0. It was the Crimson Tide's fifth-straight shutout against the Volunteers. ... Pollard concluded his Alabama career with a 21–4–5 record. Alabama finished the decade 45–23–7.

1 Wins recorded by Doc Pollard in his only other coaching stop. He coached Lehigh in 1901 before coming to Alabama, dropping the other 11 games the Mountain Hawks played. Pollard also coached baseball at both schools.

1910
4-4

Oct. 1	Birmingham Sou	Tuscaloosa	W	25-0
Oct. 8	Marion Institute	Tuscaloosa	W	26-0
Oct. 15	Georgia	Birmingham	L	22-0
Oct. 22	Georgia Tech	Tuscaloosa	L	36-0
Nov. 5	Ole Miss	Greenville	L	16-0
Nov. 12	Sewanee	Birmingham	L	30-0
Nov. 19	Tulane	New Orleans	W	5-3
Nov. 24	Washington & Lee	Birmingham	W	9-0
Coach: Guy Lowman				65-107
Captain: O.C. Gresham				

A year after Doc Pollard left Alabama, his Washington & Lee team played the Crimson Tide on Thanksgiving. Farley Moody kicked a field goal and scored a touchdown on a 50-yard run for a 9-0 Alabama victory.

1911
5-2-2

Sept. 30	Howard	Tuscaloosa	W	24-0
Oct. 7	Georgia	Birmingham	L	11-3
Oct. 14	Birmingham Sou	Birmingham	W	47-5
Oct. 21	Mississippi State	Columbus	T	6-6
Oct. 29	Georgia Tech	Atlanta	T	0-0
Nov. 4	Marion Institute	Marion	W	35-0
Nov. 11	Sewanee	Tuscaloosa	L	3-0
Nov. 18	Tulane	Tuscaloosa	W	22-0
Nov. 30	Davidson	Birmingham	W	16-6
Coach: D.V. Graves				153-31
Captain: R.H. Burmgardner				

Even though Alabama didn't defeat Georgia Tech in Atlanta, the 0-0 final was considered a big step for the program. ... Standout Charlie Joplin would be killed in France during World War I.

1912
5-3-1

Sept. 28	Marion Institute	Tuscaloosa	W	25-0
Oct. 5	Birmingham Sou	Tuscaloosa	W	62-0
Oct. 12	Georgia Tech	Atlanta	L	20-3
Oct. 18	Mississippi State	Aberdeen	L	7-0
Oct. 26	Georgia	Columbus	L	13-9
Nov. 2	Tulane	New Orleans	W	7-0
Nov. 9	Ole Miss	Tuscaloosa	W	10-9
Nov. 16	Sewanee	Birmingham	T	6-6
Nov. 28	Tennessee	Birmingham	W	7-0
Coach: D.V. Graves				156-55
Captain: Farley W. Moody				

The team featured three VandeGraaff brothers: end Hargrove, tackle Bully, and back Adrian. ... Alabama played Tennessee for the first time since 1908 and recorded its sixth straight shutout in the series.

1913
6-3

Sept. 27	Howard	Tuscaloosa	W	27-0
Oct. 4	Birmingham Sou	Tuscaloosa	W	81-0
Oct. 11	Clemson	Tuscaloosa	W	20-0
Oct. 18	Georgia	Birmingham	L	20-0
Oct. 25	Tulane	New Orleans	W	26-0
Nov. 1	Mississippi College	Jackson	W	21-3
Nov. 9	Sewanee	Birmingham	L	10-7
Nov. 14	Tennessee	Tuscaloosa	W	6-0
Nov. 27	Mississippi State	Birmingham	L	7-0
Coach: D.V. Graves				188-40
Captain: C.H. VandeGraaff				

Hargrove VandeGraaff was one of eight players to score a touchdown in the 81-0 rout of Birmingham Southern. ... Charles Long and Bully VandeGraaff kicked field goals for the only points against Tennessee. When the game lasted into the evening hours, spectators with automobiles were asked to circle the field and turn on their headlights so play could continue. It was

The Alabama-Tennessee rivalry has been heated and occasionally bloody. The Crimson Tide has an eight-win cushion on the Third Saturday in October series, but the Volunteers have been plucky in the 2000s. Here, Shaud Williams turns the corner in 2002.

also Alabama's seventh-straight shutout against Tennessee. ... Bully VandeGraaff had to be prevented by teammates from ripping his ear off against Tennessee. "What really happened is his ear got a nasty cut at its top," Tennessee's S.D. "Bull" Beyer recalled in the book *Third Saturday in October*. "It was dangling from his head a bit, bleeding a lot. He got his ear caught in the leg of my pants a play or two later, and he got so mad about it that he jumped to his feet, grabbed his ear and tried to yank it from his head. Boy, he was a tough something. He wanted to throw away his ear so he could keep playing. In all my days of football, I never saw anything like that again."

1914
5–4

Oct. 3	Howard	Tuscaloosa	W	13–0
Oct. 10	Birmingham Sou	Tuscaloosa	W	54–0
Oct. 17	Georgia Tech	Birmingham	W	13–0
Oct. 24	Tennessee	Knoxville	L	17–7
Oct. 31	Tulane	Tuscaloosa	W	58–0
Nov. 7	Sewanee	Birmingham	L	18–0
Nov. 13	Chattanooga	Tuscaloosa	W	63–0
Nov. 26	Mississippi State	Birmingham	L	9–0
Dec. 2	Carlisle	Birmingham	L	20–3
Coach: D.V. Graves				211–64
Captain: C.A. "Tubby" Long				
All-conference: W.T. VandeGraaff, tackle				

After winning the first three games by a collective score of 80–0, quarterback Charlie Joplin was ruled ineligible because he had played professional baseball. ... Alabama defeated Georgia Tech for the first time.

1915
6–2

Oct. 2	Howard	Tuscaloosa	W	44–0
Oct. 9	Birmingham Sou	Tuscaloosa	W	67–0
Oct. 16	Mississippi College	Tuscaloosa	W	40–0
Oct. 23	Tulane	Tuscaloosa	W	16–0
Oct. 30	Sewanee	Birmingham	W	23–10
Nov. 6	Georgia Tech	Atlanta	L	21–7
Nov. 13	Texas	Austin	L	20–0
Nov. 25	Ole Miss	Birmingham	W	53–0
Coach: Thomas Kelley				250–51
Captain: William L. Harsh				
All-American: First team—W.T. "Bully" VandeGraaff, tackle				
All-conference: W.T. VandeGraaff, tackle				

Through the Years

Bully VandeGraaff became Alabama's first All-American. ... The 23–10 victory over Sewanee was the Crimson Tide's first against the Southern power since 1894. VandeGraaff had a 78-yard punt and scored 17 of Alabama's 23 points. ... With Coach Thomas Kelley hospitalized with typhoid fever, athletics director Lonnie Noojin and former player Farley Moody coached the victory.

Despite missing four games with typhoid fever, Thomas Kelley is still credited with Alabama's 2–2 record in his absence. After three years with Alabama he later coached at Missouri.

1916
6–3

Sept. 30	Birmingham Sou	Tuscaloosa	W	13–0
Oct. 7	Southern University	Tuscaloosa	W	80–0
Oct. 14	Mississippi College	Tuscaloosa	W	13–7
Oct. 21	Florida	Jacksonville	W	16–0
Oct. 28	Ole Miss	Tuscaloosa	W	27–0
Nov. 4	Sewanee	Birmingham	W	7–6
Nov. 11	Georgia Tech	Atlanta	L	13–0
Nov. 18	Tulane	New Orleans	L	33–0
Nov. 30	Georgia	Birmingham	L	3–0
Coach: Thomas Kelley				156–62
Captain: Lowndes Morton				

**Goree Johnson and Cecil Creen both scored
four touchdowns against Southern University. ...
Alabama played in the Sunshine State for the first
time, beating Florida 16–0 in Jacksonville.**

1917
5–2–1

Oct. 3	2nd Ambulance Co. Ohio	Montgomery	W	7–0
Oct. 12	Marion Institute	Tuscaloosa	W	13–0
Oct. 20	Mississippi College	Tuscaloosa	W	46–0
Oct. 26	Ole Miss	Tuscaloosa	W	64–0
Nov. 3	Sewanee	Birmingham	T	3–3
Nov. 10	Vanderbilt	Birmingham	L	7–2
Nov. 17	Kentucky	Lexington	W	27–0
Nov. 29	Camp Gordon	Birmingham	L	19–6
Coach: Thomas Kelley				168–29
Captain: Jack Hovater				

**Fullback Riggs Stephenson scored a record five
touchdowns in a 64–0 win over Ole Miss. ...
Alabama traveled to Kentucky for the first time
and won 27–0 in Lexington. ... Coach Thomas
Kelley finished his three-year run with a record
of 17–7–1. ... Due to World War I, Alabama
didn't field a team in 1918 but named Dan Boone
captain.**

Alabama President George H. Denny once said that Riggs
Stephenson (left) was "the embodiment of cleanliness,
manliness, and courage." After injuries ended his football
career, Stephenson had a successful baseball career, hitting .336 with the Cleveland Indians and Chicago Cubs.

1919
8–1

Oct. 4	Birmingham Sou	Tuscaloosa	W	27–0
Oct. 11	Ole Miss	Tuscaloosa	W	49–0
Oct. 18	Howard	Tuscaloosa	W	48–0
Oct. 24	Marion Institute	Tuscaloosa	W	61–0
Nov. 1	Sewanee	Birmingham	W	40–0
Nov. 8	Vanderbilt	Nashville	L	16–12
Nov. 15	LSU	Baton Rouge	W	23–0
Nov. 22	Georgia	Atlanta	W	6–0
Nov. 27	Mississippi State	Birmingham	W	14–6
Coach: Xen Scott				280–22
Captain: Isaac J. Rogers				
All-Southern Conference: Riggs Stephenson, halfback; Mulley Lenoir, halfback; Ike Rogers, guard				

Through the Years

Only a 16–12 loss to Vanderbilt kept Alabama from winning the Southern Conference title. ... Coach Xen Scott, a former horse racing writer from Cleveland, called fullback Riggs Stephenson a "better football player than Jim Thorpe." ... Mulley Lenoir scored 13 touchdowns. ... Alabama shut out seven of nine opponents.

Riggs Stephenson was one of the finest hitters in major league history. He is 22nd all-time in career batting average, and his .336 career mark is one of the highest of any player who is not in the Hall of Fame.

1920
10–1

Sept. 25	Southern Military	Tuscaloosa	W	59–0
Oct. 2	Marion Institute	Tuscaloosa	W	49–0
Oct. 9	Birmingham Sou	Tuscaloosa	W	45–0
Oct. 16	Mississippi College	Tuscaloosa	W	57–0
Oct. 23	Howard	Tuscaloosa	W	33–0
Oct. 30	Sewanee	Birmingham	W	21–0
Nov. 6	Vanderbilt	Birmingham	W	14–7
Nov. 11	LSU	Tuscaloosa	W	21–0
Nov. 20	Georgia	Atlanta	L	21–14
Nov. 25	Mississippi State	Birmingham	W	24–7
Nov. 27	Case College	Cleveland	W	40–0
Coach: Xen Scott				377–35
Captain: Sid Johnston				
All-American: Second team—Riggs Stephenson, halfback				
All-Southern Conference: Riggs Stephenson, halfback; E.B. "Mulley" Lenoir, halfback				

Alabama recorded its first 10-win season, notching eight shutouts. ... Alabama crossed the Mason-Dixon Line for the first time and defeated Case College in Cleveland, 40–0. ... Riggs Stephenson, who went on to have a successful pro baseball career, accounted for 286 yards in a 21–0 win over Sewanee, including a 53-yard interception return for a touchdown. ... Mulley Lenoir scored at least one touchdown in each game, including four against Howard, and finished the season with 25.

1921
5-4-2

Sept. 24	Howard	Tuscaloosa	W	34-14
Oct. 1	Spring Hill	Tuscaloosa	W	27-7
Oct. 8	Marion Institute	Tuscaloosa	W	55-0
Oct. 15	Bryson (Tenn.)	Tuscaloosa	W	95-0
Oct. 22	Sewanee	Birmingham	L	17-0
Oct. 29	LSU	New Orleans	T	7-7
Nov. 5	Vanderbilt	Birmingham	L	14-0
Nov. 11	Florida	Tuscaloosa	L	9-2
Nov. 19	Georgia	Atlanta	L	22-0
Nov. 24	Mississippi State	Birmingham	T	7-7
Dec. 3	Tulane	New Orleans	W	14-7
Coach: Xen Scott				241-104
Captain: Al Clemens				

Alabama played LSU in New Orleans for the only time in the series. ... The victory against Tulane, also in New Orleans, clinched a winning record in the rebuilding season. ... Coach Xen Scott hired future Alabama legend Hank Crisp as an assistant.

1922
6-3-1

Sept. 30	Marion Institute	Tuscaloosa	W	110-0
Oct. 7	Oglethorpe	Tuscaloosa	W	41-0
Oct. 14	Georgia Tech	Atlanta	L	33-7
Oct. 21	Sewanee	Birmingham	T	7-7
Oct. 28	Texas	Austin	L	19-10
Nov. 4	Pennsylvania	Philadelphia	W	9-7
Nov. 10	LSU	Tuscaloosa	W	47-3
Nov. 18	Kentucky	Lexington	L	6-0
Nov. 25	Georgia	Montgomery	W	10-6
Nov. 30	Mississippi State	Birmingham	W	59-0
Coach: Xen Scott				300-81
Captain: Ernest E. Cooper				
All-American: Second team—Shorty Propst, center				

In front of 25,000 fans, Alabama shocked Penn 9-7 in Philadelphia thanks to center Shorty

Propst recovering Pooley Hubert's fumble in the end zone. Thousands of fans greeted the returning team at the Tuscaloosa train depot. ... Suffering from throat cancer, which would soon take his life, Coach Xen Scott tendered his resignation in October. His career concluded with a 29–9–3 record.

1923
7-2-1

Sept. 29	Union	Tuscaloosa	W	12-0
Oct. 6	Ole Miss	Tuscaloosa	W	56-0
Oct. 13	Syracuse	Syracuse	L	23-0
Oct. 20	Sewanee	Birmingham	W	7-0
Oct. 27	Spring Hill	Mobile	W	56-0
Nov. 3	Georgia Tech	Atlanta	T	0-0
Nov. 10	Kentucky	Tuscaloosa	W	16-8
Nov. 16	LSU	Montgomery	W	30-3
Nov. 24	Georgia	Montgomery	W	36-0
Nov. 29	Florida	Birmingham	L	16-6
Coach: Wallace Wade				222-50
Captain: Al Clemons				

All-Southern Conference: Al Clemens, end; Grant Gillis, quarterback

Disciplinarian Wallace Wade, who had been an assistant at Vanderbilt, replaced Xen Scott. ... After losing 23–0 at Syracuse, Wade claimed the loss taught him more about football than any other game he coached.

After coaching at both Alabama and Duke in addition to serving time in the military, Wallace Wade was commissioner of the Southern Conference for nearly the entire 1950s.

Seen here at Duke, Wallace Wade was one of the first coaching legends at Alabama. He later led Duke to a pair of undefeated regular seasons, including 1941 when the Blue Devils went undefeated before losing the Rose Bowl in their home stadium.

1924

8–1, Southern Conference champions

Sept. 27	Union	Tuscaloosa	W	55–0
Oct. 4	Furman	Greenville, S.C.	W	20–0
Oct. 11	Mississippi College	Tuscaloosa	W	55–0
Oct. 18	Sewanee	Birmingham	W	14–0
Oct. 25	Georgia Tech	Atlanta	W	14–0
Nov. 1	Ole Miss	Montgomery	W	61–0
Nov. 8	Kentucky	Tuscaloosa	W	42–7
Nov. 15	Centre College	Birmingham	L	17–0
Nov. 27	Georgia	Birmingham	W	33–0
Coach: Wallace Wade				294–24
Captain: A.T.S. "Pooley" Hubert				

All-Southern Conference: Johnny Mack Brown, back; Bull Buckler, guard; Ben Compton, guard; A.T.S. "Pooley" Hubert, back

Even with the loss to Centre College, Alabama won its first championship. Georgia was rated the No. 1 team in the region before losing to the Crimson Tide 33–0. Pooley Hubert threw touchdown passes and Johnny Mack Brown returned an interception 65 yards for a touchdown.

After his playing days, Johnny Mack Brown went on to a successful career in the pre war movie industry. He acted in many notable pictures and was featured in no less than 127 westerns.

1925

10–0, National champions,
Southern Conference champions

Sept. 26	Union College	Tuscaloosa	W	53–0
Oct. 2	Birmingham Sou	Tuscaloosa	W	50–7
Oct. 10	LSU	Baton Rouge	W	42–0
Oct. 17	Sewanee	Birmingham	W	27–0
Oct. 24	Georgia Tech	Atlanta	W	7–0
Oct. 31	Mississippi State	Tuscaloosa	W	6–0
Nov. 7	Kentucky	Birmingham	W	31–0
Nov. 14	Florida	Montgomery	W	34–0
Nov. 26	Georgia	Birmingham	W	27–0
Jan. 1	Washington	Rose Bowl	W	20–19
Coach: Wallace Wade				297–26
Captain: Bruce Jones				

All-American: First team—A.T.S. "Pooley" Hubert, quarterback
Second team—Johnny Mack Brown, halfback

All-Southern Conference: Johnny Mack Brown, back; Bill Buckler, guard; A.T.S. "Pooley" Hubert, back

Despite recording eight shutouts, Alabama wasn't the first choice of the Rose Bowl selection committee and was subsequently considered an underdog. Johnny Mack Brown caught two touchdown passes to be named MVP of the Rose Bowl, and Pooley Hubert ran for another score. ... Alabama won its first national title, sharing the honor with Dartmouth. ... Alabama allowed just one touchdown during the regular season. ... Alabama was the first Southern school to play in the Rose Bowl. Georgia Tech turned down an invitation in 1917 because players didn't want to wait any longer to enroll in the military for World War I.

Through the Years

1926

9–0–1, National champions,
Southern Conference champions

Sept. 24	Millsaps	Tuscaloosa	W	54–0
Oct. 2	Vanderbilt	Nashville	W	19–7
Oct. 9	Mississippi State	Meridian	W	26–7
Oct. 16	Georgia Tech	Atlanta	W	21–0
Oct. 23	Sewanee	Birmingham	W	2–0
Oct. 30	LSU	Tuscaloosa	W	24–0
Nov. 6	Kentucky	Birmingham	W	14–0
Nov. 13	Florida	Montgomery	W	49–0
Nov. 25	Georgia	Birmingham	W	33–6
Jan. 1	Stanford	Rose Bowl	T	7–7
Coach: Wallace Wade				249–27
Captain: Emile "Red" Barnes				

All-American: First team—Hoyt "Wu" Winslett, end; Fred Pickhard, tackle

All-Southern Conference: Emile "Red" Barnes, back; Herschel Caldwell, back; Gordon Holmes, center; Fred Pickhard, tackle; Hoyt Winslett, end

Alabama, Stanford, Navy, and Lafayette were all declared national champions by various organizations before the Crimson Tide reached Pasadena to play Stanford in the Rose Bowl. Fred Pickhard was named Rose Bowl MVP. ... Pickhard's blocked punt that went through the end zone for a safety was the difference against Sewanee. The following week against LSU he blocked two punts, both resulting in touchdowns. ... The Rose Bowl featured the first transcontinental radio broadcast of a sporting event on NBC.

1927
5-4-1

Sept. 24	Millsaps	Tuscaloosa	W	46-0
Sept. 30	So. Presbyterian U.	Tuscaloosa	W	31-0
Oct. 8	LSU	Birmingham	T	0-0
Oct. 15	Georgia Tech	Atlanta	L	13-0
Oct. 22	Sewanee	Birmingham	W	24-0
Oct. 29	Mississippi State	Tuscaloosa	W	13-7
Nov. 5	Kentucky	Birmingham	W	21-6
Nov. 12	Florida	Montgomery	L	13-6
Nov. 27	Georgia	Birmingham	L	20-6
Dec. 3	Vanderbilt	Birmingham	L	14-7
Coach: Wallace Wade				154-73
Captain: Fred Pickhard				
All-Southern Conference: Fred Pickhard.				

Alabama played at what evolved into Legion
Field in Birmingham for the first time, losing to
Georgia. The week before, Howard (which became
Samford) played Birmingham Southern there.

1928
6-3

Oct. 6	Ole Miss	Tuscaloosa	W	27-0
Oct. 13	Mississippi State	Starkville	W	46-0
Oct. 20	Tennessee	Tuscaloosa	L	15-13
Oct. 27	Sewanee	Birmingham	W	42-12
Nov. 3	Wisconsin	Madison	L	15-0
Nov. 10	Kentucky	Montgomery	W	14-0
Nov. 17	Georgia Tech	Atlanta	L	33-13
Nov. 29	Georgia	Birmingham	W	19-0
Dec. 8	LSU	Birmingham	W	13-0
Coach: Wallace Wade				187-75
Captain: Earle Smith				

Alabama traveled to play at a Big Ten school for
the first time and lost 15-0 at Wisconsin. ...
Work began on a new home for the Crimson Tide
in Tuscaloosa: Denny Stadium.

Through the Years

COACH PAUL

Today cramming more than 92,000 into its gates, Bryant-Denny Stadium got off to a modest start as Denny Stadium in 1929. Expansion started in 1937 and the stadium has been enlarged and improved upon ever since.

1929
6–3

Sept. 28	Mississippi College	Tuscaloosa	W	55-0
Oct. 5	Mississippi	Tuscaloosa	W	22-7
Oct. 12	Chattanooga	Tuscaloosa	W	46-0
Oct. 19	Tennessee	Knoxville	L	6-0
Oct. 26	Sewanee	Birmingham	W	35-7
Nov. 2	Vanderbilt	Nashville	L	13-0
Nov. 9	Kentucky	Montgomery	W	24-13
Nov. 16	Georgia Tech	Atlanta	W	13-0
Nov. 28	Georgia	Birmingham	L	12-0
Coach: Wallace Wade				196-58
Captain: Billy Hicks				
All-American: First team—Tony Holm, fullback; Fred Sington, tackle				
All-Southern Conference: Tony Holm, back; Fred Sington, tackle				

Denny Stadium, named after university president George Denny, was dedicated by Governor Bibb Graves on October 5, 1929, with Alabama defeating Ole Miss 22–7. Original capacity was 12,000. … Alabama finished the decade 72–21–6.

101,000

Approximate capacity of Bryant-Denny Stadium when the new south end zone expansion project is finished in 2010. The project was given final approval in 2009, and construction will take place through the summer of 2010.

1930

10–0, National champions,
Southern Conference champions

Sept. 27	Howard	Tuscaloosa	W	43–0
Oct. 4	Ole Miss	Tuscaloosa	W	64–0
Oct. 11	Sewanee	Birmingham	W	25–0
Oct. 18	Tennessee	Tuscaloosa	W	18–6
Oct. 25	Vanderbilt	Birmingham	W	12–7
Nov. 1	Kentucky	Lexington	W	19–0
Nov. 8	Florida	Gainesville	W	20–0
Nov. 15	LSU	Montgomery	W	33–0
Nov. 27	Georgia	Birmingham	W	13–0
Jan. 1	Washington State	Rose Bowl	W	24–0
Coach: Wallace Wade				271–13
Captain: Charles B. Clement				

All-American: First team—John Suther, halfback; Fred Sington, tackle. Second team—Johnny Cain, halfback

All-Southern Conference: Fred Sington, tackle; John Suther, back; John Miller, guard; Johnny Cain, back

Coach Wallace Wade announced in the spring that he would leave at the end of the season for Duke, and his replacement, Frank Thomas, was on hand for the trip to California for the Rose Bowl. Clyde Bolton of the *Birmingham News* called it the "greatest swan song in the history of football." ... Against Washington State Wade started his second unit, leaving his best players on the bench until the second quarter, when the opposition began to wear down. ... John "Monk" Campbell was named Rose Bowl MVP. ... Tennessee and Vanderbilt were the only teams to score against Alabama. ... Wade finished with a record of 61–13–3. ... Rudy Vallee dedicated the song "Football Freddy" to Fred Sington.

1931

9-1

Sept. 26	Howard	Tuscaloosa	W	42-0
Oct. 3	Ole Miss	Tuscaloosa	W	55-6
Oct. 10	Mississippi State	Meridian	W	53-0
Oct. 17	Tennessee	Knoxville	L	25-0
Oct. 24	Sewanee	Birmingham	W	3-0
Oct. 31	Kentucky	Tuscaloosa	W	9-7
Nov. 7	Florida	Birmingham	W	41-0
Nov. 14	Clemson	Montgomery	W	74-7
Nov. 26	Vanderbilt	Nashville	W	14-6
Dec. 2	Chattanooga	Chattanooga	W	39-0
Coach: Frank Thomas				360-51
Captain: Joe Sharpe				
All-American: First team—Johnny Cain, fullback				
All-Southern Conference: Johnny Cain, fullback				

Coach Frank Thomas implemented Notre Dame's "Box Formation" offense, which steamrolled every opponent except Tennessee. ... Alabama's 36 points per game set a team record.

1932

8-2

Sept. 24	Southwestern	Tuscaloosa	W	45-6
Oct. 1	Mississippi State	Montgomery	W	53-0
Oct. 8	George Washington	Washington D.C.	W	28-6
Oct. 15	Tennessee	Birmingham	L	7-3
Oct. 22	Ole Miss	Tuscaloosa	W	24-13
Oct. 29	Kentucky	Lexington	W	12-7
Nov. 5	Virginia Tech	Tuscaloosa	W	9-6
Nov. 12	Georgia Tech	Atlanta	L	6-0
Nov. 24	Vanderbilt	Birmingham	W	20-0
Dec. 3	St. Mary's	San Francisco	W	6-0
Coach: Frank Thomas				200-51
Captain: Johnny Cain				
All-American: First team—Johnny Cain, fullback				
All-Southern Conference: Johnny Cain, fullback; Tom Hupke, guard				

Johnny "Hurry" Cain's 81-yard touchdown run against St. Mary's in San Francisco highlighted the season. ... In a driving rainstorm against Tennessee, Cain punted 19 times, averaging 48 yards. ... Plans to create the offshoot Southeastern Conference were being formulated at a December meeting in Knoxville.

1933

7-1-1, SEC champions

Sept. 30	Oglethorpe	Tuscaloosa	W	34-0
Oct. 7	Ole Miss	Birmingham	T	0-0
Oct. 14	Mississippi State	Tuscaloosa	W	18-0
Oct. 21	Tennessee	Knoxville	W	12-6
Oct. 28	Fordham	New York	L	2-0
Nov. 4	Kentucky	Birmingham	W	20-0
Nov. 11	Virginia Tech	Tuscaloosa	W	27-0
Nov. 18	Georgia Tech	Atlanta	W	12-9
Nov. 30	Vanderbilt	Nashville	W	7-0
Coach: Frank Thomas				130-17
Captain: Foy Leach				

All-American: First team—Tom Hupke, guard. Second team—Dixie Howell, halfback; Bill Lee, tackle

All-SEC: Dixie Howell, halfback; Tom Hupke, guard

Alabama won the first SEC championship. Road wins against Tennessee, Georgia Tech, and Vanderbilt keyed the title, and UA overcame the scoreless tie against Ole Miss in Birmingham. ... Making the conference's first trip to New York, the Crimson Tide lost a controversial 2-0 game to Fordham at the Polo Grounds.

1934

10–0, National champions, SEC champions

Date	Opponent	Location		Score
Sept. 29	Howard	Tuscaloosa	W	24–0
Oct. 5	Sewanee	Montgomery	W	35–6
Oct. 13	Mississippi State	Tuscaloosa	W	41–0
Oct. 20	Tennessee	Birmingham	W	13–6
Oct. 27	Georgia	Birmingham	W	26–6
Nov. 3	Kentucky	Lexington	W	34–14
Nov. 10	Clemson	Tuscaloosa	W	40–0
Nov. 17	Georgia Tech	Atlanta	W	40–0
Nov. 29	Vanderbilt	Birmingham	W	34–0
Jan. 1	Stanford	Rose Bowl	W	29–13
Coach: Frank Thomas				316–45
Captain: Bill Lee				

All-American: First team—Millard "Dixie" Howell, back; Don Hutson, end; Bill Lee, tackle

All-SEC: Dixie Howell, halfback; Don Hutson, end; Bill Lee, tackle; Charlie Marr, guard

Alabama shared the national title with Minnesota and Pittsburgh, but Coach Frank Thomas called this his best team. ... Dixie Howell scored two touchdowns, on a 67-yard run and a 59-yard pass to Don Hutson, to be named Rose Bowl MVP. He averaged 43.8 yards a punt, gained 111 yards rushing, and 160 passing. He was also named SEC Player of the Year. ... Alabama averaged 31.4 points a game, compared to 4.5 allowed.

Dixie Howell was not only a stellar quarterback, he was a fantastic punter as well. For his exploits in the "Grandaddy of them All," Howell was named to the all-time Rose Bowl team.

1935
6-2-1

Sept. 28	Howard	Tuscaloosa	T	7-7
Oct. 5	George Washington	Washington D.C.	W	39-0
Oct. 12	Mississippi State	Tuscaloosa	L	20-7
Oct. 19	Tennessee	Knoxville	W	25-0
Oct. 26	Georgia	Athens	W	17-7
Nov. 2	Kentucky	Birmingham	W	13-0
Nov. 9	Clemson	Tuscaloosa	W	33-0
Nov. 16	Georgia Tech	Birmingham	W	38-7
Nov. 28	Vanderbilt	Nashville	L	14-6
Coach: Frank Thomas				185-55
Captain: James Walker				
All-American: First team—Riley Smith, back				
All-SEC: Riley Smith, back; James Whatley, tackle				

Despite sustaining a broken leg against Mississippi State, end Paul W. "Bear" Bryant continued to play and led a 25-0 victory against Tennessee. ... Alabama traveled to Washington D.C. for the first time and defeated George Washington 39-0. ... Riley Smith was named the first recipient of the Jacobs Trophy, awarded to the SEC's best blocker. Originally a fullback on the 7-1-1 team in 1933, he switched to quarterback the following year. The following spring Riley was the second-overall player picked in the first NFL Draft by the Boston Redskins. Jay Berwanger, the Heisman Trophy winner from Chicago, was selected first by the Philadelphia Eagles but didn't sign.

1936
8-0-1

Sept. 26	Howard	Tuscaloosa	W	34-0
Oct. 3	Clemson	Tuscaloosa	W	32-0
Oct. 10	Mississippi State	Tuscaloosa	W	7-0
Oct. 17	Tennessee	Birmingham	T	0-0
Oct. 24	Loyola (N.O.)	New Orleans	W	13-6
Oct. 31	Kentucky	Lexington	W	14-0
Nov. 7	Tulane	Birmingham	W	34-7
Nov. 14	Georgia Tech	Atlanta	W	20-16
Nov. 25	Vanderbilt	Birmingham	W	14-6
Coach: Frank Thomas				168-35
Captain: James "Bubber" Nisbet				
Ranking (AP): Preseason NR; Postseason No. 4				
All-American: First team—Arthur "Tarzan" White, guard; James "Bubber" Nesbit, fullback				
All-SEC: Arthur "Tarzan" White, guard; Riley Smith, quarterback				

In the inaugural year of the Associated Press poll, Alabama finished fourth, with a 0–0 tie against Tennessee costing the Crimson Tide any chance of a national championship and a postseason bowl. … Paul W. "Bear" Bryant joined the coaching staff as an assistant.

1937
9-1, SEC champions

Sept. 25	Howard	Tuscaloosa	W	41-0
Oct. 2	Sewanee	Birmingham	W	65-0
Oct. 9	South Carolina	Tuscaloosa	W	20-0
Oct. 16	Tennessee	Knoxville	W	14-7
Oct. 23	George Washington	Washington D.C.	W	19-0
Oct. 30	Kentucky	Tuscaloosa	W	41-0
Nov. 6	Tulane	New Orleans	W	9-6
Nov. 13	Georgia Tech	Birmingham	W	7-0
Nov. 25	Vanderbilt	Nashville	W	9-7
Jan. 1	California	Rose Bowl	L	13-0
Coach: Frank Thomas				225-33
Captain: Leroy Monsky				
Ranking (AP): Preseason No. 2; Postseason No. 4				

Through the Years

All-American: First team—Joe Kilgrow, halfback; Leroy Monsky, guard; James Ryba, tackle

All-SEC: Joe Kilgrow, halfback; Leroy Monsky, guard; Erwin "Tut" Warren, end

Leaders: Rushing—Charley Holm (607 yards, 117 carries); Passing—Joe Kilgrow (20 of 57, 302 yards)

Plagued by four lost fumbles, Alabama lost in the Rose Bowl for the only time in its history. Vic Botari had 137 yards on 34 carries and scored two touchdowns for Cal. ... Guard Leroy Monsky won the Jacobs Trophy while Joe Kilgrow was fifth in Heisman Trophy voting. ... Kicker Sandy Sanford made last-minute field goals against Tulane and Vanderbilt.

1938
7-1-1

Sept. 24	Southern California	Los Angeles	W	19–7
Oct. 1	Howard	Tuscaloosa	W	34–0
Oct. 8	NC State	Tuscaloosa	W	14–0
Oct. 15	Tennessee	Birmingham	L	13–0
Oct. 22	Sewanee	Tuscaloosa	W	32–0
Oct. 29	Kentucky	Lexington	W	26–6
Nov. 5	Tulane	Birmingham	W	3–0
Nov. 12	Georgia Tech	Atlanta	T	14–14
Nov. 24	Vanderbilt	Birmingham	W	7–0
Coach: Frank Thomas				149–40
Captain: Lew Bostick				
Ranking (AP): Preseason No. 15; Postseason No. 13				
All-SEC: Charles Holm, back				
Leaders: Rushing—Herky Mosley (465 yards, 78 carries); Passing—Herky Mosley (28 of 63, 334 yards)				

Coming off a loss in the Rose Bowl, Coach Frank Thomas took the Crimson Tide back to the West Coast, where it opened the season with a 19–7 victory against Southern California. The Trojans went on to play in the Rose Bowl and upset Duke, coached by Wallace Wade, 7–3. The Blue Devils went into the game without having given up a point.

1939
5-3-1

Sept. 30	Howard	Tuscaloosa	W	21-0
Oct. 7	Fordham	New York	W	7-6
Oct. 14	Mercer	Tuscaloosa	W	20-0
Oct. 21	Tennessee	Knoxville	L	21-0
Oct. 28	Mississippi State	Tuscaloosa	W	7-0
Nov. 4	Kentucky	Birmingham	T	7-7
Nov. 11	Tulane	New Orleans	L	13-0
Nov. 18	Georgia Tech	Birmingham	L	6-0
Nov. 30	Vanderbilt	Nashville	W	39-0
Coach: Frank Thomas				101-53
Captain: Carey Cox				
All-American: First team—Carey Cox, center Second team— Harold Newman, end				
Leaders: Rushing—Paul Spencer (514 yards, 100 carries); Passing—Herky Mosley (15 of 36, 172 yards)				

Alabama scored 39 of its 101 points in the season finale against Vanderbilt. ... Highlighting the season was a 7-6 victory in New York against Fordham, which featured the "Seven Blocks of Granite," including Vince Lombardi. ... For the decade, Alabama finished with a record of 79-11-5.

Frank Thomas never coached a losing team thanks to his commitment to defense. His defenses only allowed opponents to score 6.3 points per game, an interesting focus for a coach who had been a star quarterback at Notre Dame under Knute Rockne.

1940
7-2

Sept. 27	Spring Hill	Mobile	W	26-0
Oct. 5	Mercer	Tuscaloosa	W	20-0
Oct. 12	Howard	Tuscaloosa	W	31-0
Oct. 19	Tennessee	Birmingham	L	27-12
Nov. 2	Kentucky	Lexington	W	25-0
Nov. 9	Tulane	Birmingham	W	13-6
Nov. 16	Georgia Tech	Atlanta	W	14-13
Nov. 23	Vanderbilt	Birmingham	W	25-21
Nov. 30	Mississippi State	Tuscaloosa	L	13-0
Coach: Frank Thomas				166-80

Captain: Harold Newman

All-SEC: Fred Davis, tackle; Jimmy Nelson, back; Holt Rast, end

Leaders: Rushing—Paul Spencer (503 yards, 104 carries); Passing—Jimmy Nelson (21 of 43, 231 yards); Receiving—Holt Rast (8 catches, 110 yards)

Alabama played under the lights for the first time, defeating Spring Hill 26–0 at Murphy High School Stadium in Mobile. ... Paul W. "Bear" Bryant left Alabama to join Red Sanders' Vanderbilt staff.

1941
9-2, National champions

Sept. 27	SW Louisiana	Tuscaloosa	W	47-6
Oct. 4	Mississippi State	Tuscaloosa	L	14-0
Oct. 11	Howard	Birmingham	W	61-0
Oct. 18	Tennessee	Knoxville	W	9-2
Oct. 25	Georgia	Birmingham	W	27-14
Nov. 1	Kentucky	Tuscaloosa	W	30-0
Nov. 8	Tulane	New Orleans	W	19-14
Nov. 15	Georgia Tech	Birmingham	W	20-0
Nov. 22	Vanderbilt	Nashville	L	7-0
Nov. 28	Miami (Fla.)	Miami	W	21-7
Jan. 1	Texas A&M	Cotton Bowl	W	29-21
Coach: Frank Thomas				263-85

Captain: John Wyhonic

Ranking (AP): Preseason NR; Postseason No. 20

All-American: First team—Holt Rast, End Second team—Jimmy

Nelson, halfback

All-SEC: Jimmy Nelson, back; Holt Rast, back; John Wyhonic, guard

Leaders: Rushing—Jimmy Nelson (361 yards, 109 carries); Passing—Jimmy Nelson (25 of 54, 394 yards); Receiving—Holt Rast (13 catches, 207 yards)

Although most polls had Minnesota as the national champion, the Houlgate system had Alabama No. 1, while another service honored Texas. ... Halfback Jimmy Nelson returned a punt 72 yards for a touchdown and also scored on a 21-yard run in the Cotton Bowl. End Holt Rast returned an interception for a touchdown and Russ Craft scored twice, with all three players sharing the MVP award. ... Alabama played in Miami for the first time, defeating the Hurricanes 21–7 in the season finale.

1942
8–3

Sept. 25	SW Louisiana	Montgomery	W	54–0
Oct. 3	Mississippi State	Tuscaloosa	W	21–6
Oct. 10	Pensacola N.A.S.	Mobile	W	27–0
Oct. 17	Tennessee	Birmingham	W	8–0
Oct. 24	Kentucky	Lexington	W	14–0
Oct. 31	Georgia	Atlanta	L	21–10
Nov. 7	South Carolina	Tuscaloosa	W	29–0
Nov. 14	Georgia Tech	Atlanta	L	7–0
Nov. 21	Vanderbilt	Birmingham	W	27–7
Nov. 28	Georgia Pre-Flight	Birmingham	L	35–19
Jan. 1	Boston College	Orange Bowl	W	37–21
Coach: Frank Thomas				246–97

Captain: Joe Domnanovich

Ranking (AP): Preseason No. 4; Postseason No. 10

All-American: First team—Joe Domnanovich, center; Don Whitmire, tackle

All-SEC: Joe Domnanovich, center; Don Whitmire, tackle

Leaders: Rushing—Russ Craft (417 yards, 68 carries); Passing—Russ Mosley (24 of 48, 352 yards); Receiving—Sam Sharpe (13 catches, 240 yards)

Down 14–0 to Boston College in the Orange Bowl, center Joe Domnanovich and tackle Don Whitmire—who would both enter the Naval Academy and become All-Americans for the Midshipmen—led the comeback. Wheeler Leath and Bobby Tom Jenkins both scored two touchdowns. Holt Rast, Don Whitmire, and Jimmy Nelson shared the MVP award. ... One of the Crimson Tide's losses was to Georgia Pre-Flight, featuring players from around the country. ... Alabama didn't field a team in 1943 due to World War II.

1944
5-2-2

Sept. 30	LSU	Baton Rouge	T	27–27
Oct. 7	Howard	Birmingham	W	63–7
Oct. 14	Millsaps	Tuscaloosa	W	55–0
Oct. 21	Tennessee	Knoxville	T	0–0
Oct. 27	Kentucky	Montgomery	W	41–0
Nov. 4	Georgia	Birmingham	L	14–7
Nov. 11	Ole Miss	Mobile	W	34–6
Nov. 18	Mississippi State	Tuscaloosa	W	19–0
Jan. 1	Duke	Sugar Bowl	L	29–26
Coach: Frank Thomas				272–83
Captain: None (game-by-game)				

Leaders: Rushing—Harry Gilmer (405 yards, 72 carries); Passing—Harry Gilmer (32 of 66, 418 yards); Receiving—Hugh Morrow (10 catches, 107 yards)

Harry Gilmer led the "War Baby Tiders" and despite a 29–26 loss to Duke in the Sugar Bowl was named the game's MVP. It was Alabama's first appearance in the Sugar Bowl. ... Vaughn Mancha played all 60 minutes of the Sugar Bowl. ... Most of the team was comprised of 17-year-old boys too young to be drafted, students medically disqualified from military service, and returning veterans. The conference also waived its rule against freshman participation. ... Gilmer returned a kickoff 95 yards for a touchdown in the season opener against LSU. Legendary sportswriter Grantland Rice wrote that he was "the greatest college passer I've ever seen."

1945

10–0, SEC champions

Sept. 29	Keesler AAF	Biloxi	W	21–0
Oct. 6	LSU	Baton Rouge	W	26–7
Oct. 13	South Carolina	Montgomery	W	55–0
Oct. 20	Tennessee	Birmingham	W	25–7
Oct. 27	Georgia	Birmingham	W	28–14
Nov. 3	Kentucky	Louisville	W	60–19
Nov. 17	Vanderbilt	Nashville	W	71–0
Nov. 24	Pensacola NAS	Tuscaloosa	W	55–6
Dec. 1	Mississippi State	Tuscaloosa	W	55–13
Jan. 1	S. California	Rose Bowl	W	34–14
Coach: Frank Thomas				430–80

Captain: None (game-by-game)

Ranking (AP): Preseason No. 7; Postseason No. 3

All-American: First team—Harry Gilmer, halfback; Vaughn Mancha, center

All-SEC: Harry Gilmer, back; Vaughn Mancha, center; Rebel Steiner, end; Tom Whitley, tackle

Leaders: Rushing—Lowell Tew (715 yards, 88 carries); Passing—Harry Gilmer (57 of 88, 905 yards); Receiving—Rebel Steiner (18 catches, 315 yards)

Despite the perfect season, Alabama finished second in most polls to Army. The exceptions were the National Championship Foundation, the Cliff Morgan Foundation, and the Ray Byrne Foundation. Twenty years after Alabama became the first Southern team invited to the Rose Bowl, it became the last team to play in the bowl before an affiliation agreement with the Big Ten and Pac-8 was signed. Harry Gilmer, the SEC Player of the Year, was named Rose Bowl MVP. ... Against Kentucky, Gilmer had 216 rushing yards on six carries (for a 36-yard average), the first time in Crimson Tide history the 200-yard mark was eclipsed. ... Hugh Morrow won the NCAA title for scoring by a kicker.

Harry Gilmer (left) and Vaughn Mancha flank head coach
Frank Thomas as they arrive in California for the Rose
Bowl. The Crimson Tide's win capped off a perfect season
that fell just shy of the national championship.

1946

7-4

Sept. 20	Furman	Birmingham	W	26-7
Sept. 28	Tulane	New Orleans	W	7-6
Oct. 5	South Carolina	Columbia	W	14-6
Oct. 12	SW Louisiana	Tuscaloosa	W	54-0
Oct. 19	Tennessee	Knoxville	L	12-0
Oct. 26	Kentucky	Montgomery	W	21-7
Nov. 2	Georgia	Athens	L	14-0
Nov. 9	LSU	Baton Rouge	L	31-21
Nov. 16	Vanderbilt	Birmingham	W	12-7
Nov. 23	Boston College	Boston	L	13-7
Nov. 30	Mississippi State	Tuscaloosa	W	24-7
Coach: Frank Thomas				186-110
Captain: None (game-by-game)				
Ranking (AP): Preseason No. 6; Postseason NR				
All-SEC: Harry Gilmer, back				

Leaders: Rushing—Harry Gilmer (497 yards, 133 carries); Passing—Harry Gilmer (69 of 160, 930 yards); Receiving—Ted Cook (24 catches, 377 yards)

Harry Gilmer returned 37 punts for a team-record 436 yards. ... Due to health reasons, Coach Frank Thomas retired with a record of 115–24–7. ... Alabama's 21–7 victory against Kentucky came against Thomas' former assistant Paul W. "Bear" Bryant. ... Hal Self won the Jacobs Trophy. ... Harry Gilmer led the nation in punt returns.

21

After his stellar playing career, Hal Self got involved in coaching. He led the North Alabama Lions through some of their glory days, taking the helm for 21 seasons before retiring.

Through the Years

1947
8–3

Sept. 20	Southern Miss	Birmingham	W	34–7
Sept. 27	Tulane	New Orleans	L	21–20
Oct. 4	Vanderbilt	Nashville	L	14–7
Oct. 11	Duquesne	Tuscaloosa	W	26–0
Oct. 18	Tennessee	Birmingham	W	10–0
Oct. 25	Georgia	Athens	W	17–7
Nov. 1	Kentucky	Lexington	W	13–0
Nov. 15	Georgia Tech	Birmingham	W	14–7
Nov. 22	LSU	Tuscaloosa	W	41–12
Nov. 29	Miami (Fla.)	Miami	W	21–6
Jan. 1	Texas	Sugar Bowl	L	27–7

Coach: Harold "Red" Drew — 210–101

Captain: John Wozniak

Ranking (AP): Preseason NR; Postseason No. 6

All-American: Second team—Harry Gilmer, halfback

All-SEC: Harry Gilmer, back; John Wozniak, center

Leaders: Rushing—Lowell Tew (571 yards, 107 carries); Passing—Harry Gilmer (57 of 93, 610 yards); Receiving—Rebel Steiner (23 catches, 295 yards)

After coaching Ole Miss for one season, Coach Harold "Red" Drew took over the Crimson Tide. ... Alabama closed the regular season with a 21–6 victory against Miami, with the Auburn rivalry renewed a year later. ... Harry Gilmer ended his illustrious career as Alabama's all-time leader in rushing, passing, punt returns, kickoff returns, and interceptions.

1948
6–4–1

Sept. 25	Tulane	New Orleans	L	21–14
Oct. 2	Vanderbilt	Mobile	T	14–14
Oct. 8	Duquesne	Tuscaloosa	W	48–6
Oct. 16	Tennessee	Knoxville	L	21–6
Oct. 23	Mississippi State	Starkville	W	10–7
Oct. 30	Georgia	Birmingham	L	35–0
Nov. 6	Southern Miss	Tuscaloosa	W	27–0

Nov. 13	Georgia Tech	Atlanta	W	14-12
Nov. 20	LSU	Baton Rouge	L	26-6
Nov. 27	Florida	Tuscaloosa	W	34-28
Dec. 4	Auburn	Birmingham	W	55-0
Coach: Harold "Red" Drew				228-170
Captain: Ray Richeson				

Leaders: Rushing—Ed Salem (288 yards, 77 carries); Passing—Ed Salem (52 of 110, 597 yards); Receiving—Bob Hood (7 catches, 150 yards)

Gordon Pettus' touchdown pass to Butch Avinger started a 55-0 rout in the first meeting against Auburn since 1907, in front of 46,000 fans. Ed Salem passed for three touchdowns, ran for one, and kicked seven extra points. ... Gordon Pettus averaged a school record 20.0 yards per punt return.

1949
6-3-1

Sept. 24	Tulane	Mobile	L	28-14
Oct. 1	Vanderbilt	Nashville	L	14-7
Oct. 7	Duquesne	Tuscaloosa	W	48-8
Oct. 15	Tennessee	Birmingham	T	7-7
Oct. 22	Mississippi State	Tuscaloosa	W	35-6
Oct. 29	Georgia	Athens	W	14-7
Nov. 12	Georgia Tech	Birmingham	W	20-7
Nov. 19	Southern Miss	Tuscaloosa	W	34-26
Nov. 26	Florida	Gainesville	W	35-13
Dec. 3	Auburn	Birmingham	L	14-13
Coach: Harold "Red" Drew				227-130
Captain: Doug Lockridge				
All-SEC: Ed Holdnak, guard				

Leaders: Rushing—Tom Calvin (339 yards, 88 carries); Passing—Ed Salem (40 of 75, 558 yards); Receiving—Al Lary (17 catches, 315 yards)

Alabama was heavily favored heading into the season-ending loss to Auburn ... Butch Avinger won the Jacobs Trophy ... Alabama finished the decade 66-23-4. ... Former "War Baby Tiders" standout Hal Self began restoring the football program at Florence State, now known as the University of

North Alabama, and coached there for 21 years. His teams went 110–81, including 13 winning seasons, despite usually playing bigger schools and with a one-person coaching staff of assistant George Weeks.

1950
9–2

Sept. 23	Chattanooga	Birmingham	W	27–0
Sept. 30	Tulane	New Orleans	W	26–14
Oct. 7	Vanderbilt	Mobile	L	27–22
Oct. 13	Furman	Tuscaloosa	W	34–6
Oct. 21	Tennessee	Knoxville	L	14–9
Oct. 28	Mississippi State	Tuscaloosa	W	14–7
Nov. 4	Georgia	Birmingham	W	14–7
Nov. 11	Southern Miss	Tuscaloosa	W	53–0
Nov. 18	Georgia Tech	Atlanta	W	54–19
Nov. 25	Florida	Jacksonville	W	41–13
Dec. 2	Auburn	Birmingham	W	34–0
Coach: Harold "Red" Drew				328–107

Captain: Mike Mizerany

Ranking (AP): Preseason NR; Postseason No. 16

All-American: First team—Ed Salem, halfback Second team—Mike Mizerany, tackle; Al Lary, end

All-SEC: Al Lary, end; Mike Mizerany, offensive lineman; Pat O'Sullivan, center; Ed Salem, back

Leaders: Rushing—Bobby Marlow (882 yards, 118 carries); Passing—Ed Salem (44 of 86, 879 yards); Receiving—Al Lary (35 catches, 756 yards)

Even after crushing its final four opponents, Alabama didn't receive a bowl bid. ... Bobby Marlow had 180 rushing yards and scored four touchdowns against Georgia Tech. ... Butch Avinger was the first player to win the Jacobs Trophy in back-to-back seasons. ... Paul W. "Bear" Bryant led Kentucky to its first SEC championship, with the Wildcats ending Oklahoma's 31-game winning streak at the Sugar Bowl. However, he wound up resigning when it became obvious that school officials would always consider basketball to be a higher priority.

1951
5–6

Sept. 21	Delta State	Montgomery	W	89–0
Sept. 29	LSU	Mobile	L	13–7
Oct. 6	Vanderbilt	Nashville	L	22–20
Oct. 12	Villanova	Tuscaloosa	L	41–18
Oct. 20	Tennessee	Birmingham	L	27–13
Oct. 27	Mississippi State	Starkville	W	7–0
Nov. 3	Georgia	Athens	W	16–14
Nov. 10	Southern Miss	Tuscaloosa	W	40–7
Nov. 17	Georgia Tech	Birmingham	L	27–7
Nov. 24	Florida	Tuscaloosa	L	30–21
Dec. 2	Auburn	Tuscaloosa	W	25–7

Coach: Harold "Red" Drew · 263–188

Captain: Jack Brown

Ranking (AP): Preseason No. 9; Postseason NR

All-SEC: Bobby Marlow, back

Leaders: Rushing—Bobby Marlow (728 yards, 114 carries);
Passing—Clell Hobson (66 of 114, 847 yards); Receiving—Joe
Curtis (16 catches, 181 yards)

Through the Years

The 5–6 record marked Alabama's first losing season since 1903. ... The loss to Tennessee was
Alabama's first televised game. ... Bobby Marlow
set a school record, which would stand for 35
years, with 233 rushing yards against Auburn.
... Auburn hired Shug Jordan as head coach.
Through 1975, he compiled a 176–83–6 record.

16

Years between head coaching
jobs for "Red" Drew. Before coming to Tuscaloosa, Drew spent
a year at Ole Miss. The job in
Oxford was his first head coaching job since 1930, when he led
Chattanooga.

Alabama's Bart Starr leaps for a photo opportunity in 1953. Relatively unheralded coming out of college, Starr was not selected by the Green Bay Packers until the 17th round of the NFL Draft. Of course, he went on to a Hall of Fame, multiple championship-winning career as a pro.

1952

10–2

Sept. 19	Southern Miss	Montgomery	W	20–6
Sept. 27	LSU	Baton Rouge	W	21–20
Oct. 3	Miami (Fla.)	Miami	W	21–7
Oct. 11	Virginia Tech	Tuscaloosa	W	33–0
Oct. 18	Tennessee	Knoxville	L	20–0
Oct. 25	Mississippi State	Tuscaloosa	W	42–19
Nov. 1	Georgia	Birmingham	W	34–19
Nov. 8	Chattanooga	Tuscaloosa	W	42–28
Nov. 15	Georgia Tech	Atlanta	L	7–3
Nov. 22	Maryland	Mobile	W	27–7
Nov. 29	Auburn	Birmingham	W	21–0
Jan. 1	Syracuse	Orange Bowl	W	61–6

Coach: Harold "Red" Drew   325–139

Captain: Bobby Wilson

Ranking (AP): Preseason NR; Postseason No. 9

All-American: First team—Bobby Marlow, halfback

All-SEC: Hootie Ingram, back; Bobby Marlow, back; Jerry Watford, guard

Leaders: Rushing—Bobby Marlow (950 yards, 176 carries); Passing—Clell Hobson (33 of 63, 336 yards); Receiving—Corky Tharp (10 catches, 115 yards)

Hootie Ingram's 10 interceptions set a school record. He also had 163 return yards and two touchdowns. His 80-yard punt return for a touchdown helped spark the rout of Syracuse in the Orange Bowl. ... Bob Conway's 95-yard kickoff return for a touchdown led a 21–20 victory against LSU. ... The 27–7 victory against Maryland was against Coach Jim Tatum. ... Harold "Red" Drew was named SEC Coach of the Year.

1953
6–3–3, SEC champions

Sept. 18	Southern Miss	Montgomery	L	25–19
Sept. 26	LSU	Mobile	T	7–7
Oct. 3	Vanderbilt	Nashville	W	21–12
Oct. 10	Tulsa	Tuscaloosa	W	41–13
Oct. 17	Tennessee	Birmingham	T	0–0
Oct. 24	Mississippi State	Tuscaloosa	T	7–7
Oct. 31	Georgia	Athens	W	33–12
Nov. 7	Chattanooga	Tuscaloosa	W	21–14
Nov. 14	Georgia Tech	Birmingham	W	13–6
Nov. 21	Maryland	College Park	L	21–0
Nov. 28	Auburn	Birmingham	W	10–7
Jan. 1	Rice	Cotton Bowl	L	28–6

Coach: Harold "Red" Drew   178–152

Captain: Bud Willis

Ranking (AP): Preseason No. 5; Postseason No. 13

All-American: Second team—Corky Tharp, halfback

All-SEC: Corky Tharp, back

Leaders: Rushing—Corky Tharp (607 yards, 111 carries); Passing—Bart Starr (59 of 119, 870 yards); Receiving—Bud Willis (11 catches, 191 yards)

Bobby Luna's fourth-quarter field goal for a 10–7 victory against Auburn helped Alabama clinch the SEC title, its first in eight years. ... The Cotton Bowl was best remembered for fullback Tommy Lewis coming off the bench in the middle of a play and tackling Rice's Dicky Moegle. "I'm just too full of 'Bama," was his explanation. ... Bart Starr was picked to the first-ever Academic All-SEC team. ... Alabama's first home television game, against Tennessee, featured announcers Mel Allen and Lindsay Nelson. ... Frank Thomas and Don Hutson were elected to the College Football Hall of Fame.

1954
4-5-2

Sept. 17	Southern Miss	Montgomery	L	7-2
Sept. 25	LSU	Baton Rouge	W	12-0
Oct. 2	Vanderbilt	Mobile	W	28-14
Oct. 9	Tulsa	Tuscaloosa	W	40-0
Oct. 16	Tennessee	Knoxville	W	27-0
Oct. 23	Mississippi State	Tuscaloosa	L	12-7
Oct. 30	Georgia	Birmingham	T	0-0
Nov. 6	Tulane	New Orleans	T	0-0
Nov. 13	Georgia Tech	Atlanta	L	20-0
Nov. 19	Miami (Fla.)	Miami	L	23-7
Nov. 27	Auburn	Birmingham	L	28-0

Coach: Harold "Red" Drew   123-104

Captain: Sid Youngleman

Ranking (AP): Preseason No. 14; Postseason NR

All-American: First team—George Mason, tackle

All-SEC: Corky Tharp, back

Leaders: Rushing—Corky Tharp (641 yards, 139 carries); Passing—Albert Elmore (39 of 74, 499 yards); Receiving—Bobby Luna (16 catches, 304 yards)

Harold "Red" Drew's coaching career at Alabama ended with a 54–28–7 record. ... Former coach Frank Thomas died on May 10. ... Texas A&M went 1–9 in Coach Paul W. "Bear" Bryant's first season there, the only losing year of his career. Consequently, the Board of Trustees athletic committee selected former player J.B. "Ears" Whitworth, who was the head coach at Oklahoma State and had been a tackle on the Crimson Tide's 1931 Rose Bowl team, to replace Drew.

1955
0–10

Sept. 24	Rice	Houston	L	20-0
Oct. 1	Vanderbilt	Nashville	L	21-6
Oct. 8	Texas Christian	Tuscaloosa	L	21-0
Oct. 15	Tennessee	Birmingham	L	20-0
Oct. 22	Mississippi State	Tuscaloosa	L	26-7
Oct. 29	Georgia	Athens	L	35-14
Nov. 5	Tulane	Mobile	L	27-7
Nov. 12	Georgia Tech	Birmingham	L	26-2
Nov. 18	Miami (Fla.)	Miami	L	34-12
Nov. 26	Auburn	Birmingham	L	26-0
Coach: J.B. "Ears" Whitworth				48-256
Captain: Nick Germanos				

Leaders: Rushing—Clay Walls (164 yards, 49 carries); Passing—Bart Starr (55 of 96, 587 yards); Receiving—Noojin Walker (14 catches, 154 yards).

Alabama didn't win an SEC game en route to its worst season ever. ... Wallace Wade and Fred Sington were elected to the College Football Hall of Fame.

1956
2-7-1

Sept. 22	Rice	Houston	L	20-13
Oct. 6	Vanderbilt	Mobile	L	32-7
Oct. 13	Texas Christian	Tuscaloosa	L	23-6
Oct. 20	Tennessee	Knoxville	L	24-0
Oct. 27	Mississippi State	Tuscaloosa	W	13-12
Nov. 3	Georgia	Birmingham	L	16-13
Nov. 10	Tulane	New Orleans	W	13-7
Nov. 17	Georgia Tech	Atlanta	L	27-0
Nov. 24	Southern Miss	Tuscaloosa	T	13-13
Dec. 1	Auburn	Birmingham	L	34-7
Coach: J.B. "Ears" Whitworth				85-208
Captains: Jim Cunningham, Wes Thompson				

Leaders: Rushing—Don Comstock (316 yards, 76 carries); Passing—Bobby Smith (16 of 40, 356 yards); Receiving—Charlie Gray (7 catches, 108 yards)

Alabama ended a 20-game winless streak (0–18–2) with a 13–12 victory against Mississippi State. … With two wins, the Crimson Tide avoided the SEC basement, ahead of LSU and Georgia.

1957
2-7-1

Sept. 28	LSU	Baton Rouge	L	28-0
Oct. 5	Vanderbilt	Nashville	T	6-6
Oct. 12	Texas Christian	Fort Worth	L	28-0
Oct. 19	Tennessee	Birmingham	L	14-0
Oct. 26	Mississippi State	Tuscaloosa	L	13-25
Nov. 2	Georgia	Athens	W	14-13
Nov. 9	Tulane	Mobile	L	7-0
Nov. 16	Georgia Tech	Birmingham	L	10-7
Nov. 23	Southern Miss	Tuscaloosa	W	29-2
Nov. 30	Auburn	Birmingham	L	40-0
Coach: J.B. "Ears" Whitworth				69-173
Captains: Jim Loftin, Clay Walls				

Leaders: Rushing—Jim Loftin (477 yards, 106 carries); Passing—Bobby Smith (32 of 83, 377 yards); Receiving—Willie Beck (9 catches, 126 yards)

During the season, the decision was made not to renew the contract of coach J.D. "Ears" Whitworth, a former player who had managed to win four games over three seasons. …. Johnny Mack Brown was elected to the College Football Hall of Fame and returned to campus to be honored at homecoming. … After the 40–0 loss to Auburn, which went on to win its only national championship, it was announced that Paul W. "Bear" Bryant was leaving Texas A&M to return to Alabama. He was quoted as saying, "Mama called, and when Mama calls you come running."

Coach Paul W. "Bear" Bryant discusses tactics with quarterback Pat Trammell during practice before the 1961 season.

1958

5-4-1

Sept. 27	LSU	Mobile	L	13-3
Oct. 4	Vanderbilt	Birmingham	T	0-0
Oct. 11	Furman	Tuscaloosa	W	29-6
Oct. 18	Tennessee	Knoxville	L	14-7
Oct. 25	Mississippi State	Starkville	W	9-7
Nov. 1	Georgia	Tuscaloosa	W	12-0
Nov. 8	Tulane	New Orleans	L	13-7
Nov. 15	Georgia Tech	Atlanta	W	17-8
Nov. 22	Memphis State	Tuscaloosa	W	14-0
Nov. 29	Auburn	Birmingham	L	14-8
Coach: Paul W. "Bear" Bryant				106-75

Captains: Dave Singleton, Bobby Smith

Leaders: Rushing—Bobby Jackson (472 yards, 143 carries); Passing—Bobby Jackson (29 of 58, 408 yards); Receiving—Marlin Dyess (12 catches, 204 yards).

Upon returning to the Capstone, Paul W. "Bear" Bryant told both the incoming recruits and the holdovers from the previous teams—those who survived his brutal offseason conditioning program—that if they weren't there to win a national championship, they were in the wrong place. ... Fred Sington Jr.'s field goal vs. LSU scored the first points of the Bryant era. The Tigers, who went on to win the national championship, narrowly won 13-3. ... The 14 points scored by Tennessee and Auburn were the most allowed by Alabama.

When Bear Bryant took over at Texas A&M, he led such a tough training camp his first season in drought-ridden Junction, Texas, that barely one third of his team made it through the ten days.

1959
7-2-2

Sept. 19	Georgia	Athens	L	17-3
Sept. 26	Houston	Houston	W	3-0
Oct. 3	Vanderbilt	Nashville	T	7-7
Oct. 10	Chattanooga	Tuscaloosa	W	13-0
Oct. 17	Tennessee	Birmingham	T	7-7
Oct. 31	Mississippi State	Tuscaloosa	W	10-0
Nov. 7	Tulane	Mobile	W	19-7
Nov. 14	Georgia Tech	Birmingham	W	9-7
Nov. 21	Memphis State	Tuscaloosa	W	14-7
Nov. 28	Auburn	Birmingham	W	10-0
Dec. 19	Penn State	Liberty Bowl	L	7-0

Coach: Paul W. "Bear" Bryant   95-59

Captains: Marlin Dyess, Jim Blevins

Ranking (AP): Preseason NR; Postseason No. 10

Leaders: Rushing—Pat Trammell (525 yards, 156 carries);
Passing—Pat Trammell (21 of 49, 293 yards); Receiving—Marlin
Dyess (10 catches, 149 yards)

A 27-yard field goal by Tommy Brooker and a
27-yard pass from Bobby Skelton to Scooter
Dyess led to a 10–0 victory against Auburn and
ended a five-game losing streak to the Tigers.
... After a 7–0 loss to Penn State in the inau-
gural Liberty Bowl in frigid Philadelphia, Bear
Bryant took his team to New York City where Mel
Allen hosted a dinner that was attended by Joe
DiMaggio of the New York Yankees. ... Alabama
finished the decade 50–48–10.

1960
8-1-2

Sept. 17	Georgia	Birmingham	W	21-6
Sept. 24	Tulane	New Orleans	T	6-6
Oct. 1	Vanderbilt	Birmingham	W	21-0
Oct. 15	Tennessee	Knoxville	L	20-7
Oct. 22	Houston	Tuscaloosa	W	14-0
Oct. 29	Mississippi State	Starkville	W	7-0
Nov. 5	Furman	Tuscaloosa	W	51-0
Nov. 12	Georgia Tech	Atlanta	W	16-15

Nov. 19	Tampa	Tuscaloosa	W	34-6
Nov. 26	Auburn	Birmingham	W	3-0
Dec. 17	Texas	Bluebonnet Bowl	T	3-3

Coach: Paul W. "Bear" Bryant		183-56
Captains: Leon Fuller, Bobby Boylston		
Ranking (AP): Preseason NR; Postseason No. 9		
Leaders: Rushing—Pat Trammell (315 yards, 76 carries); Passing—Bobby Skelton (43 of 94, 575 yards); Receiving—Butch Wilson (13 catches, 204 yards)		

The highlight of the season was a 21-6 victory against Georgia, led by quarterback Fran Tarkenton, on national television. ... Quarterback Bobby Skelton came in for injured Pat Trammell to bring the Tide to within two points, and on the game's final play Richard "Digger" O'Dell kicked a winning field goal, the only one he ever tried in his college career. Tommy Booker, who kicked the lone field goal against Auburn, was injured. ... The Crimson Tide appeared to win the Bluebonnet Bowl when Skelton landed on the end zone chalk, but officials ruled him down, resulting in the 3-3 tie with Texas.

1961

11-0, National champions, SEC champions

Sept. 23	Georgia	Athens	W	32-6
Sept. 30	Tulane	Mobile	W	9-0
Oct. 7	Vanderbilt	Nashville	W	35-6
Oct. 14	N. Carolina State	Tuscaloosa	W	26-7
Oct. 21	Tennessee	Birmingham	W	34-3
Oct. 28	Houston	Houston	W	17-0
Nov. 4	Mississippi State	Tuscaloosa	W	24-0
Nov. 11	Richmond	Tuscaloosa	W	66-0
Nov. 18	Georgia Tech	Birmingham	W	10-0
Dec. 2	Auburn	Birmingham	W	34-0
Jan. 1	Arkansas	Sugar Bowl	W	10-3

Coach: Paul W. "Bear" Bryant		297-25
Captains: Pat Trammell, Billy Neighbors		
Ranking (AP): Preseason No. 3; Postseason No. 1		
All-American: First team—Billy Neighbors, defensive tackle Second team—Lee Roy Jordan, center; Pat Trammell, quar-		

terback. Academic—Tommy Brooker, end; Pat Trammell, quarterback

All-SEC: Mike Fracchia, back; Lee Roy Jordan, center; Billy Neighbors, guard; Pat Trammell, quarterback

Leaders: Rushing—Mike Fracchia (652 yards, 130 carries); Passing—Pat Trammell (75 of 133, 1,035 yards); Receiving—Richard Williamson (11 catches, 206 yards)

Led by quarterback Pat Trammell, center/linebacker Lee Roy Jordan, and two-way lineman Billy Neighbors, Alabama outscored opponents 297–25. North Carolina State, led by quarterback Roman Gabriel, scored the most points, with seven. ... Alabama was No. 1 in the Associated Press poll for the first time after defeating Georgia Tech and won its first AP national title. ... The Sugar Bowl victory was Alabama's first. Mike Fracchia was named game MVP. ... Neighbors was Alabama's first All-American since 1954.

1962
10–1

Sept. 22	Georgia	Birmingham	W	35–0
Sept. 28	Tulane	New Orleans	W	44–6
Oct. 6	Vanderbilt	Birmingham	W	17–7
Oct. 13	Houston	Tuscaloosa	W	14–3
Oct. 20	Tennessee	Knoxville	W	27–7
Oct. 27	Tulsa	Tuscaloosa	W	35–6
Nov. 3	Mississippi State	Starkville	W	20–0
Nov. 10	Miami (Fla.)	Tuscaloosa	W	36–3
Nov. 17	Georgia Tech	Atlanta	L	7–6
Dec. 1	Auburn	Birmingham	W	38–0
Jan. 1	Oklahoma	Orange Bowl	W	17–0

Coach: Paul W. "Bear" Bryant	289–39

Captains: Lee Roy Jordan, Jimmy Sharpe

Ranking (AP): Preseason No. 3; Postseason No. 5

All-American: First team—Lee Roy Jordan, center

All-SEC: Lee Roy Jordan, center

Leaders: Rushing—Eddie Versprille (373 yards, 76 carries); Passing—Joe Namath (76 of 146, 1,192); Receiving—Richard Williamson (24 catches, 492 yards)

Alabama shut out Auburn for the fourth-straight year. ... Lee Roy Jordan closed his career with 31 tackles against Oklahoma in the Orange Bowl. He placed fourth in Heisman Trophy voting (won by Terry Baker of Oregon State). ... Alabama's quarterback was sophomore Joe Namath. ... Georgia Tech got even for the previous year when linebacker Darwin Holt caught the Yellow Jackets' quarterback with an elbow on a late hit, fracturing his jaw. When Alabama came up inches short of completing a two-point conversion, it cost the Tide a shot at defending its national championship.

1963
9-2

Sept. 21	Georgia	Athens	W	32-7
Sept. 28	Tulane	Mobile	W	28-0
Oct. 5	Vanderbilt	Nashville	W	21-6
Oct. 12	Florida	Tuscaloosa	L	10-6
Oct. 19	Tennessee	Birmingham	W	35-0
Oct. 26	Houston	Tuscaloosa	W	21-13
Nov. 2	Mississippi State	Tuscaloosa	W	20-19
Nov. 16	Georgia Tech	Birmingham	W	27-11
Nov. 30	Auburn	Birmingham	L	10-8
Dec. 14	Miami (Fla.)	Miami	W	17-12
Jan. 1	Ole Miss	Sugar Bowl	W	12-7
Coach: Paul W. "Bear" Bryant				227-95

Captains: Benny Nelson, Steve Allen

Ranking (AP): Preseason No. 3; Postseason No. 8

All-American: Second team—Benny Nelson, halfback

All-SEC: Benny Nelson, back

Leaders: Rushing—Benny Nelson (612 yards, 97 carries); Passing—Joe Namath (63 of 128, 765 yards); Receiving—Jimmy Dill (19 catches, 316 yards)

The 10-6 loss to Florida was just one of two ever by a Bear Bryant team in Tuscaloosa. ... Without quarterback Joe Namath, who was suspended for two games, Alabama upset SEC champion Ole Miss in the Sugar Bowl. The game was played on the heels of a rare snowstorm in New Orleans.

Resting his feet on the seats of the Orange Bowl in Miami, Coach Bear Bryant is either taking a moment to relax or cooking up something for the Texas Longhorns. His team the loss to the Longhorns did not affect its standing.

Tim Davis became the only kicker to be named game MVP. ... Alabama's game against Miami was delayed after President John F. Kennedy was assassinated on November 22. Army-Navy was postponed to December 7, with Alabama-Miami subsequently bumped back another week, making it the Crimson Tide's latest regular season game of the modern era. ... The *Saturday Evening Post* accused Bryant and Georgia athletics director Wally Butts of fixing their game so they could bet on it. The article also alleged that Bryant had thrown the 1962 loss to the Yellow Jackets. Both sued, with Butts winning and Bryant settling for $300,000.

1964

10–1, National champions, SEC champions

Sept. 19	Georgia	Tuscaloosa	W	31–3
Sept. 26	Tulane	Mobile	W	36–6
Oct. 3	Vanderbilt	Birmingham	W	24–0
Oct. 10	N. Carolina State	Tuscaloosa	W	21–0
Oct. 17	Tennessee	Knoxville	W	19–8
Oct. 24	Florida	Tuscaloosa	W	17–14
Oct. 31	Mississippi State	Jackson	W	23–6
Nov. 7	LSU	Birmingham	W	17–9
Nov. 14	Georgia Tech	Atlanta	W	24–7
Nov. 26	Auburn	Birmingham	W	21–14
Jan. 1	Texas	Orange Bowl	L	21–17

Coach: Paul W. "Bear" Bryant	250–88

Captains: Joe Namath, Ray Ogden

Ranking (AP): Preseason No. 6; Postseason No. 1

All-American: First team—Wayne Freeman, guard; Dan Kearley, defensive tackle; Joe Namath, quarterback; David Ray, halfback Second team—Mickey Andrews, back Academic—Gaylon McCollough, center

All-SEC: Steve Bowman, back; Wayne Freeman, guard; Dan Kearley, defensive tackle; Joe Namath, quarterback; David Ray, end

Leaders: Rushing—Steve Bowman (536 yards, 106 carries); Passing—Joe Namath (64 of 100, 757 yards); Receiving—David Ray (19 catches, 271 yards)

Alabama was awarded the national championship before the controversial loss to Texas in the first nighttime Orange Bowl, where quarterback Joe Namath appeared to score on a fourth-quarter sneak only to have one official overrule another. ... Namath sustained a knee injury against North Carolina State. Backup Steve Sloan led wins against Florida, Tennessee, Mississippi State, and LSU—with Namath coming off the bench to spark a 24–7 victory against Georgia Tech (with the series taking a 15-year break). ... Ray Ogden's 108-yard kickoff return and Namath's touchdown pass to Ray Perkins keyed the Auburn victory and thanks to Notre Dame's loss to Southern California, propelled the Crimson Tide to No. 1. Notre Dame's John Huarte, who would be Namath's backup with the New York Jets, won the Heisman Trophy. ... Coach Paul W. "Bear" Bryant wore a helmet onto the field in Atlanta because of all the debris thrown by fans (which later became a famous college football photograph). ... Assistant coach Gene Stallings accepted the head coaching job at his alma mater, Texas A&M.

1965

9–1–1, National champions, SEC champions

Sept. 18	Georgia	Athens	L	18–17
Sept. 25	Tulane	Mobile	W	27–0
Oct. 2	Ole Miss	Birmingham	W	17–16
Oct. 9	Vanderbilt	Nashville	W	22–7
Oct. 16	Tennessee	Birmingham	T	7–7
Oct. 23	Florida State	Tuscaloosa	W	21–0
Oct. 30	Mississippi State	Jackson	W	10–7
Nov. 6	LSU	Baton Rouge	W	31–7
Nov. 13	South Carolina	Tuscaloosa	W	35–14
Nov. 27	Auburn	Birmingham	W	30–3
Jan. 1	Nebraska	Orange Bowl	W	39–28
Coach: Paul W. "Bear" Bryant				256–107
Captains: Steve Sloan, Paul Crane				
Ranking (AP): Preseason No. 5; Postseason No. 1				

All-American: First team—Paul Crane, center; Steve Sloan,

quarterback Second team—Steve Bowman, fullback Academic—
Dennis Homan, end; Steve Sloan, quarterback

All-SEC: Steve Bowman, fullback; Paul Crane, center; Creed
Gilmer, defensive end; Bobby Johns, defensive back; Tommy
Tolleson, split end

Leaders: Rushing—Steve Bowman (770 yards, 153 carries);
Passing—Steve Sloan (97 of 160, 1,453 yards); Receiving—
Tommy Tolleson (32 catches, 374 yards)

**The Associated Press held a final poll after the
bowl games for the first time, and Alabama took
advantage. Ranked fourth, the Crimson Tide
turned down an invitation to the Cotton Bowl to
keep alive its slim national championship hopes.
Prior to Alabama playing No. 3 Nebraska in the
Orange Bowl, No. 1 Michigan State had lost to
UCLA and No. 2 Arkansas to LSU. Bryant uti-
lized both the tackle-eligible play and more than
one onside kick to pull off the 39–28 upset.
Quarterback Steve Sloan was named game MVP,
Ray Perkins had nine catches for 159 yards, and
Alabama outgained Nebraska 518–377 in yard-
age. ... The tackle-eligible play was subsequently
declared illegal.**

1966

11–0, SEC champions

Sept. 24	Louisiana Tech	Birmingham	W	34–0
Oct. 1	Ole Miss	Jackson	W	17–7
Oct. 8	Clemson	Tuscaloosa	W	26–0
Oct. 15	Tennessee	Knoxville	W	11–10
Oct. 22	Vanderbilt	Birmingham	W	42–6
Oct. 29	Mississippi State	Tuscaloosa	W	27–14
Nov. 5	LSU	Birmingham	W	21–0
Nov. 12	South Carolina	Tuscaloosa	W	24–0
Nov. 26	Southern Miss	Mobile	W	34–0
Dec. 3	Auburn	Birmingham	W	31–0
Jan. 2	Nebraska	Sugar Bowl	W	34–7
Coach: Paul W. "Bear" Bryant				301–44
Captains: Ray Perkins, Richard Cole				
Ranking (AP): Preseason No. 1; Postseason No. 3				

All-American: First team—Richard Cole, defensive tackle; Cecil

Dowdy, tackle; Bobby Johns, defensive back; Ray Perkins, split end

All-SEC: John Calvert, guard; Cecil Dowdy, tackle; Bobby Johns, defensive back; Ray Perkins, end; Dicky Thompson, back.

Leaders: Rushing—Kenny Stabler (397 yards, 93 carries); Passing—Kenny Stabler (74 of 114, 956 yards); Receiving—Ray Perkins (33 catches, 490 yards).

Although voters opted for Notre Dame and Michigan State, which had tied, ahead of undefeated Alabama, Bryant called this his greatest team. Aided by receivers Ray Perkins and Dennis Homan, quarterback Kenny Stabler was named MVP of the Sugar Bowl after Alabama destroyed Nebraska. Bobby Johns had three interceptions in the game. ... Tennessee proved to be the toughest opponent, but Stabler rallied a comeback in the Knoxville rain. ... Alabama posted five shutouts. ... Many believe that the state's racial issues, which were a focal point of national debate— including Governor George Wallace's "Stand in the Schoolhouse Door" speech, the Rosa Parks bus incident in Montgomery, and the Selma civil rights march—were a crucial factor in the snubbing by voters. Additionally, the Crimson Tide had yet to integrate its football team.

1967
8-2-1

Sept. 23	Florida State	Birmingham	T	37–37
Sept. 30	Southern Miss	Mobile	W	25–3
Oct. 7	Ole Miss	Birmingham	W	21–7
Oct. 14	Vanderbilt	Nashville	W	35–21
Oct. 21	Tennessee	Birmingham	L	24–13
Oct. 28	Clemson	Clemson	W	13–10
Nov. 4	Mississippi State	Tuscaloosa	W	13–0
Nov. 11	LSU	Baton Rouge	W	7–6
Nov. 18	South Carolina	Tuscaloosa	W	17–0
Dec. 2	Auburn	Birmingham	W	7–3
Jan. 1	Texas A&M	Cotton Bowl	L	20–16
Coach: Paul W. "Bear" Bryant				204–131
Captains: Ken Stabler, Bobby Johns				

Ranking (AP): Preseason No. 2; Postseason No. 8

All-American: First team—Dennis Homan, split end; Bobby Johns, defensive back; Kenny Stabler, quarterback. Academic—Bob Childs, linebacker; Steve Davis, kicker

All-SEC: Mike Ford, defensive end; Mike Hall, linebacker; Dennis Homan, end; Bobby Johns, defensive back; Kenny Stabler, quarterback; Bruce Stephens, guard

Leaders: Rushing—Ed Morgan (388 yards, 103 carries); Passing—Kenny Stabler (103 of 178, 1,214 yards); Receiving—Dennis Homan (54 catches, 820 yards)

Florida State managed to match the 37 points Alabama gave up during the entire 1966 season. ... Though Auburn fans claimed there were numerous penalties not called on the play, quarterback Kenny Stabler's run in the mud provided a 7–3 victory over Auburn. ... Northport native Curley Hallman made two interceptions for Texas A&M in the Cotton Bowl. Afterward, Bryant gave Aggies Coach Gene Stallings a bear hug at midfield. ... Hank Crisp's career as an assistant coach came to a close. He was originally hired by Xen Scott in 1921 to be his line coach. ... Split end Dennis Homan was Stabler's favorite target and caught 87 passes during his three-year career, for 1,495 yards and 18 touchdowns. He was also an Academic All-American in 1965.

53

Yards scrambled by Kenny Stabler in the mud to win the Iron Bowl. After his five interceptions against Tennessee cost the Crimson Tide the SEC title, the touchdown was sweet redemption.

1968
8–3

Sept. 21	Virginia Tech	Birmingham	W	14–7
Sept. 28	Southern Miss	Mobile	W	17–14
Oct. 5	Ole Miss	Jackson	L	10–8
Oct. 12	Vanderbilt	Tuscaloosa	W	31–7
Oct. 19	Tennessee	Knoxville	L	10–9
Oct. 26	Clemson	Tuscaloosa	W	21–14
Nov. 2	Mississippi State	Tuscaloosa	W	20–13
Nov. 9	LSU	Birmingham	W	16–7
Nov. 16	Miami (Fla.)	Miami	W	14–6
Nov. 30	Auburn	Birmingham	W	24–16
Dec. 28	Missouri	Gator Bowl	L	35–10
Coach: Paul W. "Bear" Bryant				184–139

Captains: Mike Hall, Donnie Sutton

Ranking (AP): Preseason No. 10; Postseason No. 17

All-American: First team—Sam Gellerstedt, defensive lineman; Mike Hall, linebacker.

All-SEC: Mike Ford, defensive end; Mike Hall, linebacker; Sammy Gellerstedt, defensive lineman; Alvin Samples, guard

Leaders: Rushing—Ed Morgan (450 yards, 134 carries); Passing—Scott Hunter (122 of 227, 1,471 yards); Receiving—George Ranager (31 catches, 499 yards)

Despite quarterback Scott Hall's passing, Alabama struggled to run, evidenced by the 35–10 loss to Missouri in the Gator Bowl. ... Linebacker Mike Hall led the victory against Auburn, with 16 tackles and two interceptions, and slipped jersey No. 82 over his usual No. 54 to fill in at tight end. After the game, Alabama presented the game ball to former quarterback Pat Trammell, who would lose his battle with cancer a week later. Bryant called it the saddest day of his life. ... The 14–6 victory against Miami was ABC's first live prime-time game.

1969
6-5

Sept. 20	Virginia Tech	Blacksburg	W	17-13
Sept. 27	Southern Miss	Tuscaloosa	W	63-14
Oct. 4	Ole Miss	Birmingham	W	33-32
Oct. 11	Vanderbilt	Nashville	L	14-10
Oct. 18	Tennessee	Birmingham	L	41-14
Oct. 25	Clemson	Clemson	W	38-13
Nov. 1	Mississippi State	Jackson	W	23-19
Nov. 8	LSU	Baton Rouge	L	20-15
Nov. 15	Miami (Fla.)	Tuscaloosa	W	42-6
Nov. 29	Auburn	Birmingham	L	49-26
Dec. 13	Colorado	Liberty Bowl	L	47-33
Coach: Paul W. "Bear" Bryant				314-268

Captains: Danny Ford, Alvin Samples

Ranking (AP): Preseason No. 13; Postseason NR

All-American: First team—Alvin Samples, guard

All-SEC: Danny Ford, tackle; Alvin Samples, guard

Leaders: Rushing—Johnny Musso (516 yards, 157 carries); Passing—Scott Hunter (157 of 266, 2,188 yards); Receiving—David Bailey (56 catches, 781 yards)

A rare offensive showdown highlighted the season, when Alabama defeated Ole Miss 33–32 in Birmingham. Scott Hunter completed 22 of 29 passes for 300 yards, while Archie Manning was 33 of 52 for 436 yards and ran for 104 more. ... For the first time since 1958, the Crimson Tide lost to both Tennessee and Auburn. ... Guard Alvin Samples was named outstanding offensive lineman of the Liberty Bowl, although he played the entire game at linebacker due to numerous injuries. Days later center Richard Grammer drowned in a hunting accident when his boat capsized. ... Alabama signed its first two black players, Wilbur Jackson and Bo Matthews. ... Alabama finished the decade 90–16–5, with eight of the losses during the last two seasons.

1970
6–5–1

Sept. 12	Southern California	Birmingham	L	42–21
Sept. 19	Virginia Tech	Birmingham	W	51–18
Sept. 26	Florida	Tuscaloosa	W	46–15
Oct. 3	Ole Miss	Jackson	L	48–23
Oct. 10	Vanderbilt	Tuscaloosa	W	35–11
Oct. 17	Tennessee	Knoxville	L	24–0
Oct. 24	Houston	Houston	W	30–21
Oct. 31	Mississippi State	Tuscaloosa	W	35–6
Nov. 7	LSU	Birmingham	L	14–9
Nov. 14	Miami (Fla.)	Miami	W	32–8
Nov. 28	Auburn	Birmingham	L	33–28
Dec. 31	Oklahoma	Bluebonnet Bowl	T	24–24

Coach: Paul W. "Bear" Bryant — 334–264

Captains: Danny Gilbert, Dave Brungard

Ranking (AP): Preseason No. 16; Postseason NR

All-American: First team—Johnny Musso, tailback Academic—Johnny Musso, tailback

All-SEC: Johnny Musso, tailback

Leaders: Rushing—Johnny Musso (1,137 yards, 226 carries); Passing—Scott Hunter (103 of 179, 1,240 yards); Receiving—David Bailey (55 catches, 790 yards)

Senior quarterback Scott Hunter was slowed by injuries, but junior running back Johnny Musso emerged as an All-American. ... Sophomore Jeff Rouzie was the defensive MVP of the Bluebonnet Bowl, a 24–24 tie against Oklahoma. The Crimson Tide missed a short field goal on the game's final play. ... Dave Brungard transferred to Alabama and was the only player to letter under both legendary coaches Woody Hayes and Paul W. "Bear" Bryant. ... For the first time in more than a decade, Alabama failed to win at least eight games. ... Southern California halfback Sam Cunningham's 135 rushing yards and two touchdowns helped promote the integration of the football team.

1971
11–1, SEC champions

Sept. 10	Southern California	Los Angeles	W	17–10
Sept. 18	Southern Miss	Tuscaloosa	W	42–6
Sept. 25	Florida	Gainesville	W	38–0
Oct. 2	Ole Miss	Birmingham	W	40–6
Oct. 9	Vanderbilt	Nashville	W	42–0
Oct. 16	Tennessee	Birmingham	W	32–15
Oct. 23	Houston	Tuscaloosa	W	34–20
Oct. 30	Mississippi State	Jackson	W	41–10
Nov. 6	LSU	Baton Rouge	W	14–7
Nov. 13	Miami (Fla.)	Tuscaloosa	W	31–3
Nov. 27	Auburn	Birmingham	W	31–7
Jan. 1	Nebraska	Orange Bowl	L	38–6

Coach: Paul W. "Bear" Bryant — 368–122

Captains: Johnny Musso, Robin Parkhouse

Ranking (AP): Preseason No. 16; Postseason No. 4

All-American: First team—John Hannah, guard; Johnny Musso, tailback Second team—Jim Krapf, center; Robin Parkhouse, defensive end; Tom Surlas, linebacker Academic—Johnny Musso, tailback

All-SEC: David Bailey, split end; Jimmy Grammer, center; John Hannah, guard; Steve Higginbotham, defensive back; Jim Krapf, tackle; Johnny Musso, halfback; Robin Parkhouse, defensive end; Tom Surlas, linebacker

Leaders: Rushing—Johnny Musso (1,088 yards, 191 carries); Passing—Terry Davis (42 of 66, 452 yards); Receiving—David Bailey (21 catches, 286 yards)

During the offseason, Coach Paul W. "Bear" Bryant learned and installed the wishbone offense and unveiled it September 10 against Southern California at the Los Angeles Coliseum. Alabama scored two quick touchdowns against the surprised Trojans and won 17–10. ... Although Auburn's Pat Sullivan won the Heisman Trophy, he shared SEC Player of the Year honors with Crimson Tide running back Johnny Musso. Alabama won the only Iron Bowl in which both teams came in undefeated. ... Bryant, who enjoyed career win No. 200 against the Trojans, was named national coach of the year. ... For the first time since 1966, Alabama beat both Auburn and Tennessee in the same season. ... John Mitchell was Alabama's first black starter.

1972

10–2, SEC champions

Sept. 9	Duke	Birmingham	W	35–12
Sept. 23	Kentucky	Birmingham	W	35–0
Sept. 30	Vanderbilt	Tuscaloosa	W	48–21
Oct. 7	Georgia	Athens	W	25–7
Oct. 14	Florida	Tuscaloosa	W	24–7
Oct. 21	Tennessee	Knoxville	W	17–10
Oct. 28	Southern Miss	Birmingham	W	48–11
Nov. 4	Mississippi State	Tuscaloosa	W	58–14
Nov. 11	LSU	Birmingham	W	35–21
Nov. 18	Virginia Tech	Tuscaloosa	W	52–13
Dec. 2	Auburn	Birmingham	L	17–16
Jan. 1	Texas	Cotton Bowl	L	17–13
Coach: Paul W. "Bear" Bryant				406–150

Captains: Terry Davis, John Mitchell

Ranking (AP): Preseason No. 7; Postseason No. 7

All-American: First team—John Hannah, guard; Jim Krapf, center; John Mitchell, defensive end

All-SEC: Buddy Brown, tackle; Terry Davis, quarterback; Greg Gantt, punter; John Hannah, guard; Jim Krapf, center; Bobby McKinney, defensive back; John Mitchell, defensive end; Chuck Strickland, linebacker; Wayne Wheeler, split end

Leaders: Rushing—Steve Bisceglia (603 yards, 125 carries); Passing—Terry Davis (50 of 94, 777 yards); Receiving—Wayne Wheeler (30 catches, 573 yards)

At Tennessee, quarterback Terry Davis scored the game-winning touchdown on a 22-yard run after Mike DuBose stripped a fumble from Volunteers quarterback Condredge Holloway in the final minute of the game. ... After limiting Auburn to 80 yards of total offense, the Crimson Tide had two blocked punts returned for touchdowns, allowing the Tigers to pull off a stunning 17–16 upset

known on the plains as "Punt, 'Bama, Punt." ...
Alabama won the SEC title but lost 17–13 to
Texas in the Cotton Bowl. ... A year after becoming Alabama's first black starter, John Mitchell
was named an All-American and team co-captain.
He later became the Crimson Tide's first black
assistant coach and eventually the conference's
first black defensive coordinator at LSU.

1973

11–1, National champions, SEC champions

Sept. 15	California	Birmingham	W	66–0
Sept. 22	Kentucky	Lexington	W	28–14
Sept. 29	Vanderbilt	Nashville	W	44–0
Oct. 6	Georgia	Tuscaloosa	W	28–14
Oct. 13	Florida	Gainesville	W	35–14
Oct. 20	Tennessee	Birmingham	W	42–21
Oct. 27	Virginia Tech	Tuscaloosa	W	77–6
Nov. 3	Mississippi State	Jackson	W	35–0
Nov. 17	Miami	Tuscaloosa	W	43–13
Nov. 22	LSU	Baton Rouge	W	21–7
Dec. 1	Auburn	Birmingham	W	35–0
Dec. 31	Notre Dame	Sugar Bowl	L	24–23
Coach: Paul W. "Bear" Bryant				477–113

Captains: Wilbur Jackson, Chuck Strickland

Ranking (AP): Preseason No. 6; Postseason No. 4

All-American: First team—Buddy Brown, tackle; Woodrow
Lowe, linebacker; Wayne Wheeler, split end Second team—
Mike Washington, cornerback; John Croyle, defensive end; Mike
Raines, defensive tackle Academic—Randy Hall, defensive tackle

All-SEC: Buddy Brown, tackle; Greg Gantt, punter; Wilbur
Jackson, halfback; Woodrow Lowe, linebacker; David McMakin,
safety; Mike Raines, defensive tackle; Steve Sprayberry, tackle;
Mike Washington, cornerback; Wayne Wheeler, split end

Leaders: Rushing—Wilbur Jackson (752 yards, 95 carries);
Passing—Gary Rutledge (33 of 57, 897 yards); Receiving—
Wayne Wheeler (19 catches, 530 yards)

Through the Years

Linebacker Woodrow Lowe made a team record 134 solo tackles. ... Alabama opened the season with 66–0 victory against California, which was led by quarterback Steve Bartkowki and running back Chuck Muncie. Four players—Wilbur Jackson, Richard Todd, Calvin Culliver, and Jimmy Taylor—each had more than 100 rushing yards against Virginia Tech. ... The offense, which also featured quarterback Gary Rutledge and running back Randy Billingsley, scored 477 points and averaged 480.7 yards per game. ... Against unbeaten Tennessee, Alabama opened the game with an 80-yard touchdown pass from Rutledge to Wayne Wheeler, and Jackson scored on a memorable 80-yard run. ... Alabama was voted United Press International's national champion before its dramatic bowl loss to Notre Dame.

1974

11–1, SEC champions

Sept. 14	Maryland	College Park	W	21–16
Sept. 21	Southern Miss	Birmingham	W	52–0
Sept. 28	Vanderbilt	Tuscaloosa	W	23–10
Oct. 5	Ole Miss	Jackson	W	35–21
Oct. 12	Florida State	Tuscaloosa	W	8–7
Oct. 19	Tennessee	Knoxville	W	28–6
Oct. 26	Texas Christian	Birmingham	W	41–3
Nov. 2	Mississippi State	Tuscaloosa	W	35–0
Nov. 9	LSU	Birmingham	W	30–0
Nov. 16	Miami (Fla.)	Miami	W	28–7
Nov. 29	Auburn	Birmingham	W	17–13
Jan. 1	Notre Dame	Orange Bowl	L	13–11

Coach: Paul W. "Bear" Bryant   329–96

Captains: Sylvester Croom, Ricky Davis

Ranking (AP): Preseason No. 4; Postseason No. 5

All-American: First team—Leroy Cook, defensive end; Sylvester Croom, center; Woodrow Lowe, linebacker; Mike Washington, cornerback. Academic—Randy Hall, defensive tackle

All-SEC: First team—Leroy Cook, defensive end; Sylvester Croom, center; Ricky Davis, safety; Woodrow Lowe, linebacker;

Bear Bryant shakes a tambourine in time with the band as the national champion Crimson Tide arrive in New Orleans ahead of the Sugar Bowl. Alabama's loss in the game helped change the rules about the final poll of the season, which always took place before the bowl games.

John Rogers, guard; Willie Shelby, halfback; Mike Washington, cornerback

Leaders: Rushing—Calvin Culliver (708 yards, 116 yards); Passing—Richard Todd (36 of 67, 656 yards); Receiving—Ozzie Newsome (20 catches, 374 yards)

Despite injuries to quarterbacks Gary Rutledge and Richard Todd, Alabama played for the national championship but lost 13–11 to Notre Dame at the Orange Bowl in Ara Parseghian's final game with the Irish. Leroy Cook was named defensive MVP of the game. ... Senior end Mike DuBose helped preserve the 17–13 victory against Auburn by forcing a fumble from Phil Gargis late in the game. ... Ozzie Newsome became a starter and began his assault on the Crimson Tide record book. Through 1977 he caught 102 passes for 2,070 yards, with an average gain per pass of 20.3 yards, a conference record.

1975
11–1, SEC champions

Sept. 8	Missouri	Birmingham	L	20–7
Sept. 20	Clemson	Tuscaloosa	W	56–0
Sept. 27	Vanderbilt	Nashville	W	40–7
Oct. 4	Ole Miss	Birmingham	W	32–6
Oct. 11	Washington	Tuscaloosa	W	52–0
Oct. 18	Tennessee	Birmingham	W	30–7
Oct. 25	Texas Christian	Birmingham	W	45–0
Nov. 1	Mississippi State	Jackson	W	21–10
Nov. 8	LSU	Baton Rouge	W	23–10
Nov. 15	Southern Miss	Tuscaloosa	W	27–6
Nov. 29	Auburn	Birmingham	W	28–0
Dec. 31	Penn State	Sugar Bowl	W	13–6

Coach: Paul W. "Bear" Bryant   374–72

Captains: Leroy Cook, Richard Todd

Ranking (AP): Preseason No. 2; Postseason No. 3

All-American: First team—Leroy Cook, defensive end; Woodrow Lowe, linebacker Second team—Bob Baumhower, defensive tackle Academic—Danny Ridgeway, kicker

All-SEC: Bob Baumhower, defensive tackle; Leroy Cook, defensive end; Conley Duncan, linebacker; David Gerasimchuk, guard;

Tyrone King, defensive back; Woodrow Lowe, linebacker; Alan Pizzitola, safety; Wayne Rhodes, defensive back; Richard Todd, quarterback

Leaders: Rushing—Johnny Davis (820 yards, 123 carries); Passing—Richard Todd (47 of 89, 661 yards); Receiving—Ozzie Newsome (21 catches, 363 yards)

After an early 20–7 loss to Missouri, Alabama allowed only 52 points the rest of the season. ... Defensive end Leroy Cook led a 13-sack attack against Tennessee. ... The 13–6 victory against Penn State in the Sugar Bowl snapped a bowl losing streak that dated back to the 1967 Sugar Bowl. Quarterback Richard Todd was named game MVP. ... When asked after the game why he didn't wear his trademark houndstooth hat for the first Sugar Bowl played in the Louisiana Superdome, Bryant said, "My mother always taught me not to wear a hat indoors." ... Former Alabama tackle Don Whitmire, a rear admiral in the U.S. Navy, directed the evacuation of Saigon at the end of the Vietnam War, the largest evacuation in world history, with 82,000 men, women, and children escaping.

Through the Years

22

Consecutive SEC wins for Alabama at the end of the 1975 season. The conference dominance led the Tide to five straight conference titles, still an SEC record.

It was too cold for Bear Bryant's signature houndstooth hat at the 1976 Liberty Bowl, with temperatures dipping well past normal lows. The offense sizzled, however, whipping the UCLA defense for 36 points to cap off what Bryant had called a "rebuilding year."

1976
9–3

Sept. 11	Ole Miss	Jackson	L	10–7
Sept. 18	Southern Methodist	Birmingham	W	56–3
Sept. 25	Vanderbilt	Tuscaloosa	W	42–14
Oct. 2	Georgia	Athens	L	21–0
Oct. 9	Southern Miss	Birmingham	W	24–8
Oct. 16	Tennessee	Knoxville	W	20–13
Oct. 23	Louisville	Tuscaloosa	W	24–3
Oct. 30	Mississippi State	Tuscaloosa	W	34–17
Nov. 6	LSU	Birmingham	W	28–17
Nov. 13	Notre Dame	South Bend	L	21–18
Nov. 27	Auburn	Birmingham	W	38–7
Dec. 20	UCLA	Liberty Bowl	W	36–6

Coach: Paul W. "Bear" Bryant 327–140

Captains: Thad Flanagan, Charles Hannah

Ranking (AP): Preseason No. 6; Postseason No. 11

All-American: Second team—Bob Baumhower, defensive tackle; Ozzie Newsome, split end

All-SEC: Bob Baumhower, defensive tackle; David Gerasimchuk, guard; Charles Hannah, defensive tackle; Ozzie Newsome, split end

Leaders: Rushing—Johnny Davis (668 yards, 119 carries); Passing—Jeff Rutledge (62 of 109, 979 yards); Receiving—Ozzie Newsome (25 catches, 529 yards)

Coach Paul W. "Bear" Bryant warned fans that it would be a rebuilding year, and they didn't believe him until the coach lost 10–7 to Ole Miss on his 63rd birthday. ... Despite being a heavy underdog to UCLA in the Liberty Bowl, Alabama took a 24–0 lead and won 36–6. Sophomore Barry Krauss was named game MVP. Due to high winds and below-freezing temperatures, the game was nicknamed the "Refrigerator Bowl." "You gave us a good, old-fashioned butt-whipping and you know it," UCLA Coach Terry Donahue told Bryant at midfield. ... Alabama began a winning streak of 27 conference victories, which lasted until 1980 and set an SEC record.

1977

11–1, SEC champions

Sept. 10	Ole Miss	Birmingham	W	34–13
Sept. 17	Nebraska	Lincoln	L	31–24
Sept. 24	Vanderbilt	Nashville	W	24–12
Oct. 1	Georgia	Tuscaloosa	W	18–10
Oct. 8	Southern California	Los Angeles	W	21–20
Oct. 15	Tennessee	Birmingham	W	24–10
Oct. 22	Louisville	Tuscaloosa	W	55–6
Oct. 29	Mississippi State	Jackson	W	37–7
Nov. 5	LSU	Baton Rouge	W	24–3
Nov. 12	Miami (Fla.)	Tuscaloosa	W	36–0
Nov. 26	Auburn	Birmingham	W	48–21
Jan. 2	Ohio State	Sugar Bowl	W	35–6
Coach: Paul W. "Bear" Bryant				380–139

Captains: Ozzie Newsome, Mike Tucker

Ranking (AP): Preseason No. 6; Postseason No. 2

All-American: First team—Ozzie Newsome, wide receiver Second team—Bob Cryder, guard; Johnny Davis, fullback; Wayne Hamilton, defensive end

All-SEC: Jim Bunch, tackle; Johnny Davis, fullback; Mike Kramer, defensive back; Ozzie Newsome, split end; Dwight Stephenson, center

Leaders: Rushing—Johnny Davis (931 yards, 182 carries); Passing—Jeff Rutledge (64 of 107, 1,207 yards); Receiving—Ozzie Newsome (36 catches, 804 yards)

Alabama shook off an early loss at Nebraska to upset No. 1 Southern California at the Los Angeles Coliseum. Barry Krauss' interception of a two-point conversion secured the 21–20 victory. ... The 48–21 Auburn victory returned the Crimson Tide to the Sugar Bowl, where the Big Ten conference was making its debut with Ohio State. The coaching matchup of Bear Bryant and Woody Hayes drew the most attention, but after Alabama won 35–6, Bryant downplayed it by saying, "Woody is a great coach, and I ain't bad." ... Jeff Rutledge was named the Sugar Bowl MVP. ... Notre Dame's victory over No. 1 Texas gave Alabama a shot at the national championship, but voters instead elevated the Irish from No. 5 to No. 1. ... Joe Namath played his final NFL season with the Los Angeles Rams, and Bart Starr was voted into the Pro Football Hall of Fame.

1978

11–1, National champions, SEC champions

Sept. 2	Nebraska	Birmingham	W	20–3
Sept. 16	Missouri	Columbia	W	38–20
Sept. 23	Southern California	Birmingham	L	24–14
Sept. 30	Vanderbilt	Tuscaloosa	W	51–28
Oct. 7	Washington	Seattle	W	20–17
Oct. 14	Florida	Tuscaloosa	W	23–12
Oct. 21	Tennessee	Knoxville	W	30–17
Oct. 28	Virginia Tech	Tuscaloosa	W	35–0
Nov. 4	Mississippi State	Birmingham	W	35–14
Nov. 11	LSU	Birmingham	W	31–10
Dec. 2	Auburn	Birmingham	W	34–16
Jan. 1	Penn State	Sugar Bowl	W	14–7
Coach: Paul W. "Bear" Bryant				345–168

Captains: Marty Lyons, Jeff Rutledge, Tony Nathan

Ranking (AP): Preseason No. 1; Postseason No. 1

All-American: First team—Barry Krauss, linebacker; Marty Lyons, defensive tackle Second team—Dwight Stephenson, center

All-SEC: Mike Brock, tackle; Jim Bunch, tackle; Wayne Hamilton, defensive end; E.J. Junior, defensive end; Barry Krauss, linebacker; Murray Legg, safety; Marty Lyons, defensive tackle; Dwight Stephenson, center

Leaders: Rushing—Tony Nathan (770 yards, 111 carries); Passing—Jeff Rutledge (73 of 140, 1,078 yards); Receiving—Keith Pugh (20 catches, 446 yards)

Despite playing a brutal schedule, Alabama sustained only one loss, 24–14 to Southern California and arrived at the Sugar Bowl ranked second to face No. 1 Penn State. The game was essentially decided by a goal-line stand. After defensive back Don McNeal made a crucial stop short of the end zone on third-and-1, Nittany Lions quarterback Chuck Fusina went to check the line of scrimmage. "You'd better pass," defensive end

Marty Lyons said. The Nittany Lions didn't listen and Barry Krauss stopped the subsequent run up the gut. Krauss was named the game MVP. ... Alabama finished first in the final Associated Press poll, but the Trojans leapfrogged the Tide to No. 1 in United Press voting.

1979

12–0, national champions, SEC champions

Sept. 8	Georgia Tech	Atlanta	W	30–6
Sept. 22	Baylor	Birmingham	W	45–0
Sept. 29	Vanderbilt	Nashville	W	66–3
Oct. 6	Wichita State	Tuscaloosa	W	38–0
Oct. 13	Florida	Gainesville	W	40–0
Oct. 20	Tennessee	Birmingham	W	27–17
Oct. 27	Virginia Tech	Tuscaloosa	W	31–7
Nov. 3	Mississippi State	Tuscaloosa	W	24–7
Nov. 10	LSU	Baton Rouge	W	3–0
Nov. 17	Miami (Fla.)	Tuscaloosa	W	30–0
Dec. 1	Auburn	Birmingham	W	25–18
Jan. 1	Arkansas	Sugar Bowl	W	24–9

Coach: Paul W. "Bear" Bryant   383–67

Captains: Don McNeal, Steve Whitman

Ranking (AP): Preseason No. 2; Postseason No. 1

All-American: First team—Jim Bunch, tackle; Don McNeal, cornerback; Dwight Stephenson, center Second team—E.J. Junior, defensive end; Byron Braggs, defensive tackle Academic—Major Ogilvie, halfback

All-SEC: Thomas Boyd, linebacker; Byron Braggs, defensive tackle; Mike Brock, guard; Jim Bunch, tackle; David Hannah, defensive tackle; Jim Bob Harris, safety; E.J. Junior, defensive end; Don McNeal, cornerback; Major Ogilvie, halfback; Steadman Shealy, quarterback; Dwight Stephenson, center

Leaders: Rushing—Steadman Shealy (791 yards, 152 carries); Passing—Steadman Shealy (45 of 81, 717 yards); Receiving—Keith Pugh (25 catches, 433 yards)

Through the Years

Bear Bryant paces the practice field as the Tide gets ready for the Sugar Bowl in December 1979. A coaching legend, Bryant added to his legacy when Alabama beat Arkansas 24-9 for yet another national championship.

Led by backup quarterback Don Jacobs, Alabama overcame a 17–0 deficit to defeat Tennessee 27–17. ... Steadman Shealy led the late game-winning drive against Auburn to secure the conference title and a chance to play for the national championship. After the 24–9 victory against Arkansas in the Sugar Bowl, Alabama was a unanimous national champion for the first time in its history. Halfback Major Ogilvie was named game MVP. ... For the 1970s, Alabama compiled an incredible 103–16–1 record, with five of the losses in 1970. ... Safety Tommy Wilcox was named SEC Freshman of the Year. ... Ray Perkins was named head coach of the New York Giants.

1980
10–2

Sept. 6	Georgia Tech	Birmingham	W	26–3
Sept. 20	Ole Miss	Jackson	W	59–35
Sept. 27	Vanderbilt	Tuscaloosa	W	41–0
Oct. 4	Kentucky	Birmingham	W	45–0
Oct. 11	Rutgers	East Rutherford	W	17–13
Oct. 18	Tennessee	Knoxville	W	27–0
Oct. 25	Southern Miss	Tuscaloosa	W	42–7
Nov. 1	Mississippi State	Jackson	L	6–3
Nov. 8	LSU	Tuscaloosa	W	28–7
Nov. 15	Notre Dame	Birmingham	L	7–0
Nov. 29	Auburn	Birmingham	W	34–18
Jan. 1	Baylor	Cotton Bowl	W	30–2

Coach: Paul W. "Bear" Bryant   352–98

Captains: Major Ogilvie, Randy Scott

Ranking (AP): Preseason No. 2; Postseason No. 6

All-American: First team—Thomas Boyd, linebacker; E.J. Junior, defensive end Second team—Byron Braggs, defensive tackle

All-SEC: Thomas Boyd, linebacker; Byron Braggs, defensive tackle; Jim Bob Harris, safety; E.J. Junior, defensive end; Tommy Wilcox, safety

Leaders: Rushing—Billy Jackson (606 yards, 111 carries); Passing—Don Jacobs (32 of 76, 531 yards); Receiving—Bart Kraut (16 catches, 218 yards)

Alabama's 28-game winning streak came to a close with the 6–3 loss at Mississippi State. That, along with a 7–0 defeat to nemesis Notre Dame, cost any chance of winning three straight national titles. ... Despite having an inexperienced offense, the Crimson Tide pulled out an impressive 27–0 victory at Tennessee. ... Running back Major Ogilvie became the first player to score a touchdown in four successive New Year's Day bowls. ... He was named co-MVP of the Cotton Bowl along with Warren Lyles.

1981

9–2–1, SEC champions

Sept. 5	LSU	Baton Rouge	W	24–7
Sept. 12	Georgia Tech	Birmingham	L	24–21
Sept. 19	Kentucky	Lexington	W	19–10
Sept. 26	Vanderbilt	Nashville	W	28–7
Oct. 3	Ole Miss	Tuscaloosa	W	38–7
Oct. 10	Southern Miss	Birmingham	T	13–13
Oct. 17	Tennessee	Birmingham	W	38–19
Oct. 24	Rutgers	Tuscaloosa	W	31–7
Oct. 31	Mississippi State	Tuscaloosa	W	13–10
Nov. 14	Penn State	State College	W	31–16
Nov. 28	Auburn	Birmingham	W	28–17
Jan. 1	Texas	Cotton Bowl	L	14–12

Coach: Paul W. "Bear" Bryant — 296–151

Captains: Warren Lyles, Alan Gray

Ranking (AP): Preseason No. 4; Postseason No. 7

All-American: First team—Thomas Boyd, linebacker; Tommy Wilcox, safety Second team—Warren Lyles, nose guard

All-SEC: Thomas Boyd, linebacker; Jeremiah Castille, cornerback; Bob Cayavec, tackle; Jim Bob Harris, safety; Bart Krout, tight end; Warren Lyles, nose guard; Mike Pitts, defensive end; Tommy Wilcox, safety

Leaders: Rushing—Ricky Moore (347 yards, 79 carries); Passing—Walter Lewis (30 of 66, 633 yards); Receiving—Joey Jones (12 catches, 373 yards)

Alabama's first trip to Happy Valley to play Penn State was memorable. Thanks to another goal-line stand against the Nittany Lions, Bryant enjoyed career victory No. 314, which tied him with Amos Alonzo Stagg atop the all-time Division I-A coaching list. He set the new mark against Auburn after two fourth-quarter touchdowns resulted in a 28–17 victory. ... The 13th SEC championship was Bryant's last. ... The Crimson Tide used three different quarterbacks: Ken Coley, Alan Gray, and Walter Lewis. ... Auburn hired former Alabama assistant coach Pat Dye as head coach.

1982
8–4

Sept. 11	Georgia Tech	Atlanta	W	45–7
Sept. 18	Ole Miss	Jackson	W	42–14
Sept. 25	Vanderbilt	Tuscaloosa	W	24–21
Oct. 2	Arkansas State	Birmingham	W	34–7
Oct. 9	Penn State	Birmingham	W	42–21
Oct. 16	Tennessee	Knoxville	L	35–28
Oct. 23	Cincinnati	Tuscaloosa	W	21–3
Oct. 30	Mississippi State	Jackson	W	20–12
Nov. 6	LSU	Birmingham	L	20–10
Nov. 13	Southern Miss	Tuscaloosa	L	38–29
Nov. 27	Auburn	Birmingham	L	23–22
Dec. 29	Illinois	Liberty Bowl	W	21–15

Coach: Paul W. "Bear" Bryant   338–216

Captains: Eddie Lowe, Steve Mott

Ranking (AP): Preseason No. 3; Postseason NR

All-American: First team—Jeremiah Castille, cornerback; Mike Pitts, defensive end; Tommy Wilcox, safety Second team—Steve Mott, center

All-SEC: Tom Beazley, tackle; Jeremiah Castille, cornerback; Steve Mott, center; Mike Pitts, defensive end

Leaders: Rushing—Ricky Moore (600 yards, 111 carries); Passing—Walter Lewis (102 of 164, 1,515 yards); Receiving—Joey Jones (25 catches, 502 yards)

Alabama defeated eventual national champion Penn State 42–21, but lost Bryant's last game in Knoxville, 35–28. After subsequent losses to LSU, Southern Miss, and Auburn, Bryant announced his retirement on December 15. In his sendoff game, the Liberty Bowl against Illinois, Jeremiah Castille had three interceptions and caused a fumble inside the 3-yard line to help lead a 21–15 victory. Said Illinois quarterback Tony Eason: "Let's face it. Alabama just likes to hit you. They are the hardest hitting team I've ever played against." ... Bryant concluded his career with a 232–46–8 record at Alabama and 323 wins overall. He died four weeks later, on January 26, 1983.

1983
8–4

Sept. 10	Georgia Tech	Birmingham	W	20–7
Sept. 17	Ole Miss	Tuscaloosa	W	40–0
Sept. 24	Vanderbilt	Nashville	W	44–24
Oct. 1	Memphis State	Tuscaloosa	W	44–13
Oct. 8	Penn State	State College	L	34–28
Oct. 15	Tennessee	Birmingham	L	41–34
Oct. 29	Mississippi State	Tuscaloosa	W	35–18
Nov. 5	LSU	Baton Rouge	W	32–26
Nov. 12	Southern Miss	Birmingham	W	28–16
Nov. 25	Boston College	Foxboro	L	20–13
Dec. 3	Auburn	Birmingham	L	23–20
Dec. 24	Southern Methodist	Sun Bowl	W	28–7
Coach: Ray Perkins				366–229

Captains: Walter Lewis, Randy Edwards

Ranking (AP): Preseason No.13; Postseason No. 15

All-American: Second team—Walter Lewis, quarterback; Rickey Moore, fullback

All-SEC: Mike Adcock, guard; Walter Lewis, quarterback; Ricky Moore, fullback

Leaders: Rushing—Ricky Moore (947 yards, 166 carries); Passing—Walter Lewis (144 of 256, 1,991 yards); Receiving—Joey Jones (31 catches, 468 yards)

While players wore a little houndstooth hat on the back of their helmets in honor of former coach Paul W. "Bear" Bryant, former player Ray Perkins had the impossible task of replacing him. Alabama lost a controversial game at Penn State (34–28, after officials ruled Prestod Gothard out of bounds in the final seconds while replays seemed to indicate that he made a touchdown catch), a 41–34 shootout to Tennessee, and a 20–13 loss to Boston College in the middle of a New England ice storm. Bo Jackson also proved to be difficult to stop, with fans ignoring a downpour and tornado warning during Auburn's 23–20 victory. ... Quarterback Walter Lewis was named MVP of the Sun Bowl, and center Wes Neighbors earned the top lineman award.

1984
5–6

Sept. 8	Boston College	Birmingham	L	38–31
Sept. 15	Georgia Tech	Atlanta	L	16–6
Sept. 22	SW Louisiana	Tuscaloosa	W	37–14
Sept. 29	Vanderbilt	Tuscaloosa	L	30–21
Oct. 6	Georgia	Birmingham	L	24–14
Oct. 13	Penn State	Tuscaloosa	W	6–0
Oct. 20	Tennessee	Knoxville	L	28–27
Nov. 3	Mississippi State	Jackson	W	24–20
Nov. 10	LSU	Birmingham	L	16–14
Nov. 17	Cincinnati	Cincinnati	W	29–7
Dec. 1	Auburn	Birmingham	W	17–15
Coach: Ray Perkins				226–208

Captains: Paul Ott Carruth, Emanuel King

Ranking (AP): Preseason No. 9; Postseason NR

All-American: First team—Cornelius Bennett, linebacker

All-SEC: Cornelius Bennett, linebacker; Jon Hand, defensive tackle

Leaders: Rushing—Paul Carruth (782 yards, 163 carries); Passing—Vince Sutton (60 of 135, 662 yards); Receiving—Greg Richardson (22 catches, 357 yards)

Filling the shoes of the irreplaceable Bear Bryant, Ray Perkins takes charge during a 1983 practice as Ernest Carroll looks on.

After accumulating 297 all-purpose yards, Kerry Goode was lost for the season with a knee injury early in the third quarter of the opener against Boston College. ... After losing four of its first five games, Alabama had its 25-year bowl streak snapped. However, fans were able to enjoy the season-ending victory against Auburn. Late in the game, when the Tigers only needed a field goal to secure the victory, Coach Pat Dye called a run from the 1-yard line. When Bo Jackson went the wrong direction, defensive back Rory Turner stopped Brent Fullwood with a game-saving tackle. "I just waxed the dude," Turner said.

1985
9-2-1

Sept. 2	Georgia	Athens	W	20–16
Sept. 14	Texas A&M	Birmingham	W	23–10
Sept. 21	Cincinnati	Tuscaloosa	W	45–10
Sept. 28	Vanderbilt	Nashville	W	40–20
Oct. 12	Penn State	State College	L	19–17
Oct. 19	Tennessee	Birmingham	L	16–14
Oct. 26	Memphis State	Memphis	W	28–9
Nov. 2	Mississippi State	Tuscaloosa	W	44–28
Nov. 9	LSU	Baton Rouge	T	14–14
Nov. 16	Southern Miss	Tuscaloosa	W	24–13
Nov. 30	Auburn	Birmingham	W	25–23
Dec. 28	Southern California	Aloha Bowl	W	24–3
Coach: Ray Perkins				318–181

Captains: Jon Hand, Thornton Chandler

Ranking (AP): Preseason NR; Postseason No. 13

All-American: First team—Cornelius Bennett, linebacker; Jon Hand, defensive tackle Second team—Wes Neighbors, center

All-SEC: Al Bell, split end; Cornelius Bennett, linebacker; Jon Hand, defensive tackle; Curt Jarvis, nose guard; Freddie Robinson, cornerback; Mike Shula, quarterback

Leaders: Rushing—Gene Jelks (588 yards, 93 carries); Passing—Mike Shula (138 of 229, 2,009 yards); Receiving—Albert Bell (37 catches, 648 yards)

Quarterback Mike Shula's touchdown pass to junior-college transfer Al Bell in the final seconds resulted in a 20–16 upset victory at Georgia in the opener. Penn State and Tennessee both won in the final moments, leading up to the 50th meeting with Auburn. The lead changed hands four times in the fourth quarter, when Crimson Tide kicker Van Tiffin made a game-winning 52-yard field goal into the wind—"The Kick." His career-best came earlier in the season, 57 yards against Texas A&M. "A game like this, Alabama players will remember it for the rest of their lives," Tigers Coach Pat Dye said afterward. "Auburn players, it'll eat their guts out the rest of their lives." ... Gene Jelks and Cornelius Bennett were named MVPs of the Aloha Bowl.

1986
10–3

Aug. 27	Ohio State	East Rutherford	W	16–10
Sept. 6	Vanderbilt	Tuscaloosa	W	42–10
Sept. 13	Southern Miss	Birmingham	W	31–17
Sept. 20	Florida	Gainesville	W	21–7
Oct. 4	Notre Dame	Birmingham	W	28–10
Oct. 11	Memphis State	Tuscaloosa	W	37–0
Oct. 18	Tennessee	Knoxville	W	56–28
Oct. 25	Penn State	Tuscaloosa	L	23–3
Nov. 1	Mississippi State	Starkville	W	38–3
Nov. 8	LSU	Birmingham	L	14–10
Nov. 15	Temple	Tuscaloosa	W	24–14
Nov. 29	Auburn	Birmingham	L	21–17
Dec. 25	Washington	Sun Bowl	W	28–6
Coach: Ray Perkins				351–163

Captains: Mike Shula, Cornelius Bennett

Ranking (AP): Preseason No. 5; Postseason No. 9

All-American: First team—Cornelius Bennett, linebacker; Bobby Humphrey, running back; Van Tiffin, kicker Second team—Wes Neighbors, center

All-SEC: Cornelius Bennett, linebacker; Bill Condon, guard; Bobby Humphrey, tailback; Curt Jarvis, nose guard; Wes Neighbors, center; Freddie Robinson, cornerback; Van Tiffin, kicker

Van Tiffin makes contact on a field-goal attempt against Ohio State in the 1986 Kickoff Classic. Tiffin holds the school record for extra points with 135 (never missing one) and for the longest field goal in school history, a 57-yard effort against Texas A&M in 1985.

Awards: Cornelius Bennett, Lombardi Award (Most Outstanding Lineman)

Leaders: Rushing—Bobby Humphrey (1,471 yards, 236 carries); Passing—Mike Shula (127 of 235, 1,486 yards); Receiving—Albert Bell (26 catches, 315 yards)

The season was best remembered for "The Sack," when Cornelius Bennett put a brutal hit on Steve Beuerlein to help lead Alabama's first-ever victory against Notre Dame. "He knocked me woozy," Beuerlein said. "I have never been hit like that before and hopefully I'll never be hit like that again." Bennett, a three-time All-American, was voted the SEC Athlete of the Year. ... Alabama defeated Ohio State and Florida but faltered down the stretch to Penn State, LSU, and Auburn. ... After Alabama defeated Washington 28–6 in the Sun Bowl, Perkins left to coach the Tampa Bay Buccaneers. ... Van Tiffin completed his career with a perfect mark from extra-point range, 135 of 135. ... Defensive tackle Willie Ryles collapsed during an August practice period and never regained consciousness. In April running back George Scruggs was killed in a car accident that also left cornerback Vernon Wilkinson in serious condition.

1987
7-5

Sept. 5	Southern Miss	Birmingham	W	38–6
Sept. 12	Penn State	State College	W	24–13
Sept. 19	Florida	Birmingham	L	23–14
Sept. 26	Vanderbilt	Nashville	W	30–23
Oct. 3	SW Louisiana	Birmingham	W	38–10
Oct. 10	Memphis State	Memphis	L	13–10
Oct. 17	Tennessee	Birmingham	W	41–22
Oct. 31	Mississippi State	Birmingham	W	21–18
Nov. 7	LSU	Baton Rouge	W	22–10
Nov. 14	Notre Dame	South Bend	L	37–6
Nov. 27	Auburn	Birmingham	L	10–0
Jan. 2	Michigan	Hall of Fame	L	28–24
Coach: Bill Curry				268–213

Through the Years

Captains: Kerry Goode, Randy Rockwell

All-American: First team—Bobby Humphrey, running back
Second team—Derrick Thomas, linebacker; Larry Rose, guard

All-SEC: Bill Condon, guard; Howard Cross, tight end; Bobby Humphrey, tailback; Kermit Kendrick, safety; Derrick Thomas, linebacker; Willie Wyatt, nose guard

Leaders: Rushing—Bobby Humphrey (1,255 yards, 238 carries); Passing—Jeff Dunn (36 of 87, 484 yards); Receiving—Clay Whitehurst (18 catches, 278 yards)

Derrick Thomas forced a team-record seven fumbles. ... Bill Curry became the first head coach without an Alabama tie since Frank Thomas in 1937. ... Despite losing the final two games of the regular season, to Notre Dame and Auburn, Alabama was invited to play Michigan in the Hall of Fame Bowl. However, a last-second touchdown gave the Wolverines a 28–24 victory. ... Due to the stadium renovation in Tuscaloosa, all home games were played at Legion Field in Birmingham. Also, it was the final year Alabama and Auburn split tickets at the neutral-site Iron Bowl, with the series heading to the campus stadiums for good.

1988
9–3

Sept. 10	Temple	Philadelphia	W	37–0
Sept. 24	Vanderbilt	Tuscaloosa	W	44–10
Oct. 1	Kentucky	Lexington	W	31–27
Oct. 8	Ole Miss	Tuscaloosa	L	22–12
Oct. 15	Tennessee	Knoxville	W	28–20
Oct. 22	Penn State	Birmingham	W	8–3
Oct. 29	Mississippi State	Starkville	W	53–34
Nov. 5	LSU	Tuscaloosa	L	19–18
Nov. 12	SW Louisiana	Birmingham	W	17–0
Nov. 25	Auburn	Birmingham	L	15–10
Dec. 1	Texas A&M	College Station	W	30–10
Dec. 24	Army	Sun Bowl	W	29–28

Coach: Bill Curry 317–188

Captains: David Smith, Derrick Thomas

Ranking (AP): Preseason No. 14; Postseason No. 17

All-American: First team—Derrick Thomas, linebacker; Kermit

Kendrick, safety; Larry Rose, guard

All-SEC: Lee Ozmint, safety; Larry Rose, guard; Derrick Thomas, linebacker

Awards: Derrick Thomas, Dick Butkus Award (Most Outstanding Linebacker)

Leaders: Rushing—Murry Hill (778 yards, 136 carries); Passing—David Smith (135 of 223, 1,592 yards); Receiving—Greg Payne (33 catches, 442 yards)

Derrick Thomas had a team-record 39 tackles for a loss, totaling 250 yards. ... A foot injury during spring practice curtailed Bobby Humphrey's bid for the Heisman Trophy. He rebroke it during the second game of the season, a 44–10 victory against Vanderbilt. Gene Jelks sustained a season-ending knee injury in the same game. On a bad knee, quarterback David Smith led Alabama to nine wins, including a 29–28 victory over Army in the Sun Bowl. ... The star of the team was linebacker Derrick Thomas, who accumulated 27 sacks, 12 tackles for a loss, 44 quarterback hurries, and blocked two kicks. ... When Alabama didn't make it to College Station to play the September 17 game against Texas A&M due to the threat of Hurricane Gilbert, the game was rescheduled for December 1, and the Crimson Tide won 30–10. ... Renovated Bryant-Denny Stadium reopened, seating 70,123.

1989

10–2, SEC champions

Sept. 16	Memphis State	Birmingham	W	35–7
Sept. 23	Kentucky	Tuscaloosa	W	15–3
Sept. 30	Vanderbilt	Nashville	W	20–14
Oct. 7	Ole Miss	Jackson	W	62–27
Oct. 14	SW Louisiana	Tuscaloosa	W	24–17
Oct. 21	Tennessee	Birmingham	W	47–30
Oct. 28	Penn State	State College	W	17–16
Nov. 3	Mississippi State	Birmingham	W	23–10
Nov. 11	LSU	Baton Rouge	W	32–16
Nov. 18	Southern Miss	Tuscaloosa	W	37–14
Dec. 2	Auburn	Auburn	L	30–20
Jan. 1	Miami	Sugar Bowl	L	33–25
Coach: Bill Curry				357–217

Captains: Marco Battle, Willie Wyatt

Ranking (AP): Preseason No. 16; Postseason No. 9

All-American: First team—Keith McCants, linebacker; John Mangum, cornerback Second team—Siran Stacy, running back; Lamonde Russell, tight end; Philip Doyle, kicker

All-SEC: Terrill Chatman, tackle; Philip Doyle, kicker; Gary Hollingsworth, quarterback; John Mangum, cornerback; Keith McCants, linebacker; Lamonde Russell, tight end; Roger Shultz, center; Siran Stacy, running back; Efrum Thomas, cornerback; Willie Wyatt, nose guard

Leaders: Rushing—Siran Stacy (1,079 yards, 216 carries); Passing—Gary Hollingsworth (205 of 339, 2,379 yards); Receiving—Lamonde Russell (51 catches, 622 yards)

John Mangum broke up a team-record 24 passes. ... Backup quarterback Gary Hollingsworth led Alabama to its first SEC title since 1981. However, the Crimson Tide wasn't able to compensate for decades of frustration felt by Auburn, which won the first meeting on the plains, 30–20. ... After Alabama lost to Miami 33–25 in the Sugar Bowl, securing the national championship for the Hurricanes, Coach Bill Curry resigned and was later hired by Kentucky. His record at Alabama was 26–10, but he was unable to defeat Auburn. "I knew Coach Curry was leaving when he

Siran Stacy carries against Tennessee in 1989. After spending time at community college, Stacy came to Tuscaloosa and was a two-time All-SEC performer. Recently, he was the honorary captain at the 2008 Iron Bowl.

came in the squad room with a blue jacket on and in its lapels were tickets to the Kentucky Derby," center Roger Shultz joked. ... Hootie Ingram returned to the Capstone as director of athletics, and called it a "dream come true."

Through the Years

1990
7-5

Sept. 8	Southern Miss	Birmingham	L	27-24
Sept. 15	Florida	Tuscaloosa	L	17-13
Sept. 22	Georgia	Athens	L	17-16
Sept. 29	Vanderbilt	Tuscaloosa	W	59-28
Oct. 6	SW Louisiana	Lafayette	W	25-6
Oct. 20	Tennessee	Knoxville	W	9-6
Oct. 27	Penn State	Tuscaloosa	L	9-0
Nov. 3	Mississippi State	Starkville	W	22-0
Nov. 10	LSU	Tuscaloosa	W	24-3
Nov. 17	Cincinnati	Birmingham	W	45-7
Dec. 1	Auburn	Birmingham	W	16-7
Jan. 1	Louisville	Fiesta Bowl	L	34-7
Coach: Gene Stallings				260-161

Captains: Gary Hollingsworth, Efrum Thomas, Philip Doyle

All-American: First team—Phillip Doyle, kicker

All-SEC: Terrill Chatman, tackle, Phillip Doyle, kicker; Roger Shultz, center; John Sullins, linebacker; Efrum Thomas, safety; George Thornton, defensive end

Leaders: Rushing—Chris Anderson (492 yards, 106 carries); Passing—Gary Hollingsworth (140 of 282, 1,463 yards); Receiving—Lamonde Russell (28 catches, 306 yards)

The optimism created with the hiring of Gene Stallings—who said "What's wrong with people expecting excellence?"—waned when Alabama lost its first three games and Siran Stacy, Craig Sanderson, and Prince Wimbley all sustained season-ending injuries. However, the Crimson Tide won seven of its last eight regular-season games, including a 9–6 victory at Tennessee keyed by Stacy Harrison's blocked field goal and kicker Philip Doyle's last-second field goal. ... Alabama's victory against Auburn ended a four-game losing streak in the series. ... Doyle finished as the national field-goal champion.

1991
11–1

Sept. 7	Temple	Birmingham	W	41–3
Sept. 14	Florida	Gainesville	L	35–0
Sept. 21	Georgia	Tuscaloosa	W	10–0
Sept. 28	Vanderbilt	Nashville	W	48–17
Oct. 5	Tenn.-Chattanooga	Birmingham	W	53–7
Oct. 12	Tulane	Tuscaloosa	W	62–0
Oct. 19	Tennessee	Birmingham	W	24–19
Nov. 2	Mississippi State	Tuscaloosa	W	13–7
Nov. 9	LSU	Baton Rouge	W	20–17
Nov. 16	Memphis State	Memphis	W	10–7
Nov. 30	Auburn	Birmingham	W	13–6
Dec. 28	Colorado	Blockbuster Bowl	W	30–25
Coach: Gene Stallings				324–143

Captains: Siran Stacy, Robert Stewart, John Sullins, Kevin Turner

Ranking (AP): Preseason No. 22; Postseason No. 5

All-American: First team—Robert Stewart, nose tackle

All-SEC: Siran Stacy, tailback; Robert Stewart, nose tackle; John Sullins, linebacker

Leaders: Rushing—Siran Stacy (966 yards, 200 carries); Passing—Danny Woodson (64 of 101, 882 yards); Receiving—David Palmer (17 catches, 314 yards)

After an early-season loss to Florida, the season featured numerous close, last-minute wins, including Tennessee and Auburn at Legion Field. ... Jay Barker took over as starting quarterback at LSU after Danny Woodson was suspended for the rest of the season. ... Freshman David Palmer returned three punts for touchdowns during the regular season to set a school record. He had another in the 30–25 victory against defending national champion Colorado in the Blockbuster Bowl and was named game MVP. ... The university dedicated the new Hank Crisp Indoor Facility.

1992

13–0, National champions, SEC champions

Sept. 5	Vanderbilt	Tuscaloosa	W	25–8
Sept. 12	Southern Miss	Birmingham	W	17–10
Sept. 19	Arkansas	Little Rock	W	38–11
Sept. 26	Louisiana Tech	Birmingham	W	13–0
Oct. 3	South Carolina	Tuscaloosa	W	48–7
Oct. 10	Tulane	New Orleans	W	37–0
Oct. 17	Tennessee	Knoxville	W	17–10
Oct. 24	Ole Miss	Tuscaloosa	W	31–10
Nov. 7	LSU	Baton Rouge	W	31–11
Nov. 14	Mississippi State	Starkville	W	30–21
Nov. 26	Auburn	Birmingham	W	17–0
Dec. 5	Florida	SEC Championship	W	28–21
Jan. 1	Miami (Fla.)	Sugar Bowl	W	34–13
Coach: Gene Stallings				366–122

Captains: Derrick Oden, George Teague, George Wilson, Prince Wimbley

Ranking (AP): Preseason No. 9; Postseason No. 1

All-American: First team—John Copeland, defensive end; Eric Curry, defensive end; Antonio Langham, cornerback Second team—George Teague, safety

All-SEC: John Copeland, defensive end; Eric Curry, defensive end; Lemanski Hall, linebacker; Antonio Langham, cornerback; Derrick Lassic, tailback; Antonio London, linebacker; Derrick Oden, linebacker; Tobie Sheils, center; George Teague, safety

Leaders: Rushing—Derrick Lassic (905 yards, 178 carries); Passing—Jay Barker (132 of 243, 1,614 yards); Receiving—David Palmer (24 catches, 297 yards)

Alabama's centennial season also featured the first SEC Championship Game, and after the Crimson Tide won at Tennessee, with Derrick Lassic rushing for 142 yards, it emerged as a contender for both conference and national titles. Antonio Langham's interception return for a touchdown in the final minutes against Florida secured the SEC title and earned him MVP honors. Langham had done the same thing to Auburn, with the dominating defense yielding just 20 rushing yards. Against No. 1 Miami in the Sugar Bowl,

Alabama attempted just four passes and pounded out a 34–14 victory. Although safety George Teague returned an interception for a touchdown and dramatically chased down receiver Lamar Thomas—taking the ball away from him on a play that was nullified by a penalty—Lassic was named Sugar Bowl MVP. ... Stallings was named national coach of the year. ... said defensive coordinator Bill Oliver: "I wish Coach Bryant were here to see this defense play."

1993

*1–12, SEC Western Division champions

Sept. 4	Tulane	Birmingham	W	31–17
Sept. 11	Vanderbilt	Nashville	W	17–6
Sept. 18	Arkansas	Tuscaloosa	W	43–3
Sept. 25	Louisiana Tech	Birmingham	W	56–3
Oct. 2	South Carolina	Columbia	W	17–6
Oct. 16	Tennessee	Birmingham	T	17–17
Oct. 23	Ole Miss	Oxford	W	19–14
Oct. 30	Southern Miss	Tuscaloosa	W	40–0
Nov. 6	LSU	Tuscaloosa	L	17–13
Nov. 13	Mississippi State	Tuscaloosa	W	36–25
Nov. 20	Auburn	Auburn	L	22–14
Dec. 4	Florida	SEC Championship	L	28–13
Dec. 31	North Carolina	Gator Bowl	W	24–10
Coach: Gene Stallings				316–158

Captains: Chris Anderson, Lemanski Hall, Antonio Langham, Tobie Sheils

Ranking (AP): Preseason No. 2; Postseason No. 14

All-American: First team—Antonio Langham, cornerback; David Palmer, wide receiver; Michael Proctor, kicker

All-SEC: Tobie Sheils, center; David Palmer, wide receiver; Michael Proctor, kicker; Jeremy Nunley, defensive end; Lemanski Hall, linebacker; Antonio Langham, cornerback; Sam Shade, safety

Awards: Antonio Langham, Thorpe Award (Most Outstanding Defensive Back)

Leaders: Rushing—Sherman Williams (738 yards, 168 carries); Passing—Jay Barker (98 of 171, 1,524 yards); Receiving—David Palmer (61 catches, 1,000 yards)

*Alabama finished 9–3–1 but was forced to forfeit all its regular season wins when it was determined Antonio Langham should have been ruled ineligible. ... Quarterback Jay Barker was sidelined by an injury for losses to LSU, Auburn, and Florida in the SEC Championship Game. ... The tie against Tennessee was the last in Alabama history, as the NCAA adopted overtime three years later. ... Backup quarterback Brian Burgdorf was voted MVP of the Gator Bowl. ...Palmer finished third in Heisman Trophy voting. ... After winning six national title rings as an assistant coach and one as a player, Mal Moore retired from coaching and would later become athletics director.

1994

12–1, SEC Western Division champions

Sept. 3	Tenn.-Chattanooga	Birmingham	W	42–13
Sept. 10	Vanderbilt	Tuscaloosa	W	17–7
Sept. 17	Arkansas	Fayetteville	W	13–6
Sept. 24	Tulane	Birmingham	W	20–10
Oct. 1	Georgia	Tuscaloosa	W	29–28
Oct. 8	Southern Miss	Tuscaloosa	W	14–6
Oct. 15	Tennessee	Knoxville	W	17–13
Oct. 22	Ole Miss	Tuscaloosa	W	21–10
Nov. 5	LSU	Baton Rouge	W	35–17
Nov. 12	Mississippi State	Starkville	W	29–25
Nov. 19	Auburn	Birmingham	W	21–14
Dec. 3	Florida	SEC Championship	L	24–23
Jan. 2	Ohio State	Florida Citrus Bowl	W	24–17
Coach: Gene Stallings				305–190

Captains: Jay Barker, Tommy Johnson, Tarrant Lynch, San Shade

Ranking (AP): Preseason No. 12; Postseason No. 5

All-American: First team—Jay Barker, quarterback; Michael Proctor, kicker Second team—Jay Barker, quarterback; Dameian Jeffries, defensive end; Sherman Williams, tailback

All-SEC: Jay Barker, quarterback; Willie Gaston, safety; Dameian Jeffries, defensive end; Tommy Johnson, cornerback; Michael Proctor, kicker; Jon Stevenson, guard; Sherman Williams, tailback

Awards: Jay Barker, Johnny Unitas Golden Arm Award (Best Quarterback)

Leaders: Rushing—Sherman Williams (1,341 yards, 291 carries); Passing—Jay Barker (139 of 226, 1,996 yards); Receiving—Curtis Brown (39 catches, 639 yards)

Despite a bad shoulder, quarterback Jay Barker guided Alabama through a perfect regular season, including close victories against Georgia, Tennessee, Mississippi State, and Auburn. He closed his career with a touchdown pass to running back Sherman Williams as Alabama defeated talent-laden Ohio State 24–17 in the Florida Citrus Bowl. Williams was named MVP, and the game is also remembered for being delayed by a stray dog on the field. ... Dwayne Rudd returned an interception for a touchdown, but when the Crimson Tide missed a pair of potential picks, Florida won the SEC Championship Game. ... The Ole Miss game was stopped in the second quarter due to lightning and a thunderstorm. During the offseason the NCAA instituted a policy to halt all games when such inclement weather threatened participants and fans.

Through the Years

35

Wins by Jay Barker as Alabama's quarterback. The team only failed to win three times with Barker at the helm, giving him a 35-2-1 record. It is the best winning percentage by any quarterback in school history.

1995
8–3

Sept. 2	Vanderbilt	Nashville	W	33–25
Sept. 9	Southern Miss	Birmingham	W	24–20
Sept. 16	Arkansas	Tuscaloosa	L	20–19
Sept. 30	Georgia	Athens	W	31–0
Oct. 7	N. Carolina State	Tuscaloosa	W	27–11
Oct. 14	Tennessee	Birmingham	L	41–14
Oct. 21	Ole Miss	Oxford	W	23–9
Oct. 28	North Texas	Tuscaloosa	W	38–19
Nov. 4	LSU	Tuscaloosa	W	10–3
Nov. 11	Mississippi State	Tuscaloosa	W	14–9
Nov. 18	Auburn	Auburn	L	31–27
Coach: Gene Stallings				260–188

Captains: Shannon Brown, Brian Burgdorf, Tony Johnson, John Walters

Ranking (AP): Preseason No. 10; Postseason No. 21

All-American: Second team—Shannon Brown, defensive tackle

All-SEC: Shannon Brown, defensive tackle; Kevin Jackson, safety; John Walters, linebacker

Leaders: Rushing—Dennis Riddle (969 yards, 236 carries); Passing—Brian Burgdorf (96 of 162, 1,200 yards); Receiving—Curtis Brown (43 catches, 557 yards)

Alabama wasn't bowl eligible due to penalties handed down by the National Collegiate Athletic Association. ... Tennessee recorded its first victory against Alabama since 1985, and Alabama lost close controversial games to Arkansas and Auburn. Against the Razorbacks, officials failed to notice Arkansas had 12 players on the field during the final moments. An apparent touchdown catch by Curtis Brown from Freddie Kitchens was also missed at Auburn. ... Brian Burgdorf's 30-yard touchdown pass to Toderick Malone on the final play of the game gave Alabama a 24–20 victory against Southern Miss.

Gene Stallings stalks the sideline during the 1995 matchup against LSU. Running back Dennis Riddle is seen next to Stallings, and he was the key player of the game, rushing for 174 yards and the only touchdown in Alabama's 10–3 win.

1996

10–3, SEC Western Division champions

Aug. 31	Bowling Green	Birmingham	W	21–7
Sept. 7	Southern Miss	Tuscaloosa	W	20–10
Sept. 14	Vanderbilt	Tuscaloosa	W	36–26
Sept. 21	Arkansas	Little Rock	W	17–7
Oct. 5	Kentucky	Tuscaloosa	W	35–7
Oct. 12	NC State	Raleigh	W	24–19
Oct. 19	Ole Miss	Tuscaloosa	W	37–0
Oct. 26	Tennessee	Knoxville	L	20–13
Nov. 9	LSU	Baton Rouge	W	26–0
Nov. 16	Mississippi State	Starkville	L	17–16
Nov. 23	Auburn	Birmingham	W	24–23
Dec. 7	Florida	SEC Championship	L	45–30
Jan. 1	Michigan	Outback Bowl	W	17–14
Coach: Gene Stallings				316–195

Captains: John Causey, Fernando Davis

Ranking (AP): Preseason No. 15; Postseason No. 11

All-American: First team—Kevin Jackson, safety; Michael Myers, defensive end; Dwayne Rudd, linebacker

All-SEC: Kevin Jackson, safety; Michael Myers, defensive end; Dwayne Rudd, linebacker; Ralph Staten, linebacker; Deshea Townsend, cornerback

Leaders: Rushing—Dennis Riddle (1,079 yards, 242 carries); Passing—Freddie Kitchens (152 of 302, 2,124 yards); Receiving—Michael Vaughn (39 catches, 702 yards)

Freshman running back Shaun Alexander had a school-record 291 rushing yards on 20 carries against LSU. ... The Monday prior to the Auburn game, Stallings told those closest to him that he would retire at season's end. After a swing pass from Freddie Kitchens to Dennis Riddle (and Jon Brock's extra point) gave Alabama a 24–23 victory, he told the team. The distraction prior to the SEC Championship Game didn't sit well with the coach, nor did the loss to Florida, which went on to win the national championship. ... Kitchens had a 90-yard touchdown pass to Michael Vaughn against Florida. ... Dwayne Rudd returned an interception for a touchdown against Michigan and was named MVP of the Outback Bowl. ... Mike DuBose, who had just replaced Bill Oliver as defensive coordinator, (while Woody McCorvey replaced Homer Smith as offensive coordinator) was named Stallings' successor.

1997
4–7

Aug. 30	Houston	Birmingham	W	42–17
Sept. 11	Vanderbilt	Nashville	W	20–0
Sept. 20	Arkansas	Tuscaloosa	L	17–16
Sept. 27	Southern Miss	Birmingham	W	27–14
Oct. 4	Kentucky	Lexington	L OT	40–34
Oct 18	Tennessee	Birmingham	L	38–21
Oct. 25	Ole Miss	Oxford	W	29–20
Nov. 1	Louisiana Tech	Tuscaloosa	L	26–20
Nov. 8	LSU	Tuscaloosa	L	27–0
Nov. 15	Mississippi State	Tuscaloosa	L	32–20
Nov. 22	Auburn	Auburn	L	18–17
Coach: Mike DuBose				246–248

Captains: Curtis Alexander, Paul Pickett, Rod Rutledge, Deshea Townsend

Ranking (AP): Preseason No. 15; Postseason No. NR

All-American: Second team—Chris Hood, defensive end

All-SEC: Chris Hood, defensive end

Leaders: Rushing—Curtis Alexander (729 yards, 155 carries); Passing—Freddie Kitchens (121 of 237 yards, 1,545 yards); Receiving—Quincy Jackson (28 catches, 472 yards)

The emotional highs and lows under DuBose started with a low thanks to losses against Arkansas, Kentucky, and Mississippi State; blowout defeats to Tennessee and LSU; and a homecoming disaster against Louisiana Tech. Alabama had a chance to knock Auburn out of the SEC Championship Game, but a fumble on a late screen pass set up the Tigers' game-winning field goal. ... It was the first losing season

Shaun Alexander points to the sky after scoring the game-winning touchdown in overtime against Florida in 1999. Alexander had a stellar career at Alabama.

since 1984 and marked the first time Alabama didn't win a game in Tuscaloosa since 1955. ... Alabama played in its first overtime game, a loss to Kentucky.

1998
7-5

Sept. 5	Brigham Young	Tuscaloosa	W	38-31
Sept. 12	Vanderbilt	Birmingham	W	32-7
Sept. 26	Arkansas	Fayetteville	L	42-6
Oct. 3	Florida	Tuscaloosa	L	16-10
Oct. 10	Ole Miss	Tuscaloosa	W OT	20-17
Oct. 17	East Carolina	Birmingham	W	23-22
Oct. 24	Tennessee	Knoxville	L	35-18
Oct. 31	Southern Miss	Tuscaloosa	W	30-20
Nov. 7	LSU	Baton Rouge	W	22-16
Nov. 14	Mississippi State	Starkville	L	26-14
Nov. 21	Auburn	Birmingham	W	31-17
Dec. 29	Virginia Tech	Music City Bowl	L	38-7
Coach: Mike DuBose				251-287

Captains: Calvin Hall, John David Phillips, Daniel Pope, Kelvin Singler, Trevis Smith

All-SEC: Shaun Alexander, tailback; Fernando Bryant, cornerback; Daniel Pope, punter; Chris Samuels, tackle

Leaders: Rushing—Shaun Alexander (1,178 yards, 258 carries); Passing—Andrew Zow (143 of 256, 1,169 yards); Receiving—Quincy Jackson (48 catches, 621 yards)

Arvin Richard returned a team-record 25 kickoffs for 595 yards. ... Running back Shaun Alexander scored five touchdowns in the season opener against Brigham Young in newly renovated Bryant-Denny Stadium, with capacity up to 83,818. ... Alabama's victory against Ole Miss was its first overtime win. ... Despite getting pounded at Arkansas and Tennessee, and losing its third straight to Mississippi State, the Crimson Tide had a comeback victory against LSU and beat Auburn in the last Iron Bowl played at Legion Field. ... With the 38-7 loss to Virginia Tech in the Music City Bowl, Alabama set a school record for points allowed in a single season, with 287.

1999

10–3, SEC champions

Date	Opponent	Location		Score
Sept. 4	Vanderbilt	Nashville	W	28–17
Sept. 11	Houston	Birmingham	W	37–10
Sept. 18	Louisiana Tech	Birmingham	L	29–28
Sept. 25	Arkansas	Tuscaloosa	W	35–28
Oct. 2	Florida	Gainesville	W	40–39
Oct. 16	Ole Miss	Oxford	W	30–24
Oct. 23	Tennessee	Tuscaloosa	L	21–7
Oct. 30	Southern Miss	Tuscaloosa	W	35–14
Nov. 6	LSU	Tuscaloosa	W	23–17
Nov. 13	Mississippi State	Tuscaloosa	W	19–7
Nov. 20	Auburn	Auburn	W	28–17
Dec. 4	Florida	SEC Championship	W	34–7
Jan. 1	Michigan	Orange Bowl	L	35–34
Coach: Mike DuBose				380–265

Captains: Shaun Alexander, Cornelius Griffin, Miguel Merritt, Ryan Pflugner, Chris Samuels

Ranking (AP): Preseason No. 20; Postseason No. 8

All-American: First team—Chris Samuels, tackle; Shaun Alexander, tailback

All-SEC: Shaun Alexander, tailback; Paul Hogan, center; Freddie Milons, split end; Chris Samuels, tackle

Awards: Chris Samuels, Outland Trophy (best interior lineman)

Leaders: Rushing—Shaun Alexander (1,383 yards, 302 carries); Passing—Andrew Zow (148 of 264, 1,799 yards); Receiving—Freddie Milons (65 catches, 733 yards)

Running behind left tackle Chris Samuels, Shaun Alexander scored a team-record 24 touchdowns. However, an ankle injury derailed his Heisman Trophy chances, and Samuels missed the Orange Bowl. Defensively, Alabama was also without Marvin Constant, Kenny Smith, and Canary Knight against Michigan, which won in overtime. ... The Crimson Tide won at Auburn for the first time. ... Alabama rushed for 300 yards in the Florida rematch at the SEC Championship Game.

2000
3–8

Sept. 2	UCLA	Pasadena	L	35–24
Sept. 9	Vanderbilt	Birmingham	W	28–10
Sept. 16	Southern Miss	Birmingham	L	21–0
Sept. 23	Arkansas	Fayetteville	L	28–21
Sept. 30	South Carolina	Tuscaloosa	W	27–17
Oct. 14	Ole Miss	Tuscaloosa	W	45–7
Oct. 21	Tennessee	Knoxville	L	20–10
Oct. 28	Central Florida	Tuscaloosa	L	40–38
Nov. 4	LSU	Baton Rouge	L	30–28
Nov. 11	Mississippi State	Starkville	L	29–7
Nov. 18	Auburn	Tuscaloosa	L	9–0
Coach: Mike DuBose				228–246

Captains: Paul Hogan, Bradley Ledbetter, Kenny Smith

Ranking [AP]: Preseason No. 3; Postseason NR

All-SEC: Paul Hogan, center; Jarret Johnson, defensive tackle.

Leaders: Rushing—Ahmaad Galloway (659 yards, 137 carries);
Passing—Andrew Zow (120 of 249, 1,561 yards); Receiving—
Antonio Carter (45 catches, 586 yards)

An alleged affair with his secretary had DuBose
back on the ropes, but the losing season did him
in. The decision was made after Alabama lost
another homecoming game, this time to Central
Florida. His record over four seasons was 24–23.
... For the first time since 1969, the Crimson
Tide lost to LSU in Tiger Stadium. ... In November
school officials were notified that the National
Collegiate Athletic Association was investigating
Alabama for a recruiting scandal.

Through the Years

2001
7–5

Sept. 1	UCLA	Tuscaloosa	L	20–17
Sept. 8	Vanderbilt	Nashville	W	12–9
Sept. 22	Arkansas	Tuscaloosa	W	31–10
Sept. 29	South Carolina	Columbia	L	37–36
Oct. 6	Texas–El Paso	Birmingham	W	56–7
Oct. 13	Ole Miss	Oxford	L	27–24
Oct. 20	Tennessee	Tuscaloosa	L	35–24
Nov. 3	LSU	Tuscaloosa	L	35–21
Nov. 10	Mississippi State	Tuscaloosa	W	24–17
Nov. 17	Auburn	Auburn	W	31–7
Nov. 29	Southern Miss	Birmingham	W	28–15
Dec. 27	Iowa State	Independence Bowl	W	14–13
Coach: Dennis Franchione				304–219

Captains: Jarrett Johnson, Terry Jones Jr., Saleem
Rasheed, Tyler Watts, Andrew Zow

All-SEC: Alonzo Ephram, center; Jarret Johnson, defensive
tackle; Kindal Moorehead, defensive tackle; Saleem Rasheed,
linebacker

Leaders: Rushing—Ahmaad Galloway (881 yards, 174 carries);
Passing—Tyler Watts (94 of 172, 1,325 yards); Receiving—
Freddie Milons (36 catches, 626 yards)

Thanks primarily to its improving defense,
Alabama won its last four games, includ-
ing a 14–13 victory against Iowa State in the
Independence Bowl. The high point was the 31–7
victory against Auburn, which knocked the Tigers
out of the SEC Championship Game. Santonio
Beard (199 yards) and Ahmaad Galloway (127)
both exceeded 100 rushing yards, while Andrew
Zow replaced injured Tyler Watts and threw a
key 45-yard touchdown pass to Jason McAddley.
… Due to the September 11 terrorist attacks,
Southern Miss at Alabama was rescheduled to
November 29. It was played in a driving rainstorm
on a Thursday night at Legion Field.

2002
10–3

Aug. 31	Middle Tennessee St.	Birmingham	W	39–34
Sept. 7	Oklahoma	Norman	L	37–27
Sept. 14	North Texas	Tuscaloosa	W	33–7
Sept. 21	Southern Miss	Tuscaloosa	W	20–7
Sept. 28	Arkansas	Fayetteville	W	30–12
Oct. 5	Georgia	Tuscaloosa	L	27–25
Oct. 19	Ole Miss	Tuscaloosa	W	42–7
Oct. 26	Tennessee	Knoxville	W	34–14
Nov. 2	Vanderbilt	Tuscaloosa	W	30–8
Nov. 9	Mississippi State	Tuscaloosa	W	28–14
Nov. 16	LSU	Baton Rouge	W	31–0
Nov. 23	Auburn	Tuscaloosa	L	17–7
Nov. 30	Hawaii	Honolulu	W	21–16
Coach: Dennis Franchione				367–200

Captains: Lane Bearden, Ahmaad Galloway, Jarret Johnson, Kenny King, Kindal Moorehead, Tyler Watts

Ranking [AP]: Preseason NR; Postseason No. 11

All-American: Academic—Kenny King, defensive tackle

All-SEC: Wesley Britt, tackle; Alonzo Ephram, center; Jarret Johnson, defensive tackle; Kenny King, defensive tackle; Kindal Moorehead, defensive end; Marico Portis, guard

Leaders: Rushing—Shaud Williams (921 yards, 130 carries); Passing—Tyler Watts (112 of 181, 1,414 yards); Receiving—Triandos Luke (41 catches, 482 yards)

On February 1, Alabama was notified of its penalties by the NCAA for recruiting violations under Mike DuBose: a two-year bowl ban, scholarship reductions, and five years probation. ... Instead of a bowl, Alabama scheduled a season-ending game at Hawaii. ... Quarterbacks Tyler Watts and Brodie Croyle became the first quarterback combo to each pass for more than 1,000 yards in a season. ... Texas Tech transfer Shaud Williams scored on the first snap against Arkansas, an 80-yard run. ... Santonio Beard scored five touchdowns against Ole Miss, tying the school record set by Muley Lenoir (1920) and Shaun Alexander (1998). ... Rumors of Dennis Franchione's departure swelled during Auburn

Despite playing much of the 2003 season with a dislo-
cated nonthrowing shoulder while being battered behind
an inexperienced offensive line, Brodie Croyle made big
strides as a sophomore. He threw for more than 2,000
yards and tied the school record for touchdown passes in
a season with 16.

week, and at season's end he left Alabama to become the head coach at Texas A&M.

2003
4-9

Aug. 30	South Florida	Birmingham	W	40-17
Sept. 6	Oklahoma	Tuscaloosa	L	20-13
Sept. 13	Kentucky	Tuscaloosa	W	27-17
Sept. 20	Northern Illinois	Tuscaloosa	L	19-16
Sept. 27	Arkansas	Tuscaloosa	L 2OT	34-31
Oct. 4	Georgia	Athens	L	37-23
Oct. 11	Southern Miss	Tuscaloosa	W	17-3
Oct. 18	Ole Miss	Oxford	L	43-28
Oct. 25	Tennessee	Tuscaloosa	L 5OT	51-43
Nov. 8	Mississippi State	Starkville	W	38-0
Nov. 15	LSU	Tuscaloosa	L	27-3
Nov. 22	Auburn	Auburn	L	28-23
Nov. 29	Hawaii	Honolulu	L	37-29
Coach: Mike Shula				331-333

Captains: Derrick Pope, Shaud Williams

All-SEC: Wesley Britt, tackle; Antwan Odom, defensive end; Derrick Pope, linebacker; Justin Smiley, guard

Leaders: Rushing—Shaud Williams (1,367 yards, 280 carries); Passing—Brodie Croyle (186 of 341, 2,303 yards); Receiving—Zach Fletcher (21 catches, 498 yards)

Former Washington State coach Mike Price was hired to replace Dennis Franchione, but after a night of alleged indiscretions while attending a pro-am golf tournament in Pensacola, Florida, he was fired by university president Dr. Robert Witt. Just 115 days before the season opener, Mike Shula was hired. Alabama won two of its first three games and lost a 20–13 nail-biter to No. 1 Oklahoma, but the team lost eight of its last 10 games, including a dramatic five-overtime game against Tennessee. ... Despite playing with a bad shoulder, Brodie Croyle became the first Tide sophomore quarterback to pass for more than 2,000 yards. ... Running back Shaud Williams led the SEC in rushing with 1,357 yards on 278 carries. .... The 333 points allowed were the most ever by an Alabama team.

2004
6–6

Sept. 4	Utah State	Tuscaloosa	W	48–17
Sept. 11	Ole Miss	Tuscaloosa	W	28–7
Sept. 18	Western Carolina	Tuscaloosa	W	52–0
Sept. 25	Arkansas	Fayetteville	L	27–10
Oct. 2	South Carolina	Tuscaloosa	L	20–3
Oct. 9	Kentucky	Lexington	W	45–17
Oct. 16	Southern Miss	Tuscaloosa	W	27–3
Oct. 23	Tennessee	Knoxville	L	17–13
Nov. 6	Mississippi State	Tuscaloosa	W	30–14
Nov. 13	LSU	Baton Rouge	L	26–10
Nov. 20	Auburn	Tuscaloosa	L	21–13
Dec. 31	Minnesota	Music City Bowl	L	20–16
Coach: Mike Shula				295–189

Captains: Wesley Britt, Todd Bates

All-SEC: Brian Bostick, kicker; Wesley Britt, tackle; Evan Mathis, guard; Cornelius Wortham, linebacker

Leaders: Rushing—Kenneth Darby (1,062 yards, 219 carries); Passing—Spencer Pennington (82 of 152, 974 yards); Receiving—Tyrone Prothro (25 catches, 347 yards)

Alabama was bowl eligible again (following NCAA sanctions), but the season nearly unraveled when Brodie Croyle blew out his right knee against Western Carolina and was lost for the season. He would soon be joined by running back Ray Hudson and fullback Tim Castille. At one point, Alabama was down to its third-string quarterback, tailback, fullback, and tight end but still scraped together six wins to play Minnesota in the Music City Bowl. Despite sustaining a concussion, quarterback Spencer Pennington completed 22 of 36 passes for a career-high 234 yards and one touchdown and just missed Tyrone Prothro on what could have been a last-second touchdown. ... Kenneth Darby had 1,101 rushing yards on 219 carries before sustaining a sports hernia ... Led by linebacker DeMeco Ryans, the defense topped the nation in passing defense and was second in total defense.

Spencer Pennington had an odd career at Alabama. A third stringer on the football team who saw playing time due to injuries before nearly going down himself, Pennington was also a standout on the Alabama baseball team. He left the football program after the Music City Bowl to play baseball, and he is seen here celebrating a three-run homer in 2006.

2005
10–2

Sept. 3	Middle Tennessee St.	Tuscaloosa	W	26–7
Sept. 10	Southern Miss	Tuscaloosa	W	30–21
Sept. 17	South Carolina	Columbia	W	37–14
Sept. 24	Arkansas	Fayetteville	W	24–13
Oct. 1	Florida	Tuscaloosa	W	31–3
Oct. 15	Ole Miss	Oxford	W	13–10
Oct. 22	Tennessee	Tuscaloosa	W	6–3
Oct. 29	Utah State	Tuscaloosa	W	35–3
Nov. 5	Mississippi State	Starkville	W	17–0
Nov. 12	LSU	Tuscaloosa	L OT	16–13
Nov. 19	Auburn	Auburn	L	28–18
Jan. 2	Texas Tech	Cotton Bowl	W	13–10
Coach: Mike Shula				263–128

Captains: Brodie Croyle, DeMeco Ryans

Ranking (AP): Preseason NR; Postseason No. 8

All-American: First team—DeMeco Ryans, linebacker

All-SEC: First team—DeMeco Ryans, linebacker; Kenneth Darby, running back; Roman Harper, safety; Tyrone Prothro, split end.

Awards: DeMeco Ryans, Lott Trophy (Defensive Impact Player)

Leaders: Rushing—Kenneth Darby (1,242 yards, 239 carries); Passing—Brodie Croyle (202 of 339, 2,499 yards); Receiving—DJ Hall (48 catches, 676 yards)

Tyrone Prothro had the play of the year against Southern Miss when he reached around both sides of a defender to make an unbelievable long-bomb catch to set up a 1-yard touchdown at the end of the first half. ... After fumbling the first punt, Prothro scored an 87-yard touchdown on the first snap against No. 5 Florida, to spark the rout. However, he was lost for the season after horrifically breaking two bones in his leg in the fourth quarter. ... Sophomore kicker Jamie Christensen, nicknamed "Money," made last-second game-winning field goals against Ole Miss, Tennessee, and Texas Tech in the Cotton Bowl. ... Senior Roman Harper made a game-saving tackle against Tennessee, in the process knocking the ball through the end zone for a touchback. ... Alabama defeated Mississippi State without scoring an offensive touchdown.

2006

6–7

Sept. 2	Hawaii	Tuscaloosa	W	25–17
Sept. 9	Vanderbilt	Tuscaloosa	W	13–10
Sept. 16	Louisiana–Monroe	Tuscaloosa	W	41–7
Sept. 23	Arkansas	Fayetteville	L	24–23
Sept. 30	Florida	Gainesville	L	28–13
Oct. 7	Duke	Tuscaloosa	W	30–14
Oct. 14	Ole Miss	Tuscaloosa	W	26–23
Oct. 21	Tennessee	Knoxville	L	16–13
Oct. 28	Florida International	Tuscaloosa	W	38–3
Nov. 4	Mississippi State	Tuscaloosa	L	24–16
Nov. 11	LSU	Baton Rouge	L	28–14
Nov. 18	Auburn	Tuscaloosa	L	22–15
Dec. 28	Oklahoma State	Independence	L	34–31

Coach: Mike Shula [Joe Kines for Independence Bowl] 298–250

Captains: Le'Ron McLain, Juwan Simpson

Ranking [AP]: Preseason NR; Postseason NR

All-SEC: First team—Simeon Castille, defensive back

Leaders: Rushing—Kenneth Darby (835 yards, 210 carries);
Passing—John Parker Wilson (216 of 379, 2,707 yards);
Receiving—DJ Hall (62 catches, 1,056 yards)

Shortly after Alabama lost for the fifth-straight time to Auburn, Coach Mike Shula was fired, with defensive coordinator Joe Kines named interim coach for the Independence Bowl. ... With his 253 passing yards against Auburn, quarterback John Parker Wilson surpassed Bordie Croyle to become the Crimson Tide single-season passing leader. ... Sophomore kicker Jason Ricks made a 27-yard field goal with 8.9 seconds remaining to give Oklahoma State the victory in the Independence Bowl. The Cowboys outgained the Tide 419–276, but the game was also remembered for left tackle Andre Smith taking a lateral and easily scoring a 2-yard touchdown and Javier Arenas' 86-yard punt return for a score. ... Alabama finished with its first losing season since 2003, Shula's first (when the program was on NCAA probation). ... Strange

but true, when fullback Tim Castille scored on a 2-yard run against Tennessee, it was the first touchdown in the rivalry since the second quarter of the 2004 game.

2007
7–6

Sept. 1	Western Carolina	Tuscaloosa	W	52–6
Sept. 8	Vanderbilt	Nashville	W	24–10
Sept. 15	Arkansas	Tuscaloosa	W	41–38
Sept. 22	Georgia	Tuscaloosa	L OT	26–23
Sept. 29	Florida State	Jacksonville	L	21–14
Oct. 16	Houston	Tuscaloosa	W	30–24
Oct. 13	Ole Miss	Oxford	W	27–24
Oct. 20	Tennessee	Tuscaloosa	W	41–17
Nov. 3	LSU	Tuscaloosa	L	41–34
Nov. 10	Mississippi State	Starkville	L	17–12
Nov. 17	Louisiana-Monroe	Tuscaloosa	L	21–14
Nov. 24	Auburn	Auburn	L	17–10
Dec. 30	Colorado	Independence	W	30–24
Coach: Nick Saban				352–286

Captains: Antoine Caldwell, Rashad Johnson, Darren Mustin

All-SEC: First team—Andre Smith, offensive line; Wallace Gilberry, defensive end; Simeon Castille, defensive back; Rashad Johnson, defensive back

Leaders: Rushing—Terry Grant (891 yards, 180 carries); Passing—John Parker Wilson (255 of 462, 2,846 yards); Receiving—DJ Hall (67 catches, 1,005 yards)

After saying he had no interest in the Alabama job, (when the Miami Dolphins' season was still ongoing) Nick Saban was coaxed back into the collegiate game and signed a contract averaging $4 million a year. Before he even coached a game, Bryant-Denny Stadium was filled to capacity (92,138) for A-Day. ... Terry Grant scored a 47-yard touchdown on the first offensive snap of the season. ... Senior quarterback John Parker Wilson passed for a career-high 363 yards, and DJ Hall had a school-record 13 catches for 185 yards as the Crimson Tide crushed Tennessee. However, before the game five players (Antoine

Caldwell, Marlon Davis, Glen Coffee, Chris Rogers, and Marquis Johnson) were suspended for a text-book disbursement scandal. The Tide subsequently went on a four-game losing streak, including an embarrassing defeat to Louisiana-Monroe. ... After scoring two touchdowns in the final three minutes to beat Alabama, LSU went on to win the national championship. ... Alabama avoided consecutive losing seasons for the first time in 50 years by defeating Colorado in the Independence Bowl. Wilson completed 13 of his first 15 passes for 185 yards to lead the Tide to a 27-0 lead and was named game MVP.

2008

12–2, SEC Western Division champion

Aug. 30	Clemson	Atlanta	W	34–10
Sept. 6	Tulane	Tuscaloosa	W	20–6
Sept. 13	Western Kentucky	Tuscaloosa	W	41–7
Sept. 20	Arkansas	Fayetteville	W	49–14
Sept. 27	Georgia	Athens	W	41–30
Oct. 4	Kentucky	Tuscaloosa	W	17–14
Oct. 18	Ole Miss	Tuscaloosa	W	24–20
Oct. 25	Tennessee	Knoxville	W	29–9
Nov. 1	Arkansas State	Tuscaloosa	W	35–0
Nov. 8	LSU	Baton Rouge	W OT	27–21
Nov. 15	Mississippi State	Tuscaloosa	W	32–7
Nov. 29	Auburn	Tuscaloosa	W	36–0
Dec. 6	Florida	SEC Championship	L	31–20
Jan. 2	Utah	Sugar Bowl	L	31–17
Coach: Nick Saban				422–200

Captains: Antoine Caldwell, Rashad Johnson, John Parker Wilson

Ranking (AP): Preseason No. 24; Postseason No. 6

All-American: First team—Andre Smith, tackle; Antoine Caldwell, center; Terrence Cody, nose guard; Rashad Johnson, safety; Mike Johnson, guard

All-SEC: First team—Andre Smith, tackle; Glen Coffee, running back; Terrence Cody, defensive tackle; Rolando McClain, linebacker; Rashad Johnson, safety

Awards: Andre Smith, Outland Trophy (outstanding interior lineman)

Leaders: Rushing—Glen Coffee (1,383 yards, 233 carries); Passing—John Parker Wilson (187 of 323, 2,273yards); Receiving—Julio Jones (58 catches, 924 yards)

Nick Saban became the fifth person to go as an opposing head coach into the stadium of a team he previously led to a national title. The LSU game was also the first time Alabama played as No. 1 since 1980. ... Junior running back Glen Coffee's 1,383 rushing yards tied Shaun Alexander (1999) on Alabama's single-season rushing yards list. ... Senior quarterback John Parker Wilson's assault on the Alabama record book ended with 665 completions, 1,175 attempts, 7,924 yards, and 47 touchdowns. He was also named MVP of the Senior Bowl. ... The Tide snapped a six-game losing streak to rival Auburn and a five-game skid to Saban's former school, LSU. ... Julio Jones' 924 receiving yards as a freshman was fourth on the Tide's single-season list. ... Outland Trophy winner Andre Smith was suspended for the Sugar Bowl. The Tide promptly gave up a season-high eight sacks. ... Massive nose guard Terrence Cody periodically lined up with the backfield in goal-line situations.

Alabama Bowl Games

Overall Record 31–22–3

(Note: Alabama leads the NCAA in all-time bowl appearances and bowl victories.)

Jan. 1, 1926	Rose	Alabama 20, Washington 19
Jan. 1, 1927	Rose	Alabama 7, Stanford 7
Jan. 1, 1931	Rose	Alabama 24, Washington State 0
Jan. 1, 1935	Rose	Alabama 29, Stanford 13
Jan. 1, 1938	Rose	California 13, Alabama 0

ALABAMA FOOTBALL

Jan. 1, 1942	Cotton	Alabama 29, Texas A&M 21
Jan. 1, 1943	Orange	Alabama 37, Boston College 21
Jan. 1, 1945	Sugar	Duke 29, Alabama 26
Jan. 1, 1946	Rose	Alabama 34, Southern California 14
Jan. 1, 1948	Sugar	Texas 27, Alabama 7
Jan. 1, 1953	Orange	Alabama 61, Syracuse 6
Jan. 1, 1954	Cotton	Rice 28, Alabama 6
Dec. 19, 1959	Liberty	Penn State 7, Alabama 0
Dec. 17, 1960	Bluebonnet	Alabama 3, Texas 3
Jan. 1, 1962	Sugar	Alabama 10, Arkansas 3
Jan. 1, 1963	Orange	Alabama 17, Oklahoma 0
Jan. 1, 1964	Sugar	Alabama 12, Ole Miss 7
Jan. 1, 1965	Orange	Texas 21, Alabama 17
Jan. 1, 1966	Orange	Alabama 39, Nebraska 28
Jan. 1, 1967	Sugar	Alabama 34, Nebraska 7
Jan. 1, 1968	Cotton	Texas A&M 20, Alabama 16
Dec. 28, 1968	Gator	Missouri 35, Alabama 10
Dec. 13, 1969	Liberty	Colorado 47, Alabama 33
Dec. 31, 1970	Bluebonnet	Alabama 24, Oklahoma 24
Jan. 1, 1972	Orange	Nebraska 38, Alabama 6
Jan. 1, 1973	Cotton	Texas 17, Alabama 13
Dec. 31, 1973	Sugar	Notre Dame 24, Alabama 23
Jan. 1, 1975	Orange	Notre Dame 13, Alabama 11
Dec. 31, 1975	Sugar	Alabama 13, Penn State 6
Dec. 20, 1976	Liberty	Alabama 33, UCLA 6
Jan. 2, 1978	Sugar	Alabama 35, Ohio State 6
Jan. 1, 1979	Sugar	Alabama 14, Penn State 7
Jan. 1, 1980	Sugar	Alabama 24, Arkansas 9
Jan. 1, 1981	Cotton	Alabama 30, Baylor 2
Jan. 1, 1982	Cotton	Texas 14, Alabama 12
Dec. 29, 1982	Liberty	Alabama 21, Illinois 15
Dec. 24, 1983	Sun	Alabama 28, Southern Methodist 7
Dec. 28, 1985	Aloha	Alabama 24, Southern California 3
Dec. 25, 1986	Sun	Alabama 28, Washington 6
Jan. 2, 1988	Hall of Fame	Michigan 29, Alabama 24
Dec. 24, 1988	Sun	Alabama 29, Army 28
Jan. 1, 1990	Sugar	Miami 33, Alabama 25
Jan. 1, 1991	Fiesta	Louisville 34, Alabama 7
Dec. 28, 1991	Blockbuster	Alabama 30, Colorado 25

Jan. 1, 1993	Sugar	Alabama 34, Miami 13
Dec. 31, 1993	Gator	Alabama 24, North Carolina 10
Jan. 2, 1995	Florida Citrus	Alabama 24, Ohio State 17
Jan. 1, 1997	Outback	Alabama 17, Michigan 14
Dec. 29, 1998	Music City	Virginia Tech 38, Alabama 7
Jan. 1, 2000	Orange	Michigan 35, Alabama 34 (OT)
Dec. 27, 2001	Independence	Alabama 14, Iowa State 13
Dec. 31, 2004	Music City	Minnesota 20, Alabama 16
Jan. 2, 2006	Cotton	Alabama 13, Texas Tech 10
Dec. 28, 2006	Independence	Oklahoma State 34, Alabama 31
Dec. 30, 2007	Independence	Alabama 30, Colorado 24
Jan. 2, 2009	Sugar	Utah 31, Alabama 17

All-Time Record vs. Opponents

Opponent	W	L	T	Last
Alabama Southern	1	0	0	1916
#Arkansas	11	8	0	2008
Arkansas State	2	0	0	2008
Army	1	0	0	1988
Auburn	39	33	1	2008
Baylor	2	0	0	1981
Birmingham Athletic Club	2	3	0	1896
Birmingham high schools	2	0	0	1902
Birmingham-Southern	11	0	0	1925
Boston College	1	3	0	1984
Bowling Green	1	0	0	1996
Brigham Young	1	0	0	1998
Bryson College	1	0	0	1921
California	1	1	0	1973
Camp Gordon	0	1	0	1917
Carlisle	0	1	0	1914
Case College	1	0	0	1920
Central Florida	0	1	0	2000
Centre	2	1	0	1924
Chattanooga	10	0	0	1994
Cincinnati	5	0	0	1990

Clemson	12	3	0	2008
Colorado	2	1	0	2007
Cumberland	0	1	0	1903
Davidson	1	0	0	1911
Delta State	1	0	0	1951
Duke	2	1	0	2006
Duquesne	3	0	0	1949
East Carolina	1	0	0	1998
Florida	21	14	0	2008
Florida International	1	0	0	2006
Florida State	2	1	1	2007
Fordham	1	1	0	1939
Furman	5	0	0	1960
George Washington	3	0	0	1937
Georgia	36	25	4	2008
Georgia Pre-Flight	0	1	0	1942
Georgia Tech	28	21	3	1984
Haskell Institute	1	0	0	1908
Hawaii	2	1	0	2006
Houston	10	0	0	2007
Howard	20	0	1	1944
Illinois	1	0	0	1982
Iowa State	1	0	0	2001
Kentucky	34	2	1	2008
Kessler Field	1	0	0	1945
Louisiana-Monroe	1	1	0	2007
LSU	44	22	5	2008
#Louisiana Tech	2	3	0	1999
Louisville	2	1	0	1991
Loyola (La.)	1	0	0	1936
Marion Institute	9	0	0	1922
Maryland	2	1	0	1974
Maryville	3	0	0	1907
Memphis State	7	1	0	1991
Mercer	2	0	0	1940
Miami	14	3	0	1993
Michigan	1	2	0	2000
Middle Tennessee State	2	0	0	2005

Millsaps	3	0	0	1944
Minnesota	0	1	0	2004
#Ole Miss	45	9	2	2008
Mississippi College	7	0	0	1929
#Mississippi State	72	18	3	2008
Missouri	1	2	0	1978
Montgomery Athletic Club	1	0	0	1899
Nashville University	1	0	0	1904
Nebraska	3	2	0	1978
New Orleans Athletic Club	0	1	0	1899
North Carolina	1	0	0	1993
North Carolina State	5	0	0	1996
Northern Illinois	0	1	0	2003
North Texas	2	0	0	2002
Notre Dame	1	5	0	1987
Oglethorpe	2	0	0	1933
2nd Ambulance Co. of Ohio	1	0	0	1917
Ohio State	3	0	0	1986
Oklahoma	1	2	1	2003
Oklahoma State	0	1	0	2006
Pennsylvania	1	0	0	1922
Penn State	8	5	0	1990
Pensacola Athletic Club	1	0	0	1904
Pensacola N.A.S.	2	0	0	1945
Rice	0	3	0	1956
Richmond	1	0	0	1961
Rutgers	2	0	0	1980
St. Mary's	1	0	0	1932
Sewanee	17	10	3	1938
#South Carolina	10	3	0	2005
South Florida	1	0	0	2003
Southern California	5	2	0	1995
Southern Methodist	2	0	0	1983
Southern Military Institute	1	0	0	1920
#Southern Miss	34	6	2	2005
Southwestern (Tenn.)	2	0	0	1927
S.W. Louisiana	8	0	0	1990
Spring Hill	3	0	0	1940
Stanford	1	0	1	1926

Syracuse	1	1	0	1953
Tampa	1	0	0	1960
Taylor School	1	0	0	1900
Temple	3	0	0	1991
#Tennessee	46	38	8	2008
Texas	0	7	1	1981
Texas A&M	3	1	0	1988
Texas Christian	2	3	0	1975
Texas-El Paso	1	0	0	2001
Texas Tech	1	0	0	2006
#Tulane	27	11	3	2008
Tulsa	3	0	0	1962
Tuscaloosa Athletic Club	2	0	0	1899
UCLA	1	2	0	2001
Union	4	0	0	1925
Utah	0	1	0	2008
Utah State	2	0	0	2005
#Vanderbilt	58	19	4	2007
Villanova	0	1	0	1951
Virginia Tech	10	1	0	1998
Washington	4	0	0	1986
Washington & Lee	1	0	0	1910
Washington State	1	0	0	1930
Western Carolina	2	0	0	2007
Western Kentucky	1	0	0	2008
Wetumpka	1	0	0	1908
Wichita State	1	0	0	1979
Wisconsin	0	1	0	1928

#Win or tie later forfeited by NCAA action due to ineligible player.

Alabama's Longest Winning Streaks

Wins	Seasons	First win	Ended by
28	1978–80	Vanderbilt (Oct. 30, 1978)	Mississippi State (Nov. 1, 1980)
28	1991–93*	Georgia (Sept. 21, 1991)	Tennessee (Oct. 16, 1993)
20	1924–26	Georgia (Nov. 27, 1924)	Stanford (Jan. 1, 1927)
19	1961–62	Georgia (Sept. 17, 1961)	Georgia Tech (Nov. 17, 1962)
17	1965–66	Tulane (Sept. 25, 1965)	Florida State (Sept. 23, 1967)
14	1933–34	Kentucky (Nov. 4, 1933)	Howard (Sept. 28, 1935)
14	1936–37	Loyola (Oct. 24, 1936)	California (Jan. 1, 1938)
14	1945–46	Keesler AAF (Sept. 29, 1945)	Tennessee (Oct. 19, 1946)
13	2007–08	Colorado (Dec. 30, 2007)	Florida (Dec. 6, 2008)
13	1930–31	Samford (Sept. 27, 1930)	Tennessee (Oct. 17, 1931)
12	1963–64	Miami (Dec. 12, 1963)	Texas (Jan. 1, 1964)
12	1977–78	Vanderbilt (Sept. 24, 1977)	Southern California (Nov. 23, 1978)
12	1988–89	Texas A&M (Dec. 1, 1988)	Auburn (Dec. 2, 1989)
12	1993–94	N. Carolina (Dec. 31, 1993)	Florida (Dec. 3, 1994)
11	1919–20	LSU	Georgia

		(Nov. 15, 1919)	(Nov. 20, 1920)
11	1971	Southern California	Nebraska
		(Sept. 10, 1971)	(Jan. 1, 1972)
11	1973	California	Notre Dame
		(Sept. 15, 1973)	(Dec. 31, 1973)
11	1974	Maryland	Notre Dame
		(Sept. 14, 1974)	(Jan. 1, 1975)
11	1975	Clemson	Ole Miss
		(Sept. 20, 1975)	(Sept. 11, 1976)

*Alabama later had to forfeit eight regular-season victories and a tie.

The loss to Mississippi State in 1980 not only ended the longest winning streak in school history, it also ended an impressive run against the Bulldogs. The Crimson Tide had not lost to MSU since 1957.

THE GREATEST PLAYERS

Players in the College Football Hall of Fame

Pooley Hubert
Quarterback, 1922–1925
Inducted 1964

Pooley Hubert quarterbacked Alabama to its first postseason appearance ever—a 20–19 win over Washington in the 1926 Rose Bowl. The Tide torched the Huskies for three touchdowns, including a Hubert run and a scoring toss from Hubert to Johnny Mack Brown, in a seven-minute third-quarter span. In his four years as a letterman, Hubert scored 35 touchdowns for Alabama. He scored at least three times in six different games. He was All-Southern two years and All-America as a senior.

Johnny Mack Brown
Halfback, 1923–1925
Inducted 1957

Johnny Mack Brown was a hit as a cowboy in Hollywood westerns, but he was an even bigger hit as a football player. In the 1926 Rose Bowl, Brown caught two long touchdown passes, including the winning tally, as the Tide defeated a powerful Washington team and thrust Southern football into the national limelight. The "Dothan Antelope" ran with a reckless abandon that terrorized opponents. During his three years with the varsity, the Tide went 25–3–1, including the perfect 10–0 national championship campaign in 1925.

Fred Sington
Tackle, 1928–1930
Inducted 1955

Tackle Fred Sington was All-Southern, All-America, Phi Beta Kappa, and student body vice president. He was a leader of Wallace Wade's 1930 national and Rose Bowl champions. Notre Dame Coach Knute Rockne called Sington "the greatest lineman in the country." After graduating, Sington played professional baseball for the Washington Senators and Brooklyn Dodgers.

Johnny Cain
Fullback, 1930–1932
Inducted 1973

Johnny "Hurri" Cain was a two-time All-American and three-time All-Southern. Cain's most famous game came when he was a punter and dueled Tennessee's Beattie Feathers in the rain and mud of Legion Field in 1932. Cain averaged 48 yards on 19 punts that day. In 1930 he was the only sophomore starter on outgoing Coach Wallace Wade's national championship team that whitewashed Washington State 24–0 in the Rose Bowl. He missed three games with an injury as a senior after scoring nine touchdowns in the season's first four contests.

Don Hutson
End, 1932–1934
Inducted 1951

In the 1935 Rose Bowl Don Hutson caught six passes for 165 yards, including 59- and 54-yard touchdowns. Tall, fluid, and fast, Hutson was arguably the greatest pass catcher of the first half of the 20th century. Frank Thomas called Hutson "the best player I ever coached." Hutson is a charter member of the College Football Hall of Fame, and because he made

The Greatest Players

All-Pro nine times and league MVP twice during
his 11-year NFL career with the Green Bay Packers,
a shrine in his honor also can be found in the Pro
Football Hall of Fame.

Dixie Howell
Halfback, 1932–1934
Inducted 1970

The throwing component of the deadly Howell-
to-Hutson passing combo, Millard F. "Dixie" Howell
led the Crimson Tide to the national championship in
his All-America senior season of 1934. Howell's performance in a 29–13 victory over Stanford in the 1935
Rose Bowl was unforgettable. He passed for 160 yards,
rushed for 111, and averaged 44 yards on six punts.

Riley Smith
Quarterback, 1933–1935
Inducted 1985

The quarterback of Frank Thomas' 1934 juggernaut was Riley Smith, who had switched from fullback
after the 1933 season. In 1935, Smith was an All-
American and a recipient of the Jacobs Award as the
Southeastern Conference's best blocker. As a senior,
Smith led the Tide to wins over Georgia and Tennessee,
throwing a touchdown pass and running for another
score against the Vols, while playing through injuries.

Don Whitmire
Tackle, 1941–1942
Inducted 1956

Tackle Don Whitmire split his college career
between Alabama (1941–1942) and the Naval Academy
(1943–1944). His career in the navy saw him advance
to the rank of admiral. Whitmire was a key component in 'Bama's 9–2 record in 1941 and its 8–3 ledger
in 1942. He was a 6'2", 220-pound blocker and tackler

who hit like a truck. His freshman year, Alabama beat
Texas A&M 29–21 in the Cotton Bowl, and the following year the Tide rolled over Boston College 37–21 in
the Orange Bowl. Whitmire later was named to both
the Cotton Bowl and Orange Bowl all-time teams.

Harry Gilmer
Quarterback, 1944–1947
Inducted 1993

Harry Gilmer scored more touchdowns—52—than
any other player in Alabama's storied football history.
He was an All-American and SEC Player of the Year in
1945, and he concluded that season as Rose Bowl MVP
in 'Bama's 34–14 win over Southern Cal. In 1946 he led
the Crimson Tide in rushing, passing, interceptions,
punt returns, and kickoff returns. In one game against
Kentucky he rushed six times for 216 yards and passed
for 50 more. He intercepted 16 passes in his career, and
his 436 punt-return yards in 1946 still stands as the
school single-season record.

Vaughn Mancha
Center, 1944–1947
Inducted 1990

Vaughn Mancha was Alabama's starting center for
four full seasons, beginning with the first game of his
freshman year. Frank Thomas' 1945 Tide went 10–0
and beat Southern Cal in the Rose Bowl with Mancha
as an All-American. His playing career also took him to
two Sugar Bowls.

Billy Neighbors
Tackle, 1959–1961
Inducted 2003

One of Bear Bryant's best linemen, Neighbors
played on Tide teams went 26–3–4 and won a national
championship. A unanimous All-America selection

The Greatest Players

in 1961, Neighbors capped a dream season by helping Alabama to a Sugar Bowl win and a perfect 11–0
national championship season. Defensively, 'Bama
yielded just 25 points during the championship run.
Neighbors won the SEC's Jacobs Trophy in 1961, given
to the league's top blocking lineman.

Lee Roy Jordan
Linebacker, 1960–1962
Inducted 1983

Bear Bryant didn't worry too much about his
defense stopping people during Lee Roy Jordan's bril-
liant career. "If they stay inside the boundaries," the
Bear once said, "Lee Roy will get 'em." Jordan made
31 tackles in his last college game, a 17–0 'Bama win
over Oklahoma in the 1963 Orange Bowl. He was an
All-American and fourth-highest Heisman Trophy
vote-getter in 1962, was voted Alabama's Player of the
Decade for the 1960s, and is a member of both the
College Football Hall of Fame and the Dallas Cowboys
Ring of Honor.

Johnny Musso
Halfback, 1969–1971
Inducted 2000

When Bear Bryant unveiled Alabama's wishbone offense in 1971, senior halfback Johnny Musso
was called upon to carry the load. Musso, the "Italian
Stallion," was a two-year All-American and a unanimous choice as a senior, when he came in fourth in
Heisman Trophy balloting. He was also an Academic
All-American and the 1971 SEC Player of the Year.
Musso ran for more than 1,000 yards in 1970 and again
in 1971, and his 2,741 career rushing yards still rank
among the schoo's all-time leaders.

The Greatest Players

John Hannah
Guard, 1970–1972
Inducted 1999

If John Hannah isn't the best guard ever to play the game, he's certainly on the short list. Hannah was a two-year All-American for Bear Bryant's teams during the early 1970s, and he won the Jacobs Trophy as the Southeastern Conference's best blocker in 1972. From Alabama he went on to an All-Pro career with the New England Patriots. He is a member of Alabama's All-Century team, the Alabama Sports Hall of Fame, and both the College and Pro Football Halls of Fame.

Ozzie Newsome
Split End, 1974–1977
Inducted 1994

Ozzie Newsome holds the SEC career yards-per-reception record for players with a minimum of 100 catches, at 20.3 yards per reception. He started 47 consecutive games for the Tide and caught 102 balls for 2,070 yards. Newsome was instrumental in bringing three SEC titles to Tuscaloosa. He was voted Alabama's Player of the Decade for the 1970s, and after college he enjoyed a stellar 13-year NFL career with the Cleveland Browns.

Other Alabama Greats

Bobby Marlow
Halfback, 1950–1952

Bobby Marlow was the SEC's best running back of the 1950s. His three-year career rushing total of 2,560 yards was higher than any other back in the league in that decade—693 more than LSU's Billy Cannon, who won the 1959 Heisman Trophy. In 1952 Marlow was All-America and SEC Back of the Year. In the 1950 Georgia Tech game, he ran for 180 yards and four touchdowns on 13 carries in a 54–19 win. As a senior, he shredded Auburn's run defense for 233 yards. For his career, Marlow averaged 6.3 yards per rush.

Pat Trammell
Quarterback, 1959–1961

Trammell quarterbacked Alabama to the 1961 national championship, the first of six under Bear Bryant. After leading the Tide to a 10–0 regular season in 1961, Trammell scored the only touchdown on a 12-yard run in the 10–3 Sugar Bowl win over Arkansas. Trammell died from cancer at age 28.

Joe Namath
Quarterback, 1962–1964

As a sophomore in 1962, Joe Namath took the quarterback reins from Pat Trammell and succeeded to the tune of a 10–1 record, including a 17–0 win over Oklahoma in the Orange Bowl. Namath quarterbacked Alabama to a 29–4 record over his three years, and in 1964 he played through a knee injury to lead the Crimson Tide to a national title. He was MVP of the 1965 Orange Bowl and, as a New York Jet, the 1969 Super Bowl.

Steve Sloan
Quarterback, 1963–1965

Steve Sloan came of age as a quarterback on October 2, 1965. With his 1–1 Alabama team trailing Ole Miss 16–10 with five minutes to play, Sloan engineered a game-winning 89-yard drive and took it in for the score himself. He was an All-American that year, leading the nation in pass efficiency. He finished 10th in the 1965 Heisman voting and closed his career as MVP of the 39–28 Bama win over Nebraska in the 1966 Orange Bowl.

Kenny Stabler
Quarterback, 1965–1967

In 1966 Kenny Stabler guided one of the all-time great Alabama teams to a 10–0 regular-season record and followed that up with an MVP performance in the Tide's 34–7 Sugar Bowl win over Nebraska. As a senior the following year, he was an All-American and SEC Player of the Year. Stabler went on to enjoy a stellar career in the NFL with Oakland, Houston, and New Orleans.

Cornelius Bennett
Linebacker, 1983–1986

Cornelius Bennett was a three-time All-America linebacker for 'Bama from 1984 to 1986. As a senior, Bennett was chosen SEC Player of the Year, won the Lombardi Award, and finished seventh in Heisman balloting. He was Defensive Player of the Game in two different bowl games, SEC Player of the Year in 1986, a member of Alabama's All-Century team, and the school's Player of the Decade for the 1980s.

Derrick Thomas
Linebacker, 1985–1988

In 1988 Derrick Thomas compiled 27 sacks in one season. His career total was an equally imposing 52. As a senior, Thomas became the first SEC player to win the Butkus Award as the nation's top linebacker. In 1989, playing for the Kansas City Chiefs, he was named NFL Rookie of the Year. Tragically, Thomas, one of the greatest linebackers in history, died in 2000 from complications brought on in the aftermath of an automobile accident.

The Greatest Players

Antonio Langham
Cornerback, 1990–1993

Antonio Langham, a star performer on Alabama's 1992 national championship team, was a two-year All-American. Langham holds the school's career interception record with 19, including seven in his Thorpe Award–winning campaign of 1993. He was the MVP of the inaugural SEC Championship Game in 1992, a 28–21 'Bama win over Florida and a stalwart on the 1992 Tide defense, one of the greatest in history.

Jay Barker
Quarterback, 1991–1994

Jay Barker finished his career in 1994 as Alabama's all-time passing leader, capturing the Johnny Unitas Golden Arm Award as a senior. Barker established eight school career records, quarterbacked the Crimson Tide to the 1992 national championship as a sophomore, and posted a 35–2–1 record as a starter, making him the winningest quarterback in Alabama history.

David Palmer
Flanker, 1991–1993

One of the greatest all-around players in Alabama history, David Palmer finished third in the Heisman Trophy voting in 1993. Palmer could torch opponents as a receiver, runner, quarterback, and return man. He is the only player in school history with a 1,000-yard receiving season—in 1993—and his 61 catches that year were a school record. His heroics against Tennessee in 1993, when he came in at quarterback in the fourth quarter and sparked a comeback that resulted in a 17–17 tie, will live in 'Bama lore forever.

Shaun Alexander
Tailback, 1996–1999

Shaun Alexander ran for more yards (3,565) than anyone else in Alabama history. His game at LSU as a freshman, when he ran for 291 yards on 20 carries, is unforgettable, and a school record. As a senior in 1999, Alexander rushed for 1,383 yards and 19 touchdowns, finished seventh in the Heisman voting, and was named SEC Player of the Year and All-America.

Chris Samuels
Offensive Tackle, 1996–1999

Offensive tackle Chris Samuels brought the Outland Trophy to Tuscaloosa in 1999. He also won the Jacobs Award as the best blocker in the Southeastern Conference. That season he allowed opposing defenders zero sacks and zero pressures. He started 42 consecutive games during his Alabama career and was the third overall pick in the 2000 NFL Draft.

Major Awards

Heisman Trophies: None.

Maxwell Player (outstanding player): None

Walter Camp Award (player of the year): None

Dick Butkus Award (outstanding linebacker): Derrick Thomas, 1988

Outland Trophy (best interior lineman): Chris Samuels, 1999; Andre Smith, 2008

Chuck Bednarik Award (defensive player of the year): None

Davey O'Brien Award (national quarterback): None

Johnny Unitas Golden Arm Award (outstanding senior quarterback): Jay Barker, 1994

Doak Walker Award (national running back): None

Fred Biletnikoff Award (outstanding wide receiver): None

Jim Thorpe Award (outstanding defensive back): Antonio Langham, 1993

John Mackey Award (outstanding tight end): None

Lou Groza Award (collegiate kicker): None

The Greatest Players

Bronko Nagurski Award (defensive player of the year): None

Ray Guy Award (outstanding punter): None

Vince Lombardi/Rotary Award (outstanding lineman): Cornelius Bennett, 1986

Ted Hendricks Award (defensive end of the year): None

Rimington Trophy (outstanding center): None

Ronnie Lott Award (defensive impact player): DeMeco Ryans, 2005

Draddy Trophy (academic Heisman): None

First-Team All-Americans

(Source: NCAA; *consensus; #unanimous)

Hoyt Winslett, E, 1926; Tony Holm, FB, 1929; Fred Sington, T, #*1930; Johnny Cain, FB, 1931; Don Hutson, E, *1934; Bill Lee, T, *1934; Dixie Howell, B, *1934; Riley Smith, B, *1935; Arthur White, G, 1936; Leroy Monsky, G, *1937; Jim Ryba, T, 1937; Joe Kilgrow, HB, 1937; Carey Cox, G, 1939; Holt Rast, E, *1941; Joe Domnanovich, C, *1942; Don Whitmire, T, 1942; Vaughn Mancha, C, *1945; Harry Gilmer, HB, 1945; Ed Salem, HB, 1950; Billy Neighbors, T, *1961; Lee Roy Jordan, C, #*1962; Dan Kearley, OT, 1964; Wayne Freeman, OG, 1964; Paul Crane, C, *1965; Ray Perkins, SE, *1966; Cecil Dowdy, OT, #*1966; Dennis Homan, SE, 1967; Bobby Johns, DB, 1966, *1967; Mike Hall, LB, 1968; Johnny Musso, TB, *1971; John Hannah, OT, 1971, OG, #*1972; Jim Krapf, C, 1972; John Mitchell, DE, 1972; Wayne Wheeler, SE, 1973; Buddy Brown, OT, *1973; Woodrow Lowe, LB, 1973, *1974, 1975; Leroy Cook, DE, *1974, #*1975; Sylvester Croom, C, 1974; Ozzie Newsome, WR, *1977; Marty Lyons, DT, *1978; Jim Bunch, OT, *1979; E. J. Junior, DE, #*1980; Tommy Wilcox, DB, *1981; Mike Pitts, DE, *1982; Jeremiah Castille, DB, 1982; Cornelius Bennett, LB, 1985, #*1986; Bobby Humphrey, RB, 1987; Derrick Thomas, LB, #*1988; Keith McCants, LB, #*1989; Philip Doyle, PK, #*1990; Robert Stewart, DL, 1991; John Copeland, DL, *1992; Eric Curry, DL, *1992; Antonio Langham, DB, #*1993; David Palmer, KR, *1993; Michael Proctor, PK, 1993, 1994; Kevin Jackson, DB, #*1996; Michael Myers, DL, 1996; Dwayne Rudd, LB, 1996; Chris Samuels, OL, #*1999; Shaun Alexander, RB,

Ozzie Newsome lays out for a pass against Notre Dame in the 1975 Orange Bowl. A four-year starter, Newsome was an All-American and Alabama's Player of the Decade for the 1970s.

1999; DeMeco Ryans, LB, #*2005; Andre Smith, T, *#2008; Antoine Caldwell, C, *2008; Terrence Cody, DT, *2008; Rashad Johnson, S, 2008.

First-Team Academic All-Americans (CoSIDA):

Tommy Brooker, E, 1961; Pat Trammell, B, 1961; Gaylon McCollough, C, 1964; Steve Sloan, QB, 1965; Dennis Homan, HB, 1965; Steve Davis, K, 1967; Bob Childs, LB, 1967; Johnny Musso, HB, 1970–71; Randy Hall, DT, 1973–74; Danny Ridgeway, KS, 1975; Major Ogilvie, RB, 1979.

NFL Draft Selections

(Player, team, round, overall)

(F indicates a "future" pick.)

Source: The University of Alabama.

1936: Riley Smith, Boston, 1; Paul W. "Bear" Bryant, Brooklyn, 4.

1937: Arthur "Tarzan" White, NY Giants, 2.

1938: Joe Kilgrow, Brooklyn, 1A; Leroy Monsky, Brooklyn, 5.

1939: Charley Holm, Washington, 2; Lew Bostick, Cleveland, 9.

1940: Walt Merrill, Brooklyn, 5; Bob Wood, Cleveland, 4; Cary Cox, Pittsburgh, 11; Hayward Sanford, Washington 13.

1941: Fred Davis, Washington, 2; Hal Newman, Brooklyn, 5; Ed Hickerson, Washington, 8.

1942: Noah Langdale, Green Bay, 7; John Wyhonic, Philadelphia, 14; Holt Rast, Chicago Bears, 16; Jimmy Nelson, Chicago Cardinals, 19.

1943: Joe Domnanovich, Brooklyn, 4; George Hecht, Chicago Cardinals, 5; Tony Leon, Washington, 6; Sam Sharpe, Cleveland, 14; George Weeks, Philadelphia, 14; Russ Craft, Philadelphia, 15; Dave Brown, New York Giants, 23; Al Sabo, Brooklyn, 29.

1944: Don Whitmire, Green Bay, 7; Mitch Olenski, Brooklyn, 9; Bill Baughman, Green Bay, 11; Ted Cook, Brooklyn, 22; Jack McKewen, Chicago Bears, 25; Andy Bires, New York Giants, 27.

1945: Johnny August, Cleveland, 8; Jack Aland, Cleveland, 13; Hal Self, Brooklyn, 14; Bobby Jenkins, Washington, 15; Jim McWhorter, Detroit, 16; Norm Mosley, Philadelphia, 21; Jack Green, Chicago Bears, 23; Charley Compton, Cleveland, 30;

John Staples, New York Giants, 30; Ken Reese, Philadelphia, 29.

1946: Phil Tinsley, Chicago Cardinals, 8; Nick Terizzi, New York Giants, 16; D.J. Gambrell, LA Rams, 24; Fay Mills, Washington, 27.

1947: Bill Cadenhead, Detroit, 24; AAFC: Chuck Compton, Buffalo, 19, 140th.

1948: Vaughn Mancha, Boston, 1; Lowell Tew, Washington, 1; John Wozniak, Pittsburgh, 3; Ray Richeson, Philadelphia, 8; Roy "Rebel" Steiner, Detroit, 23; Harry Gilmer, Washington, Bonus Choice. 1948 AAFC: Harry Gilmer, Brooklyn, 1, 3rd; Vaughn Mancha, LA Dons, 1, 4th; Lowell Tew, NY Yankees, 1, 7th; John Woznick, Brooklyn, 16, 100th; Monk Mosely, Baltimore, 19, 123rd; Ray Richeson, Brooklyn, 26, 180th.

1949: Jim Cain, Chicago Hornets, 8, 54th; Dick Flowers, San Francisco, 10, 76th; Bill Cadenhead, Chicago Hornets, 24, 162nd; Bob Hood, New York Yankees, 24, 164th.

1950: Ed White, Washington, 19; Red Noonan, New York Bulldogs, 26.

1951: Butch Avinger, Pittsburgh, 1; Herb Hannah, New York Giants, 6; Larry Lauer, New York Yanks, 8; Al Lary, New York Yanks, 12; Mike Mizerany, Pittsburgh, 14; Elliott Speed, Washington, 22; Tommy Calvin, Pittsburgh, 25.

1952: Billy Shipp, New York Giants, 8; Bobby Wilson, Pittsburgh, 25; Harold Lutz, Chicago Cardinals, 28.

1953: Bobby Marlow, New York Giants, 1; Jesse Richardson, Philadelphia, 8; Jerry Watford, Chicago Cardinals, 8; Joe Curtis, Chicago Cardinals, 21; Bob Conway, Green Bay, 21; Travis Hunt, San Francisco, 23; Clell Hobson, Cleveland, 29.

1954: Sid Youngelman, San Francisco, 7; Tommy Lewis, Chicago Cardinals, 10; Bill Oliver, Green Bay, 12; John Smalley, Green Bay, 25; Ralph Carrigan, Chicago Cardinals, 26.

1955: George Mason, Pittsburgh, 5; Bobby Luna, San Francisco, 6; Corky Tharp, Los Angeles Rams, 6; Ed Culpepper, Green Bay, 9; Cecil Ingram, Philadelphia, 23.

1956: Jim Emmons, Pittsburgh, 14; Bart Starr, Green Bay, 17; Al Ellett, Philadelphia, 27; Wes Thompson, Pittsburgh, 29; Jim Buckler, Chicago Bears, 30.

In December 1964 Joe Namath discusses practice plans with Bear Bryant in preparation for the Orange Bowl. Namath parlayed his success at Alabama into an outspoken and successful NFL career; he was voted into the Hall of Fame in 1985.

1957: Don Comstock, Cleveland, 9; Fred Sington Jr., San Francisco, 12 (F).

1958: Jim Lofton, Detroit from Pittsburgh, 9

1959: Bobby Jackson, Green Bay, 7; Dave Sington, New York Giants, 30.

1960: Bobby Luna, Dallas Rangers expansion from Pittsburgh. AFL: Gary O'Steen, Houston, first selections; Chuck Allen, New York Titans, first selections; Don Cochran, Houston, second selections.

1961: Ed Culpepper, Minnesota expansion from St. Louis.

1962: Bill Rice, St. Louis choice to San Francisco, 5; Billy Neighbors, Washington, 4; Ray Abruzzese, Baltimore, 16; Tommy Brooker, Washington, 16. AFL: Bill Rice, Houston, 5; Billy Neighbors, Boston, 6; Tommy Brooker, Dallas Texans, 17; Ray Abruzzese, Buffalo, 23; Pat Trammell, Dallas Texans, 24.

1963: Lee Roy Jordan, Dallas, 1; Butch Wilson, Baltimore from Pittsburgh, 2; Mike Fracchia, St. Louis from Baltimore, 3; AFL: Lee Roy Jordan, Boston, 2; Butch Wilson, Oakland, 6; Dick Williamson, Boston, 7.

1964: Benny Nelson, Detroit, 5; Steve Wright, Green Bay, 5; Eddie Versprille, Cleveland, 11. AFL: Steve Wright, New York Jets, 8; Benny Nelson, Houston, 12.

1965: Joe Namath, St. Louis, 1; Ray Ogden, St. Louis, 3; Frank McClendon, Minnesota, 9; Gaylon McCullough, Dallas, 10; Bud French, St. Louis, 11. AFL: Joe Namath, New York Jets, 1; Ray Ogden, Houston, 8; Frank McClendon, Oakland, 19.

1966: Ray Perkins, Baltimore, 7; Steve Sloan, Atlanta, 11; David Ray, Cleveland, 16; Tom Tolleson, Atlanta, 15; Steve Bowman, New York Giants, 15. AFL: Billy Neighbors, Miami (Expansion); Tom Tolleson, New York Jets, 17; Steve Bowman, Oakland, 20. AFL Redshirt: Ray Perkins, Boston, 5.

1967 (first combined AFL-NFL draft): Les Kelley, New Orleans from Baltimore, 1,26th; Louis Thompson, New York Giants, 4, 82nd; Wayne Trimble, San Francisco, 4, 91st; Cecil Dowdy, Cleveland, 9, 230th; Ray Ogden, New Orleans (expansion) from St. Louis.

1968: Dennis Homan, Dallas 1, 20th; Ken Stabler, Oakland, 2, 52nd; Bobby Johns, Kansas City, 12, 320th.

1969: Mike Hall, New York Jets, 10, 260th; Bill Davis, Oakland, 16, 412th.

1970: None.

1971: Scott Hunter, Green Bay, 6, 140th.

1972: Johnny Musso, Chicago Bears, 3, 62nd; David Bailey, Green Bay, 11, 266th; Robin Parkhouse, Baltimore, 15, 386th; Steve Higginbotham, Washington, 16, 411th.

1973: John Hannah, New England, 1, 4th; John Mitchell, San Francisco, 7, 201st; Jim Krapf, Oakland, 12, 309th.

1974: Wilbur Jackson, San Francisco, 1, 9th; Wayne Wheeler, Chicago Bears from San Diego, 3, 54th; Mike Raines, San Francisco, 6, 138th; Greg Gantt, New York Jets, 8, 187th; Buddy Brown, New York Giants, 16, 392nd.

1975: Mike Washington, Baltimore, 3, 53rd; Ricky Davis, Cincinnati, 8, 195th.

1976: Richard Todd, New York Jets, 1, 6th; Wayne Rhodes, Chicago Bears from Detroit, 4, 108th; Woodrow Lowe, San Diego from New England, 5, 131st; Willie Shelby, Cincinnati from San Francisco, 5, 138th; Leroy Cook, Dallas, 10, 290th; Joe Dale Harris, Cincinnati, 12, 340th; Ricky Davis, Tampa Bay (expansion) from Cincinnati.

1977: Bob Baumhower, Miami, 2, 40th; Charley Hannah, Tampa Bay, 3, 56th; Paul Harris, Pittsburgh, 6, 159th; Calvin Culliver, Denver, 8, 212th.

1978: Bob Cryder, New England, 1, 18th; Ozzie Newsome, Cleveland from Los Angeles Rams, 1, 23rd; Johnny Davis, Tampa Bay, 2, 30th; Terry Jones, Green Bay, 11, 284th.

1979: Barry Krauss, Baltimore, 1, 6th; Marty Lyons, New York Jets, 1, 14th; Tony Nathan, Miami from Tampa Bay, 3, 61st; Rich Wingo, Green Bay from San Diego, 7, 184th; Jeff Rutledge, Los Angeles Rams, 9, 246th.

1980: Don McNeal, Miami, 1, 21st; Dwight Stephenson, Miami, 2, 48th; Wayne Hamilton, San Diego, 6, 163rd; Buddy Aydelette, Green Bay, 7, 169th; Ken Harris, New York Giants, 8, 200th; Steve Whitman, San Diego, 9, 247th.

1981: E.J. Junior, St. Louis, 1, 5th; Byron Braggs, Green Bay, 5, 117th; Billy Jackson, Kansas City, 7, 180th; James Mallard, St. Louis, 10, 253rd; Major Ogilvie, San Francisco, 12, 313th.

1982: Benny Perrin, St. Louis, 3, 65th; Thomas Boyd, Green Bay, 8, 210th; Warren Lyles, San Diego, 9, 246th.

Buried in the middle of this photo, Don McNeal made the interception in front of Penn State's Bob Bassett in the 1978 Sugar Bowl. The pick was a key play in the Crimson Tide's 14–7 win.

1983: Mike Pitts, Atlanta, 1, 16th; Jeremiah Castille, Tampa Bay, 3, 72nd; Steve Mott, Detroit, 5, 121st; Robbie Jones, New York Giants, 12, 309th.

1984: Joe Carter, Miami, 4, 109th; Jesse Bendross, San Diego, 7, 174th. Supplemental: Joey Jones, Atlanta, 1, 9th; Walter Lewis, New England, 3, 70th.

1985: Emanuel King, Cincinnati from Seattle, 1, 25th; Ricky Moore, San Francisco from New England, 3, 75th.

1986: Jon Hand, Indianapolis, 1, 4th; Larry Roberts, San Francisco, 2, 39th; Thornton Chandler, Dallas, 6, 140th; Brent Sowell, Miami, 6, 163rd.

1987: Cornelius Bennett, Indianapolis, 1, 2nd; Freddie Robinson, Indianapolis, 6, 142nd; Greg Richardson, Minnesota, 6, 156th; Curt Jarvis, Tampa Bay, 7, 169th; Wayne Davis, St. Louis, 9, 229th; Wes Neighbors, Houston, 9, 231st; Chris Goode, Indianapolis, 10, 253rd; Mike Shula, Tampa Bay, 12, 313th.

1988: Kerry Goode, Tampa Bay, 7, 167th; Bo Wright, Buffalo from San Diego, 7, 184th; Phillip Brown, Atlanta, 8, 194th.

1989: Derrick Thomas, Kansas City, 1, 4th; Greg Gilbert, Chicago, 5, 136th; Chris Mohr, Tampa Bay, 6, 146th; Howard Cross, New York Giants, 6, 158th; George Bethune, Los Angeles, 7, 188th.

1990: Keith McCants, Tampa Bay, 1, 4th; John Mangum, Chicago, 6, 144th; Thomas Rayam, Washington, 10, 270th.

1991: George Thornton, San Diego, 2, 36th; Byron Holdbrooks, San Francisco, 10, 276th; Efrum Thomas, Pittsburgh, 11, 296th.

1992: Siran Stacy, Philadelphia, 2, 48th; Robert Stewart, New Orleans, 8, 218th; Mark McMillian, Philadelphia, 10, 272nd.

1993: John Copeland, Cincinnati, 1, 5th; Eric Curry, Tampa Bay, 1, 6th; George Teague, Green Bay, 1, 29th; Antonio London, Detroit, 3, 62nd; Derrick Lassic, Dallas, 4, 94th; Derrick Oden, Philadelphia, 6, 163rd.

1994: Antonio Langham, Cleveland, 1, 9th; Kevin Lee, New England, 2, 35th; David Palmer, Minnesota from Cleveland, 2, 40th; Jeremy Nunley, Houston, 2, 60th; Roosevelt Patterson, Los Angeles Raiders from Dallas, 5, 159th; Lemanski Hall, Houston, 7, 220th.

1995: Sherman Williams, Dallas from Atlanta, 2, 46th; Sam Shade, Cincinnati, 4, 102nd; Dameian Jeffries, New Orleans, 4,

108th; Jay Barker, Green Bay, 5, 160th; Bryne Diehl, New York Giants, 7, 225th.

1996: Shannon Brown, Atlanta, 3, 84th; Brad Ford, Detroit, 4, 129th; Kendrick Burton, Houston, 4, 107th; Tony Johnson, Philadelphia from Green Bay, 6, 197th; Toderick Malone, New Orleans, 7, 204th.

1997: Dwayne Rudd, Minnesota, 1, 20th; Patrick Hape, Tampa Bay, 5, 137th; Ralph Staten, Baltimore, 7, 236th.

1998: Rod Rutledge, New England, 2, 54th; Michael Myers, Dallas, 4, 100th; Deshea Townsend, Pittsburgh, 4, 117th; Curtis Alexander, Denver, 4, 122nd.

1999: Fernando Bryant, Jacksonville, 1, 26th.

2000: Chris Samuels, Washington, 1, 3rd; Shaun Alexander, Seattle, 1, 19th; Cornelius Griffin, New York, 2nd, 42nd.

2001: Tony Dixon, Dallas (from Miami), 2, 56th; Kenny Smith, New Orleans (from Indianapolis through Dallas), 3, 81st; Shawn Draper, Miami, 5, 156th.

2002: Saleem Rasheed, San Francisco, 3, 69th; Jason McAddley, Arizona, 5, 149th; Terry Jones, Baltimore, 5, 155th; Freddie Milons, Philadelphia, 5, 162nd.

2003: Jarret Johnson, Baltimore, 4, 109th; Kenny King, Arizona, 5, 141st; Kindal Moorehead, Carolina, 5, 145th; Waine Bacon, Atlanta, 6, 202nd; Ahmaad Galloway, Denver, 7, 235th.

2004: Justin Smiley, San Francisco, 2, 40th; Antwan Odom, Tennessee, 2, 50th; Triandos Luke, Denver, 5, 160th; Derrick Pope, Miami, 7, 22th.

2005: Evan Mathis, Carolina, 3, 79th; Wesley Britt, San Diego, 5, 164; Anthony Bryant, Tampa Bay, 6,178th; Cornelius Wortham, Seattle, 7, 235th.

2006: DeMeco Ryans, Houston, 2, 33rd; Roman Harper, New Orleans, 2, 43rd; Brodie Croyle, Kansas City, 3, 85th; Charlie Peprah, N.Y. Giants, 5, 158th; Mark Anderson, Chicago, 5, 159th.

2007: Le'Ron McClain, Baltimore Ravens, 4, 137th; Kenneth Darby, Tampa Bay Buccaneers, 7th, 246th; Ramzee Robinson, Detroit Lions, 7, 255th.

2008: None.

2009: Andre Smith, Cincinnati Bengals, 1, 6th; Glen Coffee, San Francisco 49ers, 3, 74th; Antoine Caldwell, Houston Texans, 3, 77th; Rashad Johnson, Arizona Cardinals, 3, 95th.

Alabama's All-Century Team

(selected by fans)

Offense—E Don Hutson, 1932–1934; E Ozzie Newsome, 1974–77; L Fred Sington, 1928–30; L Vaughn Mancha, 1944–47; C Dwight Stephenson, 1977–79; L Billy Neighbors, 1959–61; L John Hannah, 1970–72; QB Joe Namath, 1962–64; QB Ken Stabler, 1965–67; RB Bobby Marlow, 1950–52; RB Johnny Musso, 1969–71; RB Bobby Humphrey, 1985–88; K Van Tiffin, 1983–86

Defense—L Bob Baumhower, 1973, 1976; L Marty Lyons, 1975–78; L Jon Hand, 1982–85; LB Lee Roy Jordan, 1960–62; LB Barry Kraus, 1976–78; OLB Cornelius Bennett, 1983–86; OLB Derrick Thomas, 1985–88; DB Harry Gilmer, 1944–47; DB Don McNeal, 1977–79; DB Jeremiah Castille, 1979–82; DB Tommy Wilcox, 1979–82; P Johnny Cain, 1930–32

Coach: Paul W. "Bear" Bryant.

The Greatest Players

28

Wins by Ken Stabler during his three years at the helm of the Crimson Tide. After watching from the sideline in 1964 as Alabama won the national championship, Stabler was ready to make his mark. He compiled a 28-3-2 record at Alabama before going on to a pro career. He later returned to the university as a radio color commentator.

RECORDS & LEADERS
Rushing

Game

Yards Name	Year	Carries	Opponent
1. 291 Shaun Alexander	1996	20	LSU
2. 284 Bobby Humphrey	1986	30	Mississippi State
3. 233 Bobby Marlow	1951	25	Auburn
4. 221 Johnny Musso	1970	42	Auburn
5. 220 Bobby Humphrey	1987	27	Penn State
6. 218 Glen Coffee	2008	25	Kentucky
7. 217 Bobby Humphrey	1986	36	Tennessee
8. 216 Harry Gilmer	1945	6	Kentucky
9. 214 Shaun Alexander	1999	36	Ole Miss
10. 211 Siran Stacy	1989	28	LSU

Season

Yards	Name	Carries	Year
1. 1,471	Bobby Humphrey	236	1986
2. 1,383	Shaun Alexander	302	1999
(tie) 1,383	Glen Coffee	233	2008
4. 1,367	Shaud Williams	280	2003
5. 1,341	Sherman Williams	291	1994
6. 1,255	Bobby Humphrey	238	1987
7. 1,242	Kenneth Darby	239	2005
8. 1,178	Shaun Alexander	258	1998
9. 1,137	Johnny Musso	226	1970
10. 1,088	Johnny Musso	191	1971

Career

Yards	Name	Carries	Years
1. 3,565	Shaun Alexander	727	1996–99
2. 3,420	Bobby Humphrey	615	1985–88
3. 3,324	Kenneth Darby	702	2003–06

The Greatest Players

4. 2,741	Johnny Musso	574	1969–71
5. 2,645	Dennis Riddle	612	1994–97
6. 2,560	Bobby Marlow	408	1950–52
7. 2,519	Johnny Davis	447	1974–77
8. 2,486	Sherman Williams	535	1991–94
9. 2,288	Shaud Williams	410	2002–03
10. 2,270	Ricky Moore	469	1981–84

Passing

Game

Yards	Name	Opponent	Comp/Att	Year
1. 484	Scott Hunter	Auburn	30 of 55	1969
2. 396	Jay Barker	Georgia	26 of 34	1994
3. 379	Gary Hollingsworth	Tennessee	32 of 46	1989
4. 367	Mike Shula	Memphis State	24 of 34	1985
5. 363	Gary Hollingsworth	Ole Miss	25 of 43	1989
(tie) 363	John Parker Wilson	Tennessee	32 of 46	2007
7. 340	Gary Hollingsworth	Auburn	27 of 49	1989
8. 336	Andrew Zow	Florida	28 of 40	1999
(tie) 336	Walter Lewis	Penn State	25 of 35	1983
10. 327	John Parker Wilson	Arkansas	24 of 45	2007

Season

Yards	Name	Comp/Att	Year
1. 2,846	John Parker Wilson	255 of 372	2007
2. 2,707	John Parker Wilson	216 of 379	2006
3. 2,499	Brodie Croyle	202 of 339	2005
4. 2,379	Gary Hollingsworth	205 of 339	1989
5. 2,303	Brodie Croyle	182 of 341	2003
6. 2,273	John Parker Wilson	186 of 321	2008
7. 2,188	Scott Hunter	157 of 266	1969
8. 2,124	Freddie Kitchens	152 of 302	1996
9. 2,009	Mike Shula	138 of 229	1985
10. 1,996	Jay Barker	139 of 226	1994

Career

Yards	Name	Comp/Att	Years
1. 7,924	John Parker Wilson	665 of 1,175	2005–08
2. 6,382	Brodie Croyle	488 of 869	2002–05
3. 5,983	Andrew Zow	459 of 852	1998–01
4. 5,689	Jay Barker	402 of 706	1991–94
5. 4,899	Scott Hunter	382 of 672	1968–70
6. 4,668	Freddie Kitchens	343 of 680	1993–97
7. 4,257	Walter Lewis	286 of 504	1980–83
8. 4,069	Mike Shula	313 of 578	1983–86
9. 3,842	Gary Hollingsworth	345 of 621	1989–90
10. 3,540	Tyler Watts	284 of 494	1999–02

Receiving

Game

Yards	Name	Catches	Opponent	Year
1. 217	David Palmer	8	Vanderbilt	1993
2. 187	David Bailey	9	Auburn	1969
3. 185	DJ Hall	13	Tennessee	2007
4. 173	Toderick Malone	8	Georgia	1994
5. 171	David Palmer	8	Mississippi State	1993
6. 159	Dennis Homan	6	Florida State	1967
7. 158	Siran Stacy	9	Tennessee	1989
(tie) 158	Ken MacAfee	6	Villanova	1951
9. 157	DJ Hall	11	Utah State	2005
(tie) 157	Antonio Carter	8	Ole Miss	2000

Season

Yards	Name	Catches	Year
1. 1,056	DJ Hall	62	2006
2. 1,005	DJ Hall	67	2007
3. 1,000	David Palmer	61	1993
4. 924	Julio Jones	58	2008
5. 820	Dennis Homan	54	1967
6. 804	Ozzie Newsome	36	1977

7. 790	David Bailey	55	1970
8. 781	David Bailey	56	1969
9. 756	Al Lary	35	1950
10. 733	Freddie Milons	65	1999

Career Yards	Name	Catches	Years
1. 2,923	DJ Hall	194	2004–07
2. 2,070	Ozzie Newsome	102	1974–77
3. 1,863	Keith Brown	117	2004–07
4. 1,859	Freddie Milons	152	1998–01
5. 1,857	David Bailey	132	1969–71
6. 1,611	David Palmer	102	1991–93
7. 1,568	Curtis Brown	106	1991–95
8. 1,495	Dennis Homan	87	1965–67
9. 1,386	Joey Jones	71	1980–83
10. 1,368	Toderick Malone	73	1993–95

The Greatest Players

Other Alabama Records

Points, game: 30, Santonio Beard vs. Ole Miss, Oct. 19, 2002 (5 touchdowns); Shaun Alexander vs. BYU, Sept. 5, 1998 (5 touchdowns)

Points, season: 144, Shaun Alexander, 1999 (24 touchdowns)

Points, career: 345, Philip Doyle, 1987–90 (one touchdown, 78 field goals, 105 PATs)

All-purpose yards, game: 317, Siran Stacy vs. Tennessee (125 rushing, 158 receiving, 34 kickoff returns), 1989.

All-purpose yards, season: 2,016, Bobby Humphrey (1,471 rushing, 201 receiving, 344 kickoff returns), 1986

All-purpose yards, career: 4,958, Bobby Humphrey (3,420 rushing, 523 receiving, 1,015 kickoff returns), 1985–88

Interceptions, game: 3, (tied) Bobby Wilson, Dicky Thompson, Jeremiah Castille, Kevin Jackson, Rashad Johnson

Interceptions, season: 10, Hootie Ingram, 1952

Interceptions, career: 19, Antonio Langham, 1990–93.

Tackles, game: 25, DeMeco Ryans vs. Arkansas, 2003

Tackles, season: 134, Woodrow Lane, 1973

Tackles, career: 327, Wayne Davis, 1983–86

Sacks, game: 5, Derrick Thomas vs. Texas A&M, 1988

Sacks, season: 27, Derrick Thomas, 1988

Sacks, career: 52, Derrick Thomas, 1985–88

Butkus Award winner Derrick Thomas smashed nearly every record he could while at Alabama. He was a superstar on the field and played his entire pro career for the Kansas City Chiefs. He was posthumously named to the Pro Football Hall of Fame in 2009.

THE COACHES

Wallace Wade
1923–1930

Alabama football graduated from a Deep South attraction into a national player in eight years under Wallace Wade. The son of a Tennessee farmer, Wade went to prep school in Chicago, then became a star guard at Brown University. He helped guide Vanderbilt to unbeaten seasons in 1921 and 1922 as an assistant coach, and, with the recommendation of Vanderbilt legend Dan McGugin, University of Alabama president Dr. George Hutcheson Denny lured Wade to Tuscaloosa in 1923.

The relationship between the hard-driving coach and the ambitious university president, who understood the value of a winning football program, would become strained before long, but the match nevertheless helped put Alabama football on the national radar.

After taking over for Xen Scott (1919–1922), who died of cancer within weeks of the 1922 season's conclusion, Alabama football quickly began to mirror its new boss, a former military man who was intense and goal oriented.

His first Alabama team lost only twice, including on a road trip to eastern power Syracuse, but that 1923 team set the stage for three consecutive Southern Conference championships led by players such as Johnny Mack Brown, Pooley Hubert, Grant Gillis, and Hoyt "Wu" Winslet.

Wade's 1924 team shut out seven opponents and allowed only 24 points on the season, but lost a 17–0 decision to Centre College on November 15 to block the first undefeated season in school history.

That first would come the next year, when "the greatest collection of backs in the South," according to *Birmingham News* columnist Zipp Newman, helped Alabama roll through the regular season with a 9–0 record while outscoring opponents 277–7. As a result, Alabama became the first Southern team to play in the Rose Bowl, against West Coast power Washington, a heavy favorite.

Alabama fell behind 12–0 by halftime but rallied behind Hubert and Brown to score 20 consecutive points and win 20–19. The victory, called "the Rose Bowl's greatest game" in a book written by Maxwell Stiles, legitimized Southern football in the eyes of the nation and earned Alabama a national championship.

Wade's next team went unbeaten and won another national championship but tied Stanford at the Rose Bowl, 7–7. During his final season, 1930, Alabama outscored opponents 271–13 and won its third national championship.

Wade at Alabama

Year	Record	Bowl
1923	7–2–1	
1924	8–1	
1925	10–0*	Rose
1926	9–0–1*	Rose
1927	5–4–1	
1928	6–3	
1929	6–3	
1930	10–0*	Rose
Total	61–13–3	

*Claimed national championship

Frank Thomas
1931–1946

Frank "Tommy" Thomas was a former Notre Dame player who roomed with George Gipp during the Knute Rockne years but really made a name for himself as a coach who went 115–24–7 over 15 seasons.

The Coaches

He led Alabama to four SEC championships, including the inaugural SEC season of 1933, and two national championships.

Thomas installed the Notre Dame box offense at Alabama and reeled off an amazing 34–4–1 record in his first four seasons. During the 1933 campaign, Alabama overcame a 0–0 tie with Ole Miss in week two for a championship run that included a 12–6 win at Tennessee, the Volunteers' first loss at Shields-Watkins Field in nine years. Alabama's only defeat that season came at the famed Polo Grounds in New York City with a 2–0 loss to Fordham.

A year later, Alabama featured the star tandem of quarterback Dixie Howell and end Don Hutson, who revolutionized receiving. Howell also hooked up frequently with the "other end" on that team, Paul W. "Bear" Bryant.

Alabama smoked its first eight opponents that year by a combined score of 253–32. It was 9–0 heading into its regular-season finale against Vanderbilt in Birmingham. Thomas knew the Rose Bowl was considering Alabama and unbeaten Minnesota as the opponent for Stanford, so he exhorted his players that day to "go out there and get into the Rose Bowl."

Alabama dismantled Vanderbilt 34–0 and found out upon returning to its hotel rooms that the Rose Bowl indeed would like a return trip by the Crimson Tide. Thomas guided Alabama to a 29–13 win over Stanford.

As other bowls came on the horizon in the early 1940s, Thomas' teams began making the circuit: the Cotton Bowl in 1941, the Orange Bowl in 1942, and the Sugar Bowl in 1944 after Alabama did not field a team in 1943. Thomas had a 4–2 record in bowl games.

His 1941 team, a preseason favorite as one of the best in the country, lost a stunning 14–0 game to Mississippi State in Tuscaloosa, as well as a 7–0 game at Vanderbilt, but Alabama's rough schedule earned the program's first trip to the Cotton Bowl and one of the most memorable bowl games in school history.

Alabama managed just one first down and 75 yards total offense, compared to Texas A&M's 13 first downs and 309 total yards. But Thomas' troops intercepted seven passes and recovered five fumbles and scored a 29–21 win in Dallas. The Crimson Tide was declared the national champion by Houlgate that year, even though Minnesota went unbeaten and was chosen national champion by nine other selectors.

Thomas won his final SEC championship and another Rose Bowl with a 10–0 team in 1945. Failing health forced him out after a 7–4 season in 1946.

Thomas at Alabama

Year	Record	Bowl
1931	9–1	
1932	8–2	
1933	7–1–1	
1934	10–0*	Rose
1935	6–2–1	
1936	8–0–1	
1937	9–1	Rose
1938	7–1–1	
1939	5–3–1	
1940	7–2	
1941	9–2*	Cotton
1942	8–3	Orange
1944	5–2–2	Sugar
1945	10–0	Rose
1946	7–4	
Total	115–24–7	

*Claimed national championship

Paul W. "Bear" Bryant
1958-1982

Paul W. "Bear" Bryant's name and reputation are still holding strong more than two decades following his death, thanks in part to six national championships, 13 Southeastern Conference titles, and 24 bowl appearances in 25 years coaching the Crimson Tide. More than a legend, the one true icon is remembered each and every day in Tuscaloosa, and his "Ain't never been nothing but a winner" echoes the stadium bearing his name before every game.

The native of Moro Bottom, Arkansas, earned his nickname by wrestling a bear as a youth, with the trademark houndstooth hat added much later. But he had already begun to form his legend before "Mama called," with the Junction Boys at Texas A&M and by turning moribund Kentucky into a winning program.

What prompted his return in 1958 was the program's struggling in three seasons under J. B. Whitworth, who had a 4-24-2 record. Alabama had scored just 69 points in Whitworth's final season. What was worse: Alabama had gone 0-6 against bitter rivals Auburn and Tennessee under Whitworth and had been outscored 158-7 in those games.

Bryant had a winning record against Auburn by his third season at Alabama. He began a string of six unbeaten games against Tennessee in 1961, the year of his first national championship at Alabama and would later win 11 in a row over the Volunteers.

Bryant inspired devotion in those who played for him and fear in many of his opponents. The belief that he could take his and beat yours or take yours and beat his was very real during the 1960s and 1970s.

Alabama's defenses allowed successively fewer points in each of his first four seasons, until the 1961 team gave up just 25 in an 11-0 season, the program's first unbeaten year since 1945 and its seventh overall.

Bryant led the Crimson Tide to AP national championships in 1964 and 1965 and an 11–0 season in 1966 before he fell into the biggest slump of his Alabama coaching career. His next four teams went 28–15–2, causing some to wonder if Bryant had lost his touch.

To the contrary, the adaptable Bryant flew home from a 24–24 tie with Oklahoma in the 1970 Astro-Bluebonnet Bowl with the blueprint for Alabama's domination of the 1970s: the wishbone offense.

Alabama unleashed the wishbone on unsuspecting USC to much fanfare in the 1971 season opener, touching off a 10-year record of 107–13. Bryant's forward-thinking approach to integration, after Sam Cunningham helped USC thump Alabama 42–21 in the 1970 season opener, was also fruitful in the 1970s.

The Crimson Tide won eight SEC championships in that streak, scored the UPI national championship in 1973, then won back-to-back national crowns in 1978 and 1979. Only a 9–3 mark in 1976 prevented Bryant's teams from winning at least 10 games in 10 consecutive seasons.

Bryant posted a 72–2 record at Bryant-Denny Stadium. A three-time national coach of the year, he surpassed Amos Alonzo Stagg's national record with win No. 315 against archrival Auburn in 1981. Bryant recorded career win number 323 in a 21–15 Liberty Bowl victory over Illinois on December 29, 1982, two weeks after announcing he would retire after the bowl game.

On January 26, 1983, the day after being rushed to the hospital with severe chest pains, Bryant died from coronary artery disease.

Bryant at Alabama

Year	Record	Bowl
1958	5–4–1	
1959	7–2–2	Liberty
1960	8–1–2	Bluebonnet
1961	11–0*	Sugar
1962	10–1	Orange
1963	9–2	Sugar
1964	10–1*	Orange
1965	9–1–1*	Orange
1966	11–0	Sugar
1967	8–2–1	Cotton
1968	8–3	Gator
1969	6–5	
1970	6–5–1	Bluebonnet
1971	11–1	Orange
1972	10–2	Cotton
1973	11–1*	Sugar
1974	11–1	Orange
1975	11–1	Sugar
1976	9–3	Liberty
1977	11–1	Sugar
1978	11–1*	Sugar
1979	12–0*	Sugar
1980	10–2	Cotton
1981	9–2–1	Cotton
1982	8–4	Liberty
Total	232–46–9	

*Claimed national championship

Gene Stallings
1990–1996

Although Gene Stallings brought with him a losing record as a head coach when he was tapped to replace Bill Curry following the 1989 season, Crimson Tide fans rejoiced in his selection. A true Bear Bryant

Gene Stallings roams the end zone of the Louisiana Super-dome with his son Johnny before the Sugar Bowl against Miami. One of the reasons for Stallings' retirement was to spend more time with Johnny, who suffered from Down's Syndrome.

disciple, and former assistant coach, Stallings was a surviving member of the Junction Boys from Texas A&M in 1954. "The training program was so tough that we went to camp in three buses and only one came back," Stalllings said.

As head coach at Texas A&M, Stallings beat Bryant 20–16 in the 1968 Cotton Bowl in their only head-to-head meeting. He was welcomed after Curry, who did win Alabama's first SEC championship in eight years, failed to beat Auburn.

Stallings' Tide tenure got off to an inauspicious start, as his 1990 team lost its opener to Brett Favre–led Southern Miss, then fell to Florida and Georgia. His immediate predecessors, Curry and Ray Perkins, had guided Alabama to 3-0 starts in five of their seven seasons, so the 0-3 stint had 'Bama fans in a tizzy. But Alabama won seven of its last eight regular-season games.

The Tide went 11-1 in 1991, but that was just the beginning. Stallings' 1992 team rolled out one of the stingiest defenses college football had ever seen, holding its first nine opponents to 11 points or less. It disposed of Auburn (17–0) for a third-straight season, then tripped up explosive Florida 28–21 in the inaugural SEC Championship Game.

The Crimson Tide was ranked No. 2 but was still an eight-point underdog to defending national champion Miami in the Sugar Bowl. Many thought the game would be a blowout, and it was, only for Alabama, who scored a 34-13 win for the program's 12th national championship.

Alabama took a 31-game unbeaten streak late into the 1993 season before dropping a 17-13 decision against LSU. Though Alabama's record in 1993 would officially be listed as 1–12 due to NCAA sanctions resulting from Antonio Langham's dealings with an agent after the national championship game, the Crimson Tide's on-the-field record from week three of 1991 through early 1995 was a sparkling 46–4–1, one of the greatest streaks in recent decades.

Stallings posted a 5–1 bowl record, a 4–2–1 mark against Tennessee and a 5–2 record against Auburn. However, he walked away in 1996, making a surprise announcement following the 24–23 victory against Auburn. Stallings went out with a win, 17–14 over Michigan in the Outback Bowl, to improve his record to 70–16–1.

Stallings at Alabama

Year	Record	Bowl
1990	7–5	Fiesta
1991	11–1	Blockbuster
1992	13–0*	Sugar
1993	9–3–1**	Gator
1994	12–1	Citrus
1995	8–3	
1996	10–3	Outback
Total	70–16–1	

*Claimed national championship

**Alabama later forfeited nine games for a 1–12 record

Nick Saban
2007–Present

Although the touchdown occurred at an airport instead of on a football field, it nonetheless was still considered one of the most important in Crimson Tide history.

At approximately 3:45 PM on January 3rd, 2007, Alabama's private jet landed in Tuscaloosa, where hundreds of fans had gathered in eager anticipation. They didn't even wait for the man wearing a gray suit, lavender shirt, and no tie to emerge from the open door to start celebrating and couldn't wait to give him rock-star treatment.

The following day, when Nick Saban was officially announced as the 27th head coach of the Crimson Tide, he didn't hesitate to send a clear and deliberate message to the program's fans, players, and boosters, with what instantly became the latest Alabama mantra.

"Be a champion in everything that we do," Saban said. "Every choice, every decision, everything that we do every day, we want to be a champion."

With that, the Saban era was under way at the Capstone, and approximately four months later Alabama smashed the record for A-Day attendance, with school officials having to turn people away after more than 92,000 packed Bryant-Denny Stadium to watch the final scrimmage of spring football. Even Saban was surprised.

Not surprisingly, most thought it was more a matter of *when* Saban when would turn things around, rather than *if.* They were right.

During Saban's second season, 2008, the Crimson Tide exceeded all expectations by finishing the regular season undefeated and spending five weeks at No. 1. The miraculous run came to an end in the SEC Championship Game, where Alabama lost to quarterback Tim Tebow and eventual national champion Florida, but the message had been sent: Alabama was back on top of the football world and not going anywhere.

The Coaches

Saban at Alabama

Year	Record	Bowl
2007	7–6	Independence
2008	12–2	Sugar

Coaching Awards:

Paul W. "Bear" Bryant Award: Gene Stallings, 1992

Home Depot Coach of the Year: Nick Saban, 2008

Bobby Dodd Coach of the Year: Bill Curry, 1989

Walter Camp Coach of the Year: Gene Stallings, 1992; Nick Saban, 2008

AFCA Coach of the Year: Paul W. "Bear" Bryant, 1961, 1972, 1974; Gene Stallings, 1993

Eddie Robinson Award: Gene Stallings, 1992; Nick Saban, 2008

Associated Press Coach of the Year: Nick Saban, 2008.

Liberty Mutual Coach of the Year: Nick Saban, 2008

SEC Coach of the Year: AP: Paul W. "Bear" Bryant 1959, 1961, 1964, 1965, 1971, 1973, 1978, 1979, 1981, 1989; Bill Curry, 1989; Gene Stallings, 1992, 1994; Mike DuBose, 1999; Nick Saban, 2008. Coaches: Frank Thomas, 1945; Harold Drew, 1952; Paul W. "Bear" Bryant, 1961, 1964, 1971, 1973, 1974, 1977, 1979, 1981; Bill Curry, 1989; Gene Stallings, 1992; Mike DuBose, 1999; Nick Saban (tie), 2008

The Coaches

Head coach Nick Saban has been called by *Forbes* magazine "Sport's Most Powerful Coach." He backed that up by winning several national coach of the year awards in 2008. Before he turned to coaching, he had a successful playing career at Kent State.

SOUTHEASTERN CONFERENCE

Eastern Division

Florida

Location: Gainesville, Florida
Founded: 1853
Enrollment: 51,520
Nickname: Gators
Colors: Orange and blue
Mascot: Albert and Alberta Gator
Stadium: Ben Hill Griffin Stadium at Florida Field (88,548)
Coach: Urban Meyer
National Championships (3): 1996, 2006, 2008
SEC Championships (8): 1991, 1993, 1994, 1995, 1996, 2000, 2006, 2008
First season: 1906
Heisman Winners (3): Steve Spurrier, quarterback, 1966; Danny Wuerffel, quarterback, 1996; Tim Tebow, quarterback, 2007
Retired Jerseys: None

Georgia

Location: Athens, Georgia
Founded: 1785
Enrollment: 33,405
Nickname: Bulldogs
Colors: Red and black
Mascot: Uga
Stadium: Sanford Stadium (92,746)
Coach: Mark Richt
National Championships (2): 1942, 1980
The "Other" Three: Georgia was voted No. 1 in various polls in 1927, 1946, and 1968.
SEC Championships (12): 1942, 1946, 1948, 1959, 1966, 1968, 1976, 1980, 1981, 1982, 2002, 2005
First season: 1892
Heisman Winners (2): Frank Sinkwich, halfback, 1942; Herschel Walker, running back, 1982
Retired Jerseys: 21, Frank Sinkwich; 34, Herschel Walker; 40, Theron Sapp; 62, Charley Trippi

SEC

Kentucky

Location: Lexington, Kentucky
Founded: 1865
Enrollment: 27,000
Nickname: Wildcats
Colors: Blue and white
Mascots: Wildcat and Scratch. Live mascots have included
Tom, TNT, Whiskers, Hot Tamale, Colonel, and Blue.
Stadium: Commonwealth Stadium (67,606)
Coach: Rich Brooks
National Championships: None
SEC Championships (2): 1950, 1976
First season: 1881
Heisman Winners: None
Retired Jerseys: 2 Tim Couch; 2 Ermal Allen; 8 Clyde
Johnson; 10 Vito "Babe" Parilli; 11 Rick Norton; 12 Derrick
Ramsey; 13 Bob Davis; 16 George Blanda; 19 Howard
Schnellenberger; 20 Charlie McClendon; 21 Calvin Bird; 21
Roger Bird; 22 Mark Higgs; 24 Dicky Lyons; 27 Wallace
"Wah-Wah" Jones; 32 Larry Seiple; 33 George Adams;
40 Sonny Collins; 44 John "Shipwreck" Kelly; 45 Jay Rho-
demyre; 48 Washington "Wash" Serini; 50 Jim Kovach;
50 Harry Ulinski; 51 Doug Moseley; 52 Rick Nuzum; 55
Irvin "Irv" Goode; 57 Dermontti Dawson; 59 Joe Federspiel;
65 Ray Correll; 66 Ralph Kercheval; 69 Warren Bryant;
70 Bob Gain; 70 Herschel Turner; 73 Sam Ball; 74 Dave
Roller; 79 Lou Michaels; 80 Rick Kestner; 80 Tom Hutchin-
son; 80 Steve Meilinger; 88 Jeff Van Note; 97 Art Still;
Paul "Bear" Bryant; Jerry Claiborne; Blanton Collier; Bernie
Shively

South Carolina

Location: Columbia, South Carolina
Founded: 1801
Enrollment: 23,772
Nickname: Fighting Gamecocks
Colors: Garnet and black
Mascot: Cocky
Stadium: Williams-Brice Stadium (80,250)
Coach: Steve Spurrier
National Championships: None
SEC Championships: None
First season: 1892

Heisman Winners (1): George Rogers, running back, 1980
Retired Jerseys: 2 Sterling Sharpe; 37 Steve Wadiak; 38
George Rogers; 56 Mike Johnson

Tennessee

Location: Knoxville, Tennessee
Founded: 1794
Enrollment: 25,515
Nickname: Volunteers
Colors: Orange and white
Mascot: Smokey
Stadium: Neyland Stadium/Shields-Watkins Field
(104,079)
Coach: Lane Kiffin
National Championships (2): 1951, 1998
The "Other" Four: The *Official NCAA Football Records Book*
also recognizes Tennessee as producing national champi-
ons in 1938, 1940, 1950, and 1967.
SEC Championships (13): 1938, 1939, 1940, 1946,
1951, 1956, 1967, 1969, 1985, 1989, 1990, 1997,
1998
First season: 1891
Heisman Winners: None
Retired Jerseys: 16 Peyton Manning; 32 Bill Nowling; 49
Rudy Klarer; 61 Willis Tucker; 62 Clyde Fuson, 91 Doug
Atkins, 92 Reggie White

Vanderbilt

Location: Nashville, Tennessee
Founded: 1873
Enrollment: 6,241
Nickname: Commodores
Colors: Black and gold
Mascot: A costumed commodore, though there once was
George the basset hound, followed by Samantha.
Stadium: Dudley Field/Vanderbilt Stadium (39,773)
Coach: Bobby Johnson
National Championships: None
SEC Championships: None
First season: 1890
Heisman Winners: None
Retired Jerseys: None

Western Division

Alabama

Location: Tuscaloosa, Alabama
Founded: 1831
Enrollment: 27,052
Nickname: Crimson Tide
Colors: Crimson and white
Mascot: Big Al (the elephant)
Stadium: Bryant-Denny Stadium (92,138, but being reno-
vated to bring capacity over 101,000)
Coach: Nick Saban
National Championships (12): 1925, 1926, 1930, 1934,
1941, 1961, 1964, 1965, 1973, 1978, 1979, 1992
The "Other" Five: The *Official NCAA Football Records Book*
also recognizes Alabama as producing national champions
in 1945, 1962, 1966, 1975, and 1977
SEC Championships (21): 1933, 1934, 1937, 1945,
1953, 1961, 1964, 1965, 1966, 1971, 1972, 1973,
1974, 1975, 1977, 1978, 1979, 1981, 1989, 1992,
1999
First season: 1892
Heisman Trophies: None
Retired Jerseys: None

Arkansas

Location: Fayetteville, Arkansas
Founded: 1871
Enrollment: 18,648
Nickname: Razorbacks
Colors: Cardinal and white
Mascot: Tusk (a Russian boar)
Stadium: Donald W. Reynolds Razorback Stadium (72,000)
Coach: Bobby Petrino
National Championship (1): 1964
SEC Championships: None
First season: 1894
Heisman Winners: None
Retired Jerseys: 12 Clyde Scott, 12 Steve Little; 77 Bran-
don Burlsworth

Nick Saban encourages his players from the sideline during a 2007 game. Saban, who came to Alabama after a brief stint in the NFL, has helped to breathe new life into the Alabama program in just a few short seasons.

Auburn

Location: Auburn, Alabama
Founded: 1856
Enrollment: 24,137
Nickname: Tigers
Colors: Burnt orange and navy blue
Battle cry/Mascot: War Eagle (The eagle is named Tiger; the cartoonish costumed tiger mascot is named Aubie.)
Stadium: Jordan-Hare Stadium (87,451)
Coach: Gene Chizik
National Championships (1): 1957
SEC Championships (6): 1957, 1983, 1987, 1988, 1989, 2004
First season: 1892
Heisman Winners (2): Pat Sullivan, quarterback, 1971; Bo Jackson, running back, 1985
Retired Jerseys: 34 Bo Jackson; 7 Pat Sullivan; 88 Terry Beasley

LSU

Location: Baton Rouge, Louisiana
Founded: 1860
Enrollment: 31,234
Nickname: Tigers
Colors: Purple and gold
Mascot: Mike the Tiger
Stadium: Tiger Stadium (92,400)
Coach: Les Miles
National Championships (3): 1958, 2003, 2007
SEC Championships (9): 1935, 1936, 1958, 1961, 1970, 1986, 1988, 2001, 2003
First season: 1893
Heisman Winner (1): Billy Cannon, halfback, 1959
Retired Jersey: 20 Billy Cannon

Ole Miss

Location: Oxford, Mississippi
Founded: 1848
Enrollment: 17,325
Nickname: Rebels
Colors: Cardinal red and navy blue

Mascot: Colonel Rebel (unofficial since 2003)
Stadium: Vaught-Hemingway Stadium/Hollingsworth Field (60,580)
Coach: Houston Nutt
National Championships (1): 1960
SEC Championships (6): 1947, 1954, 1955, 1960, 1962, 1963
First season: 1893
Heisman Winners: None
Retired Jerseys: 18 Archie Manning

Mississippi State

Location: Starkville, Mississippi
Founded: 1878
Enrollment: 17,039
Nickname: Bulldogs
Colors: Maroon and white
Mascot: Bully
Stadium: Davis Wade Stadium at Scot Field (55,082)
Coach: Dan Mullen
National Championships: None
SEC Championships (1): 1941
First season: 1895
Heisman Winners: None
Retired Jerseys: None

SEC

SEC Football Champions, 1933–1999

Year	Champion	SEC	Overall	Coach
1933	Alabama	5-0-1	7-1-1	Frank Thomas
1934	Tulane	8-0	10-1	Ted Cox
	Alabama	7-0	10-0	Frank Thomas
1935	LSU	5-0	9-2	Bernie Moore
1936	LSU	6-0	9-1-1	Bernie Moore
1937	Alabama	6-0	9-1	Frank Thomas
1938	Tennessee	7-0	11-0	Bob Neyland
1939	Tennessee	6-0	10-1	Bob Neyland
	Georgia Tech	6-0	8-2	Bill Alexander
	Tulane	5-0	8-1-1	"Red" Dawson
1940	Tennessee	5-0	10-1	Bob Neyland
1941	Mississippi State	4-0-1	8-1-1	Allyn McKeen
1942	Georgia	6-1	11-1	Wally Butts
1943	Georgia Tech	3-0	7-4	Bill Alexander
1944	Georgia Tech	4-0	9-2	Bill Alexander
1945	Alabama	6-0	10-0	Frank Thomas
1946	Georgia	5-0	11-0	Wally Butts
	Tennessee	5-0	9-2	Bob Neyland
1947	Ole Miss	6-1	9-2	John Vaught
1948	Georgia	6-0	9-2	Wally Butts
1949	Tulane	5-1	7-2-1	Henry Frnka
1950	Kentucky	5-1	11-1	Paul "Bear" Bryant
1951	Georgia Tech	7-0	11-0-1	Bobby Dodd
	Tennessee	5-0	10-1	Bob Neyland
1952	Georgia Tech	6-0	12-0	Bobby Dodd
1953	Alabama	4-0-3	6-3-3	Red Drew
1954	Ole Miss	5-1	9-2	John Vaught
1955	Ole Miss	5-1	10-1	John Vaught
1956	Tennessee	6-0	10-1	Bowden Wyatt
1957	Auburn	7-0	10-0	Ralph Jordan
1958	LSU	6-0	11-0	Paul Dietzel
1959	Georgia	7-0	10-1	Wally Butts
1960	Ole Miss	5-0-1	10-0-1	John Vaught
1961	Alabama	7-0	11-0	Paul "Bear" Bryant
	LSU	6-0	10-1	Paul Dietzel

1962	Ole Miss	6-0	10-0	John Vaught
1963	Ole Miss	5-0-1	7-1-2	John Vaught
1964	Alabama	8-0	10-1	Paul "Bear" Bryant
1965	Alabama	6-1-1	9-1-1	Paul "Bear" Bryant
1966	Alabama	6-0	11-0	Paul "Bear" Bryant
	Georgia	6-0	10-1	Vince Dooley
1967	Tennessee	6-0	9-2	Doug Dickey
1968	Georgia	5-0-1	8-1-2	Vince Dooley
1969	Tennessee	5-1	9-2	Doug Dickey
1970	LSU	5-0	9-3	Charlie McClendon
1971	Alabama	7-0	11-1	Paul "Bear" Bryant
1972	Alabama	7-1	10-2	Paul "Bear" Bryant
1973	*Alabama	8-0	11-1	Paul "Bear" Bryant
1974	Alabama	6-0	11-1	Paul "Bear" Bryant
1975	Alabama	6-0	11-1	Paul "Bear" Bryant
1976	Georgia	5-1	10-2	Vince Dooley
	Kentucky	5-1	9-3	Fran Curci
1977	Alabama	7-0	11-1	Paul "Bear" Bryant
1978	Alabama	6-0	11-1	Paul "Bear" Bryant
1979	Alabama	6-0	12-0	Paul "Bear" Bryant
1980	Georgia	6-0	12-0	Vince Dooley
1981	Georgia	6-0	10-2	Vince Dooley
	Alabama	6-0	9-2-1	Paul "Bear" Bryant
1982	Georgia	6-0	11-1	Vince Dooley
1983	Auburn	6-0	11-1	Pat Dye
1984	Vacated			
1985	Tennessee	5-1	9-1-2	Johnny Majors
1986	LSU	5-1	9-3	Bill Arnsparger
1987	Auburn	5-0-1	9-1-2	Pat Dye
1988	Auburn	6-1	10-2	Pat Dye
	LSU	6-1	8-4	Mike Archer
1989	Alabama	6-1	10-2	Bill Curry
	Tennessee	6-1	11-1	Johnny Majors
	Auburn	6-1	10-2	Pat Dye
1990	Tennessee	5-1-1	9-2-2	Johnny Majors
1991	Florida	7-0	10-2	Steve Spurrier
1992	Alabama	8-0	13-0	Gene Stallings
1993	Florida	7-1	11-2	Steve Spurrier

SEC

Mike DuBose fires up his team as it prepares to receive the kickoff from Houston on September 11, 1999, at Legion Field in Birmingham. The Crimson Tide would go on to win the SEC in 1999 with a 34–7 demolition of Florida in the title game.

1994	Florida	7-1	10-2-1	Steve Spurrier
1995	Florida	8-0	12-1	Steve Spurrier
1996	Florida	8-0	12-1	Steve Spurrier
1997	Tennessee	7-1	11-2	Phillip Fulmer
1998	Tennessee	8-0	13-0	Phillip Fulmer
1999	Alabama	7-1	10-3	Mike DuBose

SEC Summary 2000

EASTERN DIVISION

| School | Conference | | | | Overall | | | |
	W-L-T	Pct.	Pts.	Opp.	W-L-T	Pct.	Pts.	Opp.
Florida	7-1	.875	318	181	10-2	.833	448	236
Georgia	5-3	.625	213	164	7-4	.636	294	198
South Carolina	5-3	.625	173	152	7-4	.636	259	174
Tennessee	5-3	.625	251	176	8-3	.727	359	212
Vanderbilt	1-7	.125	120	223	3-8	.273	193	273
Kentucky	0-8	.000	152	300	2-9	.182	254	383

WESTERN DIVISION

| School | Conference | | | | Overall | | | |
	W-L-T	Pct.	Pts.	Opp.	W-L-T	Pct.	Pts.	Opp.
Auburn	6-2	.750	178	144	9-3	.750	288	235
LSU	5-3	.625	196	195	7-4	.636	292	221
Ole Miss	4-4	.500	187	210	7-4	.636	314	280
Mississippi State	4-4	.500	225	199	7-4	.636	347	265
Arkansas	3-5	.375	136	221	6-5	.545	264	258
Alabama	3-5	.375	166	150	3-8	.273	228	246

SEC Championship Game:
Florida 28, Auburn 6

Bowl Games: Las Vegas (UNLV 31, Arkansas 14), Oahu (Georgia 37, Virginia 14), Music City (West Virginia 49, Ole Miss 38), Peach (LSU 28, Georgia Tech 14), Independence (Mississippi State 43, Texas A&M 41-OT), Outback (South Carolina 24, Ohio State 7), Cotton (Kansas State 35, Tennessee 21), Florida Citrus (Michigan 31, Auburn 28), Sugar (Miami, Fla. 37, Florida 20)

SEC

Dennis Franchione proudly hoists the Independence Bowl trophy after his Crimson Tide beat Iowa State 14–13 in 2001. It was Alabama's first bowl win in five seasons and tapped a nice turnaround from a 3–8 finish the year before.

All-SEC

Offense: TE Derek Smith, Kentucky; TE Robert Royal, LSU; OL Kenyatta Walker, Florida; OL Terrence Metcalf, Ole Miss; OL Mike Pearson, Florida; OL Kendall Simmons, Auburn; OL Jonas Jennings, Georgia; OL Pork Chop Womack, Mississippi State; C Paul Hogan, Alabama; WR Jabar Gaffney, Florida; WR Josh Reed, LSU; QB Josh Booty, LSU; RB Rudi Johnson, Auburn; RB Travis Henry, Tennessee; PK Alex Walls, Tennessee

Defense: DL Alex Brown, Florida; DL John Henderson, Tennessee; DL Richard Seymour, Georgia; OLB Kalimba Edwards, South Carolina; OLB Eric Westmoreland, Tennessee; ILB Quinton Caver, Arkansas; ILB Jamie Winborn, Vanderbilt; DB Lito Sheppard, Florida; DB Fred Smoot, Mississippi State; DB Tim Wansley, Georgia; DB Rodney Crayton, Auburn; DB Ken Lucas, Ole Miss; P Damon Duval, Auburn

SEC Summary 2001

EASTERN DIVISION

School	Conference				Overall			
	W-L-T	Pct.	Pts.	Opp.	W-L-T	Pct.	Pts.	Opp.
Tennessee	7-1	.875	225	148	10-2	.833	355	234
Florida	6-2	.750	341	122	9-2	.818	482	155
South Carolina	5-3	.625	189	160	8-3	.727	279	202
Georgia	5-3	.625	204	167	8-3	.727	315	208
Kentucky	1-7	.125	206	285	2-9	.182	259	367
Vanderbilt	0-8	.000	128	315	2-9	.182	226	402

WESTERN DIVISION

School	Conference				Overall			
	W-L-T	Pct.	Pts.	Opp.	W-L-T	Pct.	Pts.	Opp.
LSU	5-3	.625	231	203	9-3	.750	371	268
Auburn	5-3	.625	152	193	7-4	.636	244	265
Alabama	4-4	.500	203	177	6-5	.545	304	219
Arkansas	4-4	.500	208	220	7-4	.636	291	269
Ole Miss	4-4	.500	262	262	7-4	.636	391	310
Mississippi State	2-6	.250	119	216	3-8	.273	196	288

SEC Championship Game:
LSU 31, Tennessee 20

Bowls: Independence (Alabama 14, Iowa State 13), Music City (Boston College 20, Georgia 16), Peach (North Carolina 16, Auburn 10), Cotton (Oklahoma 10, Arkansas 3), Outback (South Carolina

31, Ohio State 28), Florida Citrus (Tennessee 45, Michigan 17),
Orange (Florida 56, Maryland 23), Sugar (LSU 47, Illinois 34)

All-SEC

Offense: TE Randy McMichael, Georgia; OL Terrence Metcalf, Ole
Miss; OL Fred Weary, Tennessee; OL Mike Pearson, Florida; OL
Kendall Simmons, Auburn; C Zac Zedalis, Florida; WR Jabar Gaffney,
Florida; WR Josh Reed, LSU; QB Rex Grossman, Florida; RB Travis
Stephens, Tennessee; RB LaBrandon Toefield, LSU; PK Damon Duval,
Auburn

Defense: DL Alex Brown, Florida; DL John Henderson, Tennessee; DL
Will Overstreet, Tennessee; OLB Kalimba Edwards, South Carolina;
OLB Bradie James, LSU; ILB Trev Faulk, LSU; ILB Saleem Rasheed,
Alabama; DB Lito Sheppard, Florida; DB Syniker Taylor, Ole Miss;
DB Tim Wansley, Georgia; DB Andre Lott, Tennessee; DB Sheldon
Brown, South Carolina; P Damon Duval, Auburn

SEC Summary 2002

EASTERN DIVISION

	Conference				Overall			
School	W-L-T	Pct.	Pts.	Opp.	W-L-T	Pct.	Pts.	Opp.
Georgia	7-1	.875	226	144	12-1	.923	424	199
Florida	6-2	.750	191	160	8-4	.667	306	241
Tennessee	5-3	.625	182	147	8-4	.667	293	197
South Carolina	3-5	.375	108	156	5-7	.417	225	262
Vanderbilt	0-8	.000	121	260	2-10	.167	221	368
#Kentucky	3-5	.375	215	228	7-5	.583	385	301

WESTERN DIVISION

	Conference				Overall			
School	W-L-T	Pct.	Pts.	Opp.	W-L-T	Pct.	Pts.	Opp.
Arkansas	5-3	.625	223	184	9-4	.692	356	248
Auburn	5-3	.625	213	150	8-4	.667	375	222
LSU	5-3	.625	179	160	8-4	.667	303	203
Ole Miss	3-5	.375	175	230	6-6	.500	324	308
Mississippi State	0-8	.000	123	265	3-9	.250	227	339
#Alabama	6-2	.750	227	99	10-3	.769	377	200

#On probation, banned from bowl games

SEC Championship Game:
Georgia 30, Arkansas 3

Bowls: Independence (Ole Miss 27, Nebraska 23), Music City (Minnesota 29, Arkansas 14), Peach (Maryland 30, Tennessee 3), Outback (Michigan 38, Florida 30), Cotton (Texas 35, LSU 20), Capital One (Auburn 13, Penn State 9), Sugar (Georgia 26, Florida State 13)

All-SEC

Offense: TE Jason Witten, Tennessee; OL Shawn Andrews, Arkansas; OL Jon Stinchcomb, Georgia; OL Antonio Hall, Kentucky; OL Stephen Peterman, LSU; OL Marico Portis, Alabama; OL Wesley Britt, Alabama; C Ben Nowland, Auburn; WR Taylor Jacobs, Florida; WR Terrence Edwards, Georgia; QB David Greene, Georgia; RB Artose Pinner, Kentucky; RB Fred Talley, Arkansas

Defense: DL David Pollack, Georgia; DL Kindal Moorehead, Alabama; DL Kenny King, Alabama; OLB Boss Bailey, Georgia; OLB Karlos Dansby, Auburn; ILB Bradie James, LSU; ILB Eddie Strong, Ole Miss; ILB Hunter Hillenmeyer, Vanderbilt; DB Ken Hamlin, Arkansas; DB Corey Webster, LSU; DB Travaris Robinson, Auburn; DB Matt Grier, Ole Miss; DB Julian Battle, Tennessee; DB Rashad Baker, Tennessee

Special Teams: P Glenn Pakulak, Kentucky; PK Billy Bennett, Georgia; RS Derek Abney, Kentucky

SEC Summary 2003
EASTERN DIVISION

School	Conference				Overall			
	W-L-T	Pct.	Pts.	Opp.	W-L-T	Pct.	Pts.	Opp.
Georgia	6-2	.750	215	102	10-3	.769	337	176
Tennessee	6-2	.750	260	170	10-2	.833	351	212
Florida	6-2	.750	178	152	8-4	.667	373	234
South Carolina	2-6	.250	164	227	5-7	.417	268	314
Vanderbilt	1-7	.125	126	261	2-10	.167	235	358
Kentucky	1-7	.125	198	244	4-8	.333	328	321

WESTERN DIVISION

School	Conference				Overall			
	W-L-T	Pct.	Pts.	Opp.	W-L-T	Pct.	Pts.	Opp.
LSU	7-1	.875	228	90	12-1	.923	454	140
Ole Miss	7-1	.875	218	150	9-3	.750	411	257
Auburn	5-3	.625	190	148	7-5	.583	314	198
Arkansas	4-4	.500	247	223	8-4	.667	409	291
Mississippi State	1-7	.125	93	329	2-10	.167	225	471
#Alabama	2-6	.250	216	237	4-9	.308	331	333

#On probation, banned from bowls

SEC Championship Game:
LSU 34, Georgia 13

Bowls: Music City (Auburn, 28, Wisconsin 14), Independence (Arkansas 27, Missouri 14), Outback (Iowa 37, Florida 17), Capital One (Georgia 34, Purdue 27, OT), Cotton (Ole Miss 31, Oklahoma State 28), Peach (Clemson 27, Tennessee 14) Sugar (LSU 21, Oklahoma 14)

All-SEC

Offense: TE Ben Troupe, Florida; OL Shawn Andrews, Arkansas; OL Max Starks, Florida; OL Antonio Hall, Kentucky; OL Wesley Britt, Alabama; C Scott Wells, Tennessee; WR Michael Clayton, LSU; WR Chris Collins, Ole Miss; QB Eli Manning, Ole Miss; RB Carnell Williams, Auburn; RB Cedric Cobbs, Arkansas

Defense: DL David Pollack, Georgia; DL Chad Lavalais, LSU; DL Antwan Odom, Alabama; OLB Karlos Dansby, Auburn; OLB Derrick Pope, Alabama; ILB Dontarrious Thomas, Auburn; ILB Odell Thurman, Georgia; DB Keiwan Ratliff, Florida; DB Corey Webster, LSU; DB Ahmad Carroll, Arkansas; DB Tony Bua, Arkansas; DB Sean Jones, Georgia

Special Teams: P Dustin Colquitt, Tennessee; PK Jonathan Nichols, Ole Miss; RS Derek Abney, Kentucky

In a moment most offensive linemen don't find them-
selves in, Wesley Britt (left) gets forced into attempting
a tackle after an Alabama fumble in the 2004 Music City
Bowl. Minnesota won 20–16.

SEC Summary 2004

EASTERN DIVISION

School	Conference				Overall			
	W-L-T	Pct.	Pts.	Opp.	W-L-T	Pct.	Pts.	Opp.
Tennessee	7-1	.875	215	199	9-3	.750	340	288
Georgia	6-2	.750	231	133	9-2	.818	311	177
Florida	4-4	.500	251	187	7-4	.636	372	226
South Carolina	4-4	.500	185	190	6-5	.545	243	229
Kentucky	1-7	.125	106	253	2-9	.182	173	341
Vanderbilt	1-7	.125	133	213	2-9	.182	212	286

WESTERN DIVISION

School	Conference				Overall			
	W-L-T	Pct.	Pts.	Opp.	W-L-T	Pct.	Pts.	Opp.
Auburn	8-0	1.000	247	96	12-0	1.000	401	134
LSU	6-2	.750	220	131	9-2	.818	319	175
Arkansas	3-5	.375	196	215	5-6	.455	328	270
Alabama	3-5	.375	152	149	6-5	.545	279	169
Ole Miss	3-5	.375	142	200	4-7	.364	215	278
#Mississippi State	2-6	.250	125	237	3-8	.273	173	280

#On probation, banned from bowl games

SEC Championship Game:
Auburn 38, Tennessee 28

Bowls: Music City (Minnesota 20, Alabama 16), Peach (Miami, Fla., 27, Florida 10), Outback (Georgia 24, Wisconsin 21), Cotton (Tennessee 38, Texas A&M 7), Capital One (Iowa 30, LSU 25), Sugar (Auburn 16, Virginia Tech 13)

All-SEC

Offense: TE Leonard Pope, Georgia; OL Wesley Britt, Alabama; OL Marcus McNeill, Auburn; OL Max Jean-Gilles, Georgia; OL Mo Mitchell, Florida; OL Andrew Whitworth, LSU; C Ben Wilkerson, LSU; WR Fred Gibson, Georgia; WR Reggie Brown, Georgia; QB Jason Campbell, Auburn; RB Carnell Williams, Auburn; RB Ronnie Brown, Auburn

Defense: DL Marcus Spears, LSU; DL David Pollack, Georgia; DL Jeb Huckeba, Arkansas; LB Kevin Burnett, Tennessee; LB Travis Williams, Auburn; LB Cornelius Wortham, Alabama; LB Channing Crowder, Florida; LB Moses Osemwegie, Vanderbilt; LB Odell Thurman, Georgia; LB Lionel Turner, LSU; DB Jason Allen,

Tennessee; DB Thomas Davis, Georgia; DB Carlos Rogers, Auburn; DB Junior Rosegreen, Auburn

Special Teams: P Jared Cook, Mississippi State; PK Brian Bostick, Alabama; RS Carnell Williams, Auburn

SEC Summary 2005

EASTERN DIVISION

School	Conference				Overall			
	W-L-T	Pct.	Pts.	Opp.	W-L-T	Pct.	Pts.	Opp.
Georgia	6-2	.750	209	134	10-2	.833	349	175
South Carolina	5-3	.625	175	193	7-4	.636	253	241
Florida	5-3	.625	205	178	8-3	.727	312	202
Vanderbilt	3-5	.375	223	271	5-6	.455	299	321
Tennessee	3-5	.375	147	138	5-6	.455	205	205
Kentucky	2-6	.250	160	277	3-8	.273	239	375

WESTERN DIVISION

School	Conference				Overall			
	W-L-T	Pct.	Pts.	Opp.	W-L-T	Pct.	Pts.	Opp.
LSU	7-1	.875	214	114	10-2	.833	343	182
Auburn	7-1	.875	262	122	9-2	.818	376	162
Alabama	6-2	.750	159	87	9-2	.818	250	118
Arkansas	2-6	.250	173	169	4-7	.364	283	271
Mississippi State	1-7	.125	78	211	3-8	.273	153	259
Ole Miss	1-7	.125	97	208	3-8	.273	148	245

SEC Championship Game:
Georgia 34, LSU 14

Bowls: Independence (Missouri 38, South Carolina 31), Chick-fil-A (LSU 40, Miami, Fla. 3), Outback (Florida 31, Iowa 24), Cotton (Alabama 13, Texas Tech 10), Capital One (Wisconsin 24, Auburn 10), Sugar (West Virginia 38, Georgia 35)

All-SEC

Offense: Leonard Pope, TE, Georgia; Marcus McNeill, OL, Auburn; Max Jean-Gilles, OL, Georgia; Andrew Whitworth, OL, LSU; Tre' Stallings OL, Ole Miss; Arron Sears, OL, Tennessee; Mike Degory, C, Florida; Sidney Rice, WR, South Carolina; Earl Bennett, WR, Vanderbilt; Jay Cutler, QB, Vanderbilt; Kenny Irons, RB, Auburn; Kenneth Darby, RB, Alabama; Darren McFadden, RB, Arkansas

Former Alabama fan favorite Jimmy Johns digs for more yards against Florida International in 2006. Johns later converted to linebacker before legal troubles ended his football career.

Defense: Willie Evans, DL, Mississippi State; Quentin Moses, DL, Georgia; Claude Wroten, DL, LSU; DeMeco Ryans, LB, Alabama; Patrick Willis, LB, Ole Miss; Moses Osemwegie, LB, Vanderbilt; Sam Olajubutu, LB, Arkansas; Greg Blue, DB, Georgia; Roman Harper, DB, Alabama; LaRon Landry, DB, LSU; Ko Simpson, DB, South Carolina

Special Teams: Kody Bliss, P, Auburn; Brandon Coutu, K, Georgia; Skyler Green, RS, LSU

SEC Summary 2006

EASTERN DIVISION

School	Conference				Overall			
	W-L-T	Pct.	Pts.	Opp.	W-L-T	Pct.	Pts.	Opp.
Florida	7-1	.875	178	126	13-1	.929	416	189
Tennessee	5-3	.625	212	172	9-4	.692	362	254
Kentucky	4-4	.500	163	207	8-5	.615	347	369
Georgia	4-4	.500	185	168	9-4	.692	327	229
South Carolina	3-5	.375	147	146	8-5	.615	346	243
Vanderbilt	1-7	.125	131	206	4-8	.333	264	284

WESTERN DIVISION

School	Conference				Overall			
	W-L-T	Pct.	Pts.	Opp.	W-L-T	Pct.	Pts.	Opp.
Arkansas	7-1	.875	221	134	10-4	.714	404	256
Auburn	6-2	.750	162	133	11-2	.846	322	181
LSU	6-2	.750	220	131	11-2	.846	438	164
Alabama	2-6	.250	133	175	6-7	.462	298	250
Ole Miss	2-6	.250	123	182	4-8	.333	188	275
Mississippi State	1-7	.125	127	222	3-9	.250	221	309

SEC Championship Game:
Florida 38, Arkansas 28

Bowls: Independence (Oklahoma State 34, Alabama 31); Music City (Kentucky 28, Clemson 20); AutoZone (South Carolina 44, Houston 36; Chick-fil-A (Georgia 31, Virginia Tech 24); Outback (Penn State 20, Tennessee 10); Cotton (Auburn 17, Nebraska 14); Capital One (Wisconsin 17, Arkansas 14); Sugar (LSU 41, Notre Dame 14); BCS Championship (Florida 41, Ohio State 14)

SEC

All-SEC

Offense: TE Martrez Milner, Georgia; TE Jacob Tamme, Kentucky; OL Arron Sears, Tennessee; OL Zac Tubbs, Arkansas; OL Tim Duckworth, Auburn; OL Tony Ugoh, Arkansas; C Jonathan Luigs, Arkansas; C Steve Rissler, Florida; WR Robert Meachem, Tennessee; WR Dwayne Bowe, LSU; WR Dallas Baker, Florida; QB JaMarcus Russell, LSU; RB Darren McFadden, Arkansas; RB Kenny Irons, Auburn

Defense: DL Glenn Dorsey, LSU; DL Quentin Groves, Auburn; DL Jamaal Anderson, Arkansas; DL Ray McDonald, Florida; LB Patrick Willis, Ole Miss; LB Quinton Culberson, Mississippi State; LB Sam Olajubutu, Arkansas; LB Earl Everett, Florida; LB Wesley Woodyard, Kentucky; DB Reggie Nelson, Florida; DB Tra Battle, Georgia; DB Simeon Castille, Alabama; DB LaRon Landry, LSU

Special Teams: P Britton Colquitt, Tennessee; PK John Vaughn, Auburn; PK James Wilhoit, Tennessee; RS Mikey Henderson, Georgia

SEC Summary 2007

EASTERN DIVISION

School	Conference				Overall			
	W-L-T	Pct.	Pts.	Opp.	W-L-T	Pct.	Pts.	Opp.
Tennessee	6-2	.750	243	246	10-4	.714	455	382
Georgia	6-2	.750	228	171	11-2	.846	424	262
Florida	5-3	.625	305	224	9-4	.692	552	331
South Carolina	3-5	.375	205	227	6-6	.500	313	282
Kentucky	3-5	.375	249	276	8-5	.615	475	385
Vanderbilt	2-6	.250	198	203	5-7	.417	260	271

WESTERN DIVISION

School	Conference				Overall			
	W-L-T	Pct.	Pts.	Opp.	W-L-T	Pct.	Pts.	Opp.
LSU	6-2	.750	298	215	12-2	.857	541	279
Auburn	5-3	.625	156	138	9-4	.692	315	220
Arkansas	4-4	.500	274	249	8-5	.615	485	345
Mississippi State	4-4	.500	157	215	8-5	.615	279	301
Alabama	4-4	.500	212	190	7-6	.538	352	286
Ole Miss	0-8	.000	131	252	3-9	.250	241	342

One of the most popular players on Alabama's team during his tenure, Simeon Castille was also valuable on the field. He is shown here after intercepting a pass against Vanderbilt in 2006. His dad and brother both played for the Crimson Tide as well.

SEC Championship Game:
LSU 21, Tennessee 14

Bowls: Liberty (Mississippi State 10, Central Florida 3);
Independence (Alabama 30, Colorado 24); Music City (Kentucky 35,
Florida State 28); Chick-fil-A (Auburn 23, Clemson 20, OT); Cotton
(Missouri 38, Arkansas 7); Outback (Tennessee 21, Wisconsin 17);
Capital One (Michigan 41, Florida 35); Sugar (Georgia 41, Hawaii
10); BCS Championship (LSU 38, Ohio State)

All-SEC

Offense: TE Jacob Tamme, Kentucky; OL Robert Felton, Arkansas; OL
Andre Smith, Alabama; OL Anthony Parker, Tennessee; OL Herman
Johnson, LSU; OL Michael Oher, Ole Miss; OL Chris Williams,
Vanderbilt; C Jonathan Luigs, Arkansas; WR Kenny McKinley, South
Carolina; WR Earl Bennett, Vanderbilt; QB Tim Tebow, Florida; RB
Darren McFadden, Arkansas; RB Knowshon Moreno, Georgia

Defense: DL Glenn Dorsey, LSU; DL Wallace Gilberry, Alabama; DL
Quentin Groves, Auburn; DL Greg Hardy, Ole Miss; DL Eric Norwood,
South Carolina; LB Ali Highsmith, LSU; LB Wesley Woodyard,
Kentucky; LB Jerod Mayo, Tennessee; LB Brandon Spikes, Florida;
DB Craig Steltz, LSU; DB Chevis Jackson, LSU; DB Simeon Castille,
Alabama; DB Rashad Johnson, Alabama; DB Jonathan Hefney,
Tennessee; DB Captain Munnerlyn, South Carolina

Special Teams: PK Colt David, LSU; P Patrick Fisher, LSU; RS Felix
Jones, Arkansas

SEC Summary 2008

EASTERN DIVISION

| School | Conference | | | | Overall | | | |
	W-L-T	Pct.	Pts.	Opp.	W-L-T	Pct.	Pts.	Opp.
Florida	7-1	.875	359	100	13-1	.929	611	181
Georgia	6-2	.750	215	214	10-3	.769	409	319
Vanderbilt	4-4	.500	144	174	7-6	.538	249	255
South Carolina	4-4	.500	163	186	7-6	.538	270	274
Tennessee	3-5	.375	129	149	5-7	.417	208	201
Kentucky	2-6	.250	143	238	7-6	.538	294	279

SEC

WESTERN DIVISION

School	Conference				Overall			
	W-L-T	Pct.	Pts.	Opp.	W-L-T	Pct.	Pts.	Opp.
Alabama	8-0	1.000	255	115	12-2	.857	422	200
Ole Miss	5-3	.625	208	149	9-4	.692	417	247
LSU	3-5	.375	207	254	8-5	.615	402	314
Arkansas	2-6	.250	167	248	5-7	.417	263	374
Auburn	2-6	.250	93	149	5-7	.417	208	216
Mississippi State	2-6	.250	97	204	4-8	.333	183	296

SEC Championship Game:
Florida 31, Alabama 20

Bowls: Music City (Vanderbilt 16, Boston College 14), Chick-fil-A (LSU 38, Georgia Tech 3), Outback (Iowa 31, South Carolina 10), Capital One (Georgia 23, Michigan State 12), Cotton (Ole Miss 47, Texas Tech 34), Liberty (Kentucky 25, East Carolina 19), Sugar (Utah 31, Alabama 17), BCS Championship (Florida 24, Oklahoma 17)

All-SEC

Offense: QB Tim Tebow, Florida; RB Knowshon Moreno, Georgia; RB Charles Scott, LSU; WR Percy Harvin, Florida; WR Mohamed Massaquoi, Georgia; TE Jared Cook, South Carolina; C Antoine Caldwell, Alabama; OL Michael Oher, Ole Miss; OL Andre Smith, Alabama; OL Herman Johnson, LSU; OL Phil Trautwein, Florida

Defense: DE Antonio Coleman, Auburn; DE Robert Ayers, Tennessee; DT Terrence Cody, Alabama; DT Peria Jerry, Ole Miss; LB Brandon Spokes, Auburn; LB Rennie Curran, Georgia; LB Eric Norwood, South Carolina; LB Rolando McClain, Alabama; LB Micah Johnson, Kentucky; DB D.J. Moore, Vanderbilt; DB Trenard Lindley, Kentucky; DB Eric Berry, Tennessee; DB Rashad Johnson, Alabama

Special Teams: PK Colt David, LSU; P Tim Masthay, Kentucky; RS Brandon James, Florida

Jay Barker scrambles for yards against Florida in the 1994 SEC Championship. Barker had a distinguished career at Alabama: in addition to winning the national title in 1992, Barker won the Johnny Unitas Golden Arm Award in 1994, a year in which he finished fifth in Heisman Trophy voting.

SEC Awards

MVPs

1934: Dixie Howell, tailback

1945: Harry Gilmer, tailback

1961: Pat Trammell, quarterback

1965: Steve Sloan, quarterback

1971: Johnny Musso, tailback

1972: Terry Davis, quarterback

1986: Cornelius Bennett, linebacker

1994: Jay Barker, quarterback

1999: Shaun Alexander, running back

2005: DeMeco Ryans, linebacker (defense)

SEC Jacobs Award (best blocker)

1935 Riley Smith

1937 Leroy Monsky

1946 Hal Self

1949 Butch Avinger

1950 Butch Avinger

1961 Billy Neighbors

1962 Butch Wilson

1966 Cecil Dowdy

1972 John Hannah

1973 Buddy Brown

1974 Sylvester Croom

1977 Bob Cryder

1979 Dwight Stephenson

1986 Wes Neighbors

1988 Howard Cross

1993 Tobie Sheils

1999 Chris Samuels

2004 Wesley Britt

2007 Andre Smith (tied with Jonathan Luigs, Arkansas)

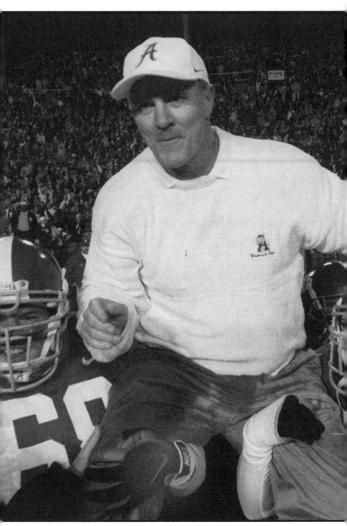

Mike DuBose and his players were all smiles after this Iron Bowl win at Legion Field. Perhaps the most heated rivalry in college football, the Iron Bowl divides the state and shuts down businesses across Alabama for one magical Saturday every fall.

THE RIVALRIES

Alabama vs. Auburn
The Iron Bowl

Named for the abundant ore found in central Alabama, the Iron Bowl between rivals Alabama and Auburn was a Birmingham staple for decades. The series ran uninterrupted at Legion Field from 1948 through 1989, when Alabama officials finally agreed to play the game on each campus.

Though the game site has settled on a rotation between the two campuses since 1999, the Iron Bowl nickname lives on. As part of the pre-Thanksgiving holiday calendar, the Alabama-Auburn series burns brightly in households across the Heart of Dixie and the nation. When various publications poll fans on their favorite college rivalries, Alabama-Auburn typically finishes at the top.

Want a peaceful, sparsely attended wedding in Alabama? Schedule it on the Saturday of the Iron Bowl (if you can find any place willing to be open). The indoctrination into declaring allegiance in this rivalry starts at an early age, as elementary school children across the state are encouraged to draw sides during Iron Bowl week. The fondest memories of many men across the state are of being taken to attend their first Iron Bowl as young boys. The same holds true for a growing number of women. The Alabama-Auburn rivalry defines the state of Alabama as much as any other political, geographic, or business ideals.

Alabama holds an edge in the series, though Auburn recently won six straight under Tommy Tuberville (but when that streak ended, so did his reign with the Tigers).

The Alabama-Auburn series dates back to February 22, 1893, the winter after both schools had started the sport the previous year. Auburn led the series by a 7–4–1 margin when it abruptly drew to a halt following

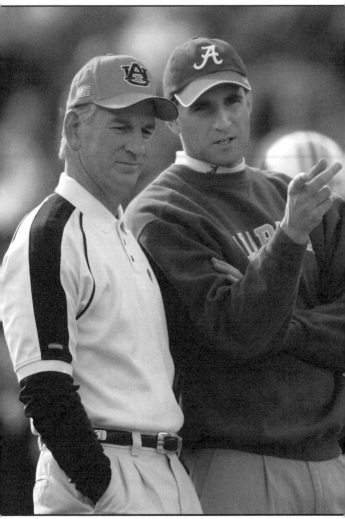

Alabama Coach Mike Shula and Auburn's Tommy Tuberville
share words before the 2004 Iron Bowl. Shula quarterbacked the Tide to one of the most memorable Iron Bowl
wins in history, marching the team downfield to set up
Van Tiffin's game-winning field goal in 1985.

a 6–6 tie in 1907. Various accounts exist as to why the in-state rivals abandoned their annual clash, but suffice it to say there was plenty of animosity on both sides. The series was set aside for 31 years, a period during which Alabama became a southern titan and a national power while Auburn football mostly languished in mediocrity.

The series resumed in 1948 with Harold "Red" Drew at the helm in Tuscaloosa and Earl Brown in Auburn. Alabama quickly established superiority in the revived series, winning five of the next six games. However, Auburn Coach Ralph "Shug" Jordan, who took over in 1951, reversed that trend starting in 1954. Jordan guided the Tigers to four consecutive wins over Alabama by a combined margin of 128–7. The last of those lopsided losses, a 40–0 rout, signaled the end of the J. B. "Ears" Whitworth era of Alabama football and ushered in the coming legend, Paul W. "Bear" Bryant, in 1958.

Bryant posted a 19–6 record against the school he dubbed "that cow college," including a nine-game winning streak from 1973 to 1981 and a string of four consecutive shutouts from 1959 to 1962. However, one of Alabama's greatest Iron Bowl moments came in 1985, when future Tide coach Mike Shula quarterbacked the team down the field in the closing moments to set up Van Tiffin's 52-yard field goal on the final play for a 25–23 victory.

The Rivalries

Alabama vs. Auburn

[Alabama leads series 39-33-1]

Date	Winner	Score	Location
Feb. 22, 1893	Auburn	33–22	Lakeview Park, Birmingham
Nov. 30, 1893	Auburn	60–16	Riverside Park, Montgomery
Nov. 29, 1894	Alabama	18–0	Riverside Park, Montgomery
Nov. 23, 1895	Auburn	48–0	Tuscaloosa
Nov. 17, 1900	Auburn	53–5	Montgomery

Nov. 15, 1901	Auburn	17–0	Tuscaloosa
Oct. 18, 1902	Auburn	23–0	West End Park, Birmingham
Oct. 23, 1903	Alabama	18–6	Highland Park, Montgomery
Nov. 12, 1904	Auburn	29–5	West End Park, Birmingham
Nov. 18, 1905	Alabama	30–0	West End Park, Birmingham
Nov. 17, 1906	Alabama	10–0	Birmingham Fair Grounds
Nov. 16, 1907	Tie	6–6	Birmingham Fair Grounds
Dec. 4, 1948	Alabama	55–0	Legion Field, Birmingham
Dec. 3, 1949	Auburn	14–13	Legion Field, Birmingham
Dec. 2, 1950	Alabama	34–0	Legion Field, Birmingham
Dec. 1, 1951	Alabama	25–7	Legion Field, Birmingham
Nov. 29, 1952	Alabama	21–0	Legion Field, Birmingham
Nov. 28, 1953	Alabama	10–7	Legion Field, Birmingham
Nov. 27, 1954	Auburn	28–0	Legion Field, Birmingham
Nov. 26, 1955	Auburn	26–0	Legion Field, Birmingham
Dec. 1, 1956	Auburn	34–7	Legion Field, Birmingham
Nov. 30, 1957	Auburn	40–0	Legion Field, Birmingham
Nov. 29, 1958	Auburn	14–8	Legion Field, Birmingham
Nov. 28, 1959	Alabama	10–0	Legion Field, Birmingham
Nov. 26, 1960	Alabama	3–0	Legion Field, Birmingham
Dec. 2, 1961	Alabama	34–0	Legion Field, Birmingham
Dec. 1, 1962	Alabama	38–0	Legion Field, Birmingham
Nov. 30, 1963	Auburn	10–8	Legion Field, Birmingham
Nov. 26, 1964	Alabama	21–14	Legion Field, Birmingham
Nov. 27, 1965	Alabama	30–3	Legion Field, Birmingham
Dec. 3, 1966	Alabama	31–0	Legion Field, Birmingham
Dec. 2. 1967	Alabama	7–3	Legion Field, Birmingham
Dec. 3, 1968	Alabama	24–16	Legion Field, Birmingham
Nov. 29, 1969	Auburn	49–26	Legion Field, Birmingham
Nov. 28, 1970	Auburn	33–28	Legion Field, Birmingham
Nov. 27, 1971	Alabama	31–7	Legion Field, Birmingham
Dec. 2, 1972	Auburn	17–16	Legion Field, Birmingham
Dec. 1, 1973	Alabama	35–0	Legion Field, Birmingham
Nov. 29, 1974	Alabama	17–13	Legion Field, Birmingham
Nov. 29, 1975	Alabama	28–0	Legion Field, Birmingham

Nov. 27, 1976	Alabama	38–7	Legion Field, Birmingham
Nov. 26, 1977	Alabama	48–21	Legion Field, Birmingham
Dec. 2, 1978	Alabama	34–16	Legion Field, Birmingham
Dec. 1, 1979	Alabama	25–18	Legion Field, Birmingham
Nov. 29, 1980	Alabama	34–18	Legion Field, Birmingham
Nov. 28, 1981	Alabama	28–17	Legion Field, Birmingham
Nov. 27, 1982	Auburn	23–22	Legion Field, Birmingham
Dec. 3, 1983	Auburn	23–20	Legion Field, Birmingham
Dec. 1, 1984	Alabama	17–15	Legion Field, Birmingham
Nov. 30, 1985	Alabama	25–23	Legion Field, Birmingham
Nov. 29, 1986	Auburn	21–17	Legion Field, Birmingham
Nov. 27, 1987	Auburn	10–0	Legion Field, Birmingham
Nov. 25, 1988	Auburn	15–10	Legion Field, Birmingham
Dec. 2, 1989	Auburn	30–20	Jordan-Hare Stadium, Auburn
Dec. 1, 1990	Alabama	16–7	Legion Field, Birmingham
Nov. 30, 1991	Alabama	13–6	Legion Field, Birmingham
Nov. 26, 1992	Alabama	17–0	Legion Field, Birmingham
Nov. 20, 1993	Auburn	22–14	Jordan-Hare Stadium, Auburn
Nov. 19, 1994	Alabama	21–14	Legion Field, Birmingham
Nov. 18, 1995	Auburn	31–27	Jordan-Hare Stadium Auburn
Nov. 23, 1996	Alabama	24–23	Legion Field, Birmingham
Nov. 22, 1997	Auburn	18–17	Jordan-Hare Stadium, Auburn
Nov. 21, 1998	Alabama	31–17	Legion Field, Birmingham
Nov. 20, 1999	Alabama	28–17	Jordan-Hare Stadium, Auburn
Nov. 18, 2000	Auburn	9–0	Bryant-Denny Stadium, Tuscaloosa
Nov. 17, 2001	Alabama	31–7	Jordan-Hare Stadium, Auburn
Nov. 23, 2002	Auburn	17–7	Bryant-Denny Stadium, Tuscaloosa
Nov. 22, 2003	Auburn	28–23	Jordan-Hare Stadium, Auburn
Nov. 20, 2004	Auburn	21–13	Bryant-Denny Stadium, Tuscaloosa
Nov. 19, 2005	Auburn	28–18	Jordan-Hare Stadium, Auburn
Nov. 18, 2006	Auburn	22–15	Bryant-Denny Stadium, Tuscaloosa
Nov. 24, 2007	Auburn	17–10	Jordan-Hare Stadium, Auburn
Nov. 29, 2008	Alabama	36–0	Bryant-Denny Stadium, Tuscaloosa

The Rivalries

Alabama vs. Tennessee
The Third Saturday in October

The Third Saturday in October, Alabama vs. Tennessee, still reigns as one of the most colorful, most hotly contested, most debated rivalries in the nation.

This gridiron version of the Hatfields and McCoys, to no one's surprise, kicked off with animosity in 1901. There had, in fact, been several disputes during that first game, which was held in Birmingham. Fans made a habit of storming onto the field to have their say, halting play on numerous occasions. After a penalty was called against Alabama in the second half, the boys from Tuscaloosa objected and swore they would not continue unless the penalty was waved off.

Fans encroached the gridiron once again. Chaos ensued. With the scene deadlocked and darkness on the way, the game, tied 6–6 at the time, hung in the balance. That's the way it would end; the finish not resolved and as many as 2,000 fans on the field arguing.

Fast forward 105 years. NCAA regulations, advances in fan decorum, and game-day security now dissuade the unruly from swarming the field during Alabama-Tennessee football games. But don't think there aren't times when fans from both teams would like to shuck off the shackles of convention, reach back a century to join hands with ancestors, and throw down a throatful of malice toward their border rival.

Perhaps the apex of hostilities between the two Southern football powers has been the NCAA infractions case adjudicated against Alabama in early 2002. Alabama fans were irate at Tennessee Coach Phillip Fulmer for providing information against Alabama

The Rivalries

to the NCAA and perhaps even helping trigger the NCAA's investigation of Crimson Tide football recruiting. In the summer of 2004, Fulmer, acting on the advice of his lawyer, chose not to attend SEC Media Days in Birmingham for fear of being served a subpoena by Alabama-based attorneys (in 2008 he was subpoenaed).

Alabama had been hit with severe NCAA sanctions, which included scholarship restrictions over a three-year period, a five-year probation, and a two-year postseason ban. Alabama fans were also enraged by eight losses to Tennessee in a nine-year span.

Few other rivalries of this magnitude are colored by the streaky nature that dominates Alabama-Tennessee. When one team breaks a losing streak, it has usually sparked a roll. There have been 12 winning streaks of three or more games in the series, including Crimson Tide rolls of seven games (1905–1913), 11 games (1971–1981), and seven games (1986–1992) and Tennessee streaks of four games (1955–1958, 1967–1970, and 1982–1985), and seven games (1995–2001).

On only three occasions have the Crimson Tide and Volunteers exchanged wins in three successive seasons (1903–1905, 1945–1947, and 2001–2003)—such are the dramatic swings in the rivalry.

Oh, and although the teams will no longer openly admit it, the winning side breaks out cigars after each meeting, a tradition started by the person who loved to beat Tennessee the most, Paul W. "Bear" Bryant.

The Rivalries

Alabama vs. Tennessee

(Alabama leads series 45–38–7)

Year	Location	Winner	Score
1901	Birmingham	Tie	6–6
1903	Birmingham	Alabama	24–0
1904	Birmingham	Tennessee	5–0
1905	Birmingham	Alabama	29–0
1906	Birmingham	Alabama	51–0

Roy Upchurch runs for a first down against Tennessee cornerback Eric Berry in Knoxville in the October 2008 installment of the rivalry game.

1907	Birmingham	Alabama	5–0
1908	Birmingham	Alabama	4–0
1909	Knoxville	Alabama	10–0
1912	Birmingham	Alabama	7–0
1913	Tuscaloosa	Alabama	6–0
1914	Knoxville	Tennessee	17–7
1928	Tuscaloosa	Tennessee	15–13
1929	Knoxville	Tennessee	6–0
1930	Tuscaloosa	Alabama	18–6
1931	Knoxville	Tennessee	25–0
1932	Birmingham	Tennessee	7–3
1933	Knoxville	Alabama	12–6
1934	Birmingham	Alabama	13–6
1935	Knoxville	Alabama	25–0
1936	Birmingham	Tie	0–0
1937	Knoxville	Alabama	14–7
1938	Birmingham	Tennessee	13–0
1939	Knoxville	Tennessee	21–0
1940	Birmingham	Tennessee	27–12
1941	Knoxville	Alabama	9–2
1942	Birmingham	Alabama	8–0
1944	Knoxville	Tie	0–0
1945	Birmingham	Alabama	25–7
1946	Knoxville	Tennessee	12–0
1947	Birmingham	Alabama	10–0
1948	Knoxville	Tennessee	21–6
1949	Birmingham	Tie	7–7
1950	Knoxville	Tennessee	14–9
1951	Birmingham	Tennessee	27–13
1952	Knoxville	Tennessee	20–0
1953	Birmingham	Tie	0–0
1954	Knoxville	Alabama	27–0
1955	Birmingham	Tennessee	20–0
1956	Knoxville	Tennessee	24–0
1957	Birmingham	Tennessee	14–0

The Rivalries

Javier Arenas knocks the ball away from Tennessee receiver Josh Briscoe in 2008. Arenas was called for pass interference on the play, but Tennessee was unable to capitalize on Alabama mistakes in the 29-9 Crimson Tide win.

1958	Knoxville	Tennessee	14–7
1959	Birmingham	Tie	7–7
1960	Knoxville	Tennessee	20–7
1961	Birmingham	Alabama	34–3
1962	Knoxville	Alabama	27–7
1963	Birmingham	Alabama	35–0
1964	Knoxville	Alabama	19–8
1965	Birmingham	Tie	7–7
1966	Knoxville	Alabama	11–10
1967	Birmingham	Tennessee	24–13
1968	Knoxville	Tennessee	10–9
1969	Birmingham	Tennessee	41–14
1970	Knoxville	Tennessee	24–0
1971	Birmingham	Alabama	32–15
1972	Knoxville	Alabama	17–10
1973	Birmingham	Alabama	42–21
1974	Knoxville	Alabama	28–6
1975	Birmingham	Alabama	30–7
1976	Knoxville	Alabama	20–13
1977	Birmingham	Alabama	24–10
1978	Knoxville	Alabama	30–17
1979	Birmingham	Alabama	27–17
1980	Knoxville	Alabama	27–0
1981	Birmingham	Alabama	38–19
1982	Knoxville	Tennessee	35–28
1983	Birmingham	Tennessee	41–34
1984	Knoxville	Tennessee	28–27
1985	Birmingham	Tennessee	16–14
1986	Knoxville	Alabama	56–28
1987	Birmingham	Alabama	41–22
1988	Knoxville	Alabama	28–20
1989	Birmingham	Alabama	47–30
1990	Knoxville	Alabama	9–6
1991	Birmingham	Alabama	24–19
1992	Knoxville	Alabama	17–10

The Rivalries

Simeon Castille breaks up a pass in the end zone intended for Tennessee's Austin Rogers in October 2007 in Tuscaloosa.

1993	Birmingham	Tie–x	17–17
1994	Knoxville	Alabama	17–13
1995	Birmingham	Tennessee	41–14
1996	Knoxville	Tennessee	20–13
1997	Birmingham	Tennessee	38–21
1998	Knoxville	Tennessee	35–18
1999	Tuscaloosa	Tennessee	21–7
2000	Knoxville	Tennessee	20–10
2001	Tuscaloosa	Tennessee	35–24
2002	Knoxville	Alabama	34–14
2003	Tuscaloosa (5OT)	Tennessee	51–43
2004	Knoxville	Tennessee	17–13
2005	Tuscaloosa	Alabama	6–3
2006	Knoxville	Tennessee	16–13
2007	Tuscaloosa	Alabama	41–17
2008	Knoxville	Alabama	29–9

x-Game later forfeited to Tennessee as a result of NCAA sanctions.

The Rivalries

5

Times the Third Saturday in October has actually been played on the third Saturday in October between 1995 and 2008. The traditional calendar date has been difficult to schedule for the teams since the SEC split into two divisions in 1992.

TRADITIONS

The Crimson Tide

Lacking an official nickname, the Alabama football teams of the 19th century were simply referred to as "The Varsity" or "Crimson White." Soon thereafter, the nickname "The Thin Red Line" was used as an official moniker until 1907. In his write-up of that year's Alabama-Auburn game, *Birmingham Age-Herald* sportswriter Hugh Roberts coined the term "Crimson Tide" to describe 'Bama's style of play in a 6–6 tie with the heavily favored cross-state rival in a quagmire of red mud. *Birmingham News* sports editor Zipp Newman took the nickname and ran with it, popularizing it for posterity.

Red Elephants

Alabama's mascot, Big Al, is an elephant. Why does a team nicknamed for an oceanic phenomenon have an elephant for a mascot?

Everett Strupper was a game official for the Southern Conference and chronicled the games he officiated in a weekly column for the *Atlanta Journal*. Strupper worked the Alabama-Ole Miss game on October 4, 1930, when 'Bama Coach Wallace Wade started his second team and took a first-quarter lead against the outmanned Rebels. Strupper penned these words for his newspaper's October 8 edition: "At the end of the quarter, the earth started to tremble, there was a distant rumble that continued to grow. Some excited fan in the stands bellowed, 'Hold your horses, the elephants are coming,' and out stampeded this Alabama varsity. It was the first time that I had seen it, and the size of the entire 11 nearly knocked me cold, men that I had seen play last year looking like they had nearly doubled in size." 'Bama won the game 64–0 and went on to a 10–0 record and a national championship.

The Alabama mascot was born when newspaper writer
Everett Strupper compared the 1930 varsity squad to a
herd of elephants because of their considerable bulk.

The pachyderm reference caught on and soon evolved into "red elephants" to include the crimson jerseys.

The Million Dollar Band

The University of Alabama Million Dollar Band is one of the sparkling gems of college football halftime tradition. More than 330 students, representing a variety of majors, comprise the group.

It began as a military band in 1914 and soon assumed its function as the centerpiece of halftime festivities under the direction of Col. Carleton K. Butler, the "Father of the Million Dollar Band." In the early days, the organization had to use all the resourcefulness at its command to raise travel funds—thus the name "Million Dollar Band" was coined in 1922 by W. C. "Champ" Pickens, an Alabama alumnus and former football manager.

Bryant-Denny Stadium

Alabama's home football stadium was christened The George Hutcheson Denny Stadium with a 55–0 victory over Mississippi College on September 28, 1929. It was officially dedicated the following week, as the Crimson Tide defeated Ole Miss 22–7. The original seating capacity was 12,000. Periodic expansion projects over the years have increased that number to its current 92,138.

Currently a total of 85 skyboxes adorn the upper deck, which is now being expanded beyond the south end zone.

In 1975 the historic facility was renamed Bryant-Denny Stadium in honor of legendary Coach Bear Bryant. It's fitting that Bryant's name should adorn the stadium; the legendary coach sported an astonishing record of 72–2 within its confines. Since the stadium's opening three-quarters of a century ago, the Crimson

Traditions

Tide has compiled a home record of 203–45–3.

On the Quad

The Quad in Tuscaloosa provides a central location for fans to tailgate, enjoy pregame festivities, pass the time before kickoff, and generally revel in the atmosphere of Alabama football.

The Crimson Tide tailgate party takes center stage on the Quad on football Saturdays, with the Alabama cheerleaders, Big Al, and the Million Dollar Band providing scenery and sounds. The Quad is also home to the Homecoming pep rally and traditional bonfire, held on the Friday night before the homecoming game.

There was a time when the Crimson Tide played its games on the Quad, and like its successor, Bryant-Denny Stadium, it was the scene of many 'Bama triumphs. From 1893 to 1914, the Tide compiled a 44–9 record there.

The Quad is also home to one of the most beloved landmarks on the Alabama campus—Denny Chimes. Dedicated in 1929 and named for George H. Denny, president of the university from 1912 to 1936. Dedicated in 1941, Denny Chimes stands on the south side of the Quad adjacent to University Boulevard. At the base lies the Alabama football captains Walk of Fame, which bears hand and foot impressions of each captain from Tide teams dating back to the 1940s.

Fight Song "Yea Alabama"

Yea Alabama! Drown 'em Tide,
Every Bama man's behind you,
Hit your stride...
Go teach the Bulldogs to behave,
Send the Yellow Jackets to a watery grave,
And if a man starts to weaken,
That's a shame,
Cause Bama's pluck and grit have
Writ her name in Crimson Flame.

Traditions

Fight on, Fight on, Fight on, men!
Remember the Rose Bowl we'll win then.
Go, roll to victory, Hit your stride!
You're Dixie's football pride,
Crimson Tide!

"Alma Mater"
Alabama, listen, mother,
To our vows of love,
To thyself and to each other,
Faithful friends we'll prove.
Faithful, loyal, firm and true,
Heart bound to heart will beat
Year by year, the ages through,
Until in heaven we meet.
College days are swiftly fleeting,
Soon we'll leave their halls,
Ne'er to join another meeting
'Neath their hallowed walls.
Faithful, loyal, firm and true,
Heart bound to heart will beat
Year by year, the ages through,
Until in heaven we meet.
So, farewell, dear Alma Mater.
May thy name, we pray,
Be rev'renced ever, pure and stainless
As it is today.
Faithful, loyal, firm and true,
Heart bound to heart will beat
Year by year, the ages through,
Until in heaven we meet.

Traditions

Twin Alabama fans cheer on the Crimson Tide during their game against Georgia in September 2007.

THE CHAMPIONSHIPS

There are almost too many national champion-ships to fully elaborate on them all. According to NCAA official records, Alabama has won at least part of 17 national titles, six of them consensus. Two of those, in 1979 and 1992, were unanimous. And though Minnesota garnered the lion's share of the national championship recognition in 1934, Coach Frank Thomas' Crimson Tide that year was undeniably one of the greatest college football teams ever fielded. 'Bama also shared national titles with Michigan State in 1965, with Notre Dame in 1973, and with USC in 1978. In 1966, an 11–0 Crimson Tide finished third in both polls behind Notre Dame and Michigan State, who had played each other to a tie.

1925 (10–0)

There was a hint that the boys down South could play football with the best of them when Alabama, under Coach Xen Scott, defeated Pennsylvania 9–7 on November 4, 1922, in Philadelphia. Three years later, when Wallace Wade's Crimson Tide prevailed over national power Washington 20–19 in the Rose Bowl to cap off the 1925 season, southern football came of age as a force to be reckoned with. With star players in Pooley Hubert and Johnny Mack Brown, the Crimson Tide had just repeated its title as Southern Conference champion with a 9–0 regular season before the trip out West. 'Bama had rolled up 277 points and allowed just one score all year—in a 50–7 win over Birmingham Southern.

1926 (9-0-1)

Hubert and Brown were gone, but Wade was still at the helm, and there was no lack of star power with end Hoyt "Wu" Winslett and tackle Fred Pickhard leading the way as All-Americans. The Crimson Tide stormed through the 1926 regular season 9–0 and returned to the Rose Bowl, playing Western champion Stanford to a 7–7 tie. That 1926 'Bama juggernaut scored 249 points against just 27 for its opponents.

1934 (10-0)

It's a shame Minnesota didn't have to play Alabama in 1934, or the national title picture that season might have had a Crimson tint to it. With Frank Thomas in his fourth year at the helm in Tuscaloosa, the Tide finished the season with a perfect 10–0 record, including a dominating 29–13 Rose Bowl win over Stanford. Halfback Dixie Howell, end Don Hutson, and tackle Bill Lee were All-Americans headlining a star-studded lineup that also included quarterback Riley Smith, end Paul Bryant, tackle Jim Whatley, and guards Arthur "Tarzan" White and Charlie Marr. Hutson led 'Bama to a 13–6 victory over previously unbeaten Tennessee, and the Tide finished the regular season with three-straight shutouts—40–0 over Clemson, 40–0 over Georgia Tech, and 34–0 over Vanderbilt—to punch its ticket to Pasadena.

1961 (11-0)

In 1961 Alabama outscored its opponents 297–25 and finished 11–0, including five-straight shutouts to end the regular season, giving Bear Bryant the first of his six national championships. Pat Trammell piloted the offense at quarterback, with All-America tackle Billy Neighbors paving the way. Lee Roy Jordan, one of the game's all-time great linebackers, put teeth in the Tide defense. A 34–0 rout of Auburn sent the Tide to New Orleans for the holidays, where Trammell's

12-yard first-quarter touchdown run was all the scoring 'Bama needed in its 10–3 Sugar Bowl win over Arkansas.

1964 (10–1)

Quarterback Joe Namath led the 1964 Crimson Tide to a 10–0 regular season and yet another national championship. Namath scored three touchdowns in a 31–3 season-opening win over Georgia. In Game 4, a 21–0 win over NC State, Namath sustained a knee injury that would dog him throughout his career. On November 7 in Birmingham, Bryant had put in an order for dry conditions to aid in his team's effort against unbeaten LSU. During pregame warm-ups, the field was wet and rain was falling—until the Bear emerged from the tunnel. At that moment, the rain relented and the sun came out, and Alabama beat the Bayou Bangals 17–9. A 21–14 win over Auburn sealed a perfect regular season. Namath's fourth-quarter touchdown on a six-inch sneak that would have beaten Texas in the Orange Bowl was ruled short, though one official and Namath's teammates saw him score. The final score stood at 21–17 Texas, but 'Bama already had been awarded the title by both the AP and UPI.

1965 (9–1–1)

Despite a season-opening one-point loss to Georgia and a rare red-zone blunder by Kenny Stabler (subbing for an injured Steve Sloan that led to a 7–7 tie) with Tennessee, Alabama captured the Associated Press portion of the 1965 national title. Sloan's heroics in overcoming a 16–7 fourth-quarter deficit against Ole Miss to win 17–16 kept the Tide's title hopes alive. Alabama added emphasis to the 1965 campaign by routing Auburn 30–3 to conclude the regular season. Bryant's club proceeded to overwhelm a big, bulky 10–0 Nebraska team with speed and quickness in the Orange Bowl. Ray Perkins was on the receiving end of two Sloan touchdown passes in the 39–28 victory over the Cornhuskers that wasn't as close as the score indicated.

1978 (11–1)

Alabama entered the 1978 season as the No. 1 team in the nation. The Crimson Tide avenged the previous season's loss to Nebraska—the only smudge on an otherwise perfect record—by whipping the Huskers 20–3 to open the campaign. Then the Tide hit a speed bump in Game 3 with a 24–14 loss to Southern Cal in the L.A. Coliseum. But Bear Bryant's men captured their seventh SEC crown in eight years with a 7–0 league mark, culminating in a 34–16 victory over Auburn. By this time 'Bama had climbed back to No. 2 in the polls, while Penn State was No. 1. The Sugar Bowl would decide the issue. 'Bama prevailed over the Nittany Lions 14–7 in a game for the ages. The most famous goal-line stand in history, with All-American Barry Krauss making the tackle, preserved the win—and the national title in the AP poll.

1979 (12–0)

After sharing the title with Southern Cal in 1978, Bryant's 1979 squad took on all comers on the way to 12–0 and a No. 1 final ranking in both polls. All-America offensive linemen Dwight Stephenson and Jim Bunch led the way for quarterback Steadman Shealy and halfback Major Ogilvie as the Tide racked up 383 points to 67 for its opponents. End E. J. Junior, linebacker Thomas Boyd, and cornerback Don McNeal solidified the defense. The only close call all year was a 3–0 win at LSU. Ogilvie took Sugar Bowl MVP honors, notching a pair of touchdown runs and returning a punt 50 yards to set up a field goal in a 24–9 triumph over Arkansas.

The Championships

1992 (13–0)

Alabama celebrated its football centennial with a national championship. Gene Stallings, a former Bryant player and assistant, was now in command in Tuscaloosa. Sophomore Jay Barker took over at quarterback to start the season and would end his career as the winningest signal caller in school history. But it was defense that separated this team from the rest of the pack. Antonio Langham and George Teague each picked off six passes. Langham and defensive linemen John Copeland and Eric Curry were All-Americans. The Tide tamed the Tigers in the Iron Bowl, disposed of the Gators in the first-ever SEC Championship Game, and handled the Hurricanes in a 34–13 Sugar Bowl triumph.

100

The 1992 national championship was a perfect cap to the season that saw the celebration of 100 years of Alabama football. The season was also the 20th in which the Crimson Tide won the Southeastern Conference.

The Championships

THE GREATEST BOWL GAMES

1926 Rose Bowl
Alabama 20, Washington 19

Consensus held Washington as the nation's best team. When Alabama accepted a bid to take on the Huskies in the Rose Bowl, sportswriters scoffed at the Tide's chances. When Coach Wallace Wade's Crimson Tide emerged from the contest a 20–19 victor, the world was aware of a new phenomenon—southern football. Trailing 12–0 at the half, 'Bama knocked Washington's All-America halfback George Wilson out of the game in the third quarter and quickly took advantage, scoring three touchdowns in less than seven minutes. Pooley Hubert and Johnny Mack Brown wowed the 45,000 fans in attendance and inspired Grantland Rice–esque hyperbole in the next day's sports pages.

1931 Rose Bowl
Alabama 24, Washington State 0

Alabama's first five bowl appearances, between 1926 and 1938, were all in Pasadena. Number three in the sequence was a 24–0 whitewashing of Washington State in the 1931 classic. Monk Campbell ran for two scores, including a 43-yard gallop, and Jimmy Moore hit John "Flash" Suther on a 61-yard scoring pass—all in a six-minute stretch of the second quarter. It was Wallace Wade's last game before he left for Duke.

Coach Frank Thomas talks strategy with some of his offensive players during Sugar Bowl preparations for a 1944, matchup with Duke..

1935 Rose Bowl
Alabama 29, Stanford 13

Coach Frank Thomas took one of the greatest football teams of all time to Pasadena for a meeting with unbeaten Stanford. The Indians led 7–0 after the first period, and then the immortal pass-catch combo of Dixie Howell and Don Hutson went to work. They ignited a 256-yard, 22-point second quarter that put Stanford down for good. Hutson caught touchdown passes of 54 and 59 yards, and Howell scored on 67- and five-yard runs. Stanford had no answer for 'Bama's speed.

1946 Rose Bowl
Alabama 34, Southern California 14

Alabama's sixth and last trip to the Rose Bowl, on New Year's Day, 1946, ended with the mighty Trojans vanquished by a score of 34–14. With All-America quarterback Harry Gilmer spearheading the attack, the Tide built a 20–0 halftime lead and never looked back. Bama led 27–0 in the third quarter before USC managed as much as a first down. Coach Frank Thomas' team outgained the Trojans 351 yards to 41. It was Southern Cal's ninth Rose Bowl appearance—and its first loss. Alabama closed the book on its New Year's Day-in-Pasadena tradition at 4–1–1.

1953 Orange Bowl
Alabama 61, Syracuse 6

Alabama set an Orange Bowl record of 586 total yards—286 on the ground, 300 through the air—in its 61–6 demolition of Syracuse, the champions of the East, in the 1953 Orange Bowl. The Tide led 7–6 after one quarter and 21–6 at intermission. In the second half Coach Red Drew's Tide scored 20 points in both the third and fourth periods. "I just couldn't stop them," Drew remarked.

1963 Orange Bowl
Alabama 17, Oklahoma 0

President John F. Kennedy was in attendance to see sophomore quarterback Joe Namath work his magic in the 1963 Orange Bowl. Namath's deft ball-handling and his 25-yard touchdown pass to end Dick Williamson sparked Alabama to a 17–0 win over Oklahoma. 'Bama's defense stifled the Sooner attack all day, with linebacker Lee Roy Jordan compiling an amazing 31 tackles.

1966 Orange Bowl
Alabama 39, Nebraska 28

Alabama parlayed a dominating performance over undefeated Nebraska in Miami on January 1, 1966, into a repeat national championship. 'Bama's speed and quickness were just too much for the Huskers as the Tide won 39–28. And it wasn't that close. The Tide ran twice as many plays and outgained the Cornhuskers by 141 yards in the one-sided affair. Steve Sloan connected with receiver Ray Perkins on two scoring tosses.

1967 Sugar Bowl
Alabama 34, Nebraska 7

In a rematch of the previous season's Orange Bowl, Alabama made an even more emphatic statement than before, beating Coach Bob Devaney's Cornhuskers by a score of 34–7. The Tide rolled in at 10–0; Nebraska had been beaten once—by one point (10–9 at Oklahoma) in the season finale. 'Bama's first play from scrimmage was a 45-yard pass completion from Kenny Stabler to Ray Perkins. Seven plays later, Les Kelly rammed in from the 1. The Tide led 17–0 after the first quarter, and the game was never in doubt. "This was the greatest college team I've ever seen" were Bear Bryant's words.

Alabama, quarterback Steve Sloan speaks at a reception in Tuscaloosa honoring the 1965 squad. Sloan had led the team to a national championship while Joe Namath missed time due to injury, and he stepped up his game even further after Namath left for the pro ranks.

But his 11–0 squad finished third in both polls behind
Notre Dame and Michigan State, which had played
each other to a tie in November.

1973 Sugar Bowl
Notre Dame 24, Alabama 23

Notre Dame and Alabama had never met until the
night of December 31, 1973, in the Sugar Bowl. Ara
Parseghian versus Bear Bryant. Both teams coming off
perfect regular seasons. The pregame hype was unprec-
edented, and fittingly, a national championship hung in
the balance. Both teams deserved to win, but the Irish
preserved their one-point victory when, in the game's
waning moments, Tom Clements fired a third-down
pass from his own end zone to Robin Weber, who made
the only catch of his college career for a first down. The
Irish vaulted to No. 1 in the final AP poll with the Tide
already voted No. 1 by UPI.

1979 Sugar Bowl
Alabama 14, Penn State 7

The 1979 Sugar Bowl featured the most memorable
goal-line stand in college football history. The second-
ranked Crimson Tide had broken a scoreless tie with
top-ranked Penn State on a 30-yard Jeff Rutledge-to-
Bruce Bolton touchdown pass with eight seconds left
before intermission. Each team added a TD in the third
quarter. In the fourth quarter, the Nittany Lions faced
third-and-goal from the 1. Matt Suhey was stopped six
inches short, and on fourth down All-America linebacker Barry Krauss met Mike Guman head-on for no
gain, sealing the win and another national title for the
Crimson Tide.

1993 Sugar Bowl
Alabama 34, Miami 13

The similarities to the 1979 Sugar Bowl were striking. The host city was New Orleans. Second-ranked Alabama beat the nation's No. 1 team to claim the national championship. But there was one big difference—in the 1993 classic, 'Bama romped. The Tide took a 13–6 halftime lead, that snowballed from there to a 34–13 rout. Coach Gene Stallings' club scored two third-quarter touchdowns in 16 seconds, the second on a 31-yard interception return by George Teague. 'Bama kept Heisman Trophy–winning Hurricane quarterback Gino Torretta on his heels all night, outrushed Miami 267 yards to 48, and came home with another national title.

1995 Citrus Bowl
Alabama 24, Ohio State 17

A scoreless first quarter was highlighted by a stray dog wandering onto the field. After the wayward pooch was scooted away through a portal, the Tide and the Buckeyes scored two touchdowns each in the second period and a 14-all deadlock at intermission. 'Bama's points came off touchdown runs by Tarant Lynch and Sherman Williams; Ohio State kept it even with a pair of Bobby Hoying–to–Joey Galloway TD tosses. Both teams again posted goose eggs in the third quarter. Tied at 17–17 with less than a minute to play, Jay Barker hooked up with Williams on a 50-yard pass-and-run for the 24–17 win. Williams captured game MVP honors with 166 rushing yards, eight catches, and two touchdowns.

1997 Outback Bowl
Alabama 17, Michigan 14

Two huge fourth-quarter plays lifted the Crimson Tide to a 17–14 win over Michigan in the 1997 Outback Bowl. Alabama trailed 6–3 at the half. After a scoreless third quarter, Alabama's Kelvin Sigler blindsided Brian Griese, forcing an errant throw from the Wolverine quarterback into the hands of Dwayne Rudd. The Tide's All-America linebacker and game MVP returned the pick 88 yards to pay dirt for a 10–6 Bama lead. A second fourth-period score—a 46-yard run by Shaun Alexander—put the game out of reach as the Tide hung on for the victory.

Wins Gene Stallings lost because of NCAA-sanctioned forfeits. Officially, his record sits at 62–25. Unofficially, Stallings led the Crimson Tide to a 70–16–1 record in his time as head coach.

THE GREATEST MOMENTS

The 1985 Iron Bowl
November 30, 1985

Alabama fans consider this game—won on Van Tiffin's 52-yard field goal as time expired—the greatest in Iron Bowl history and one of the best in Alabama annals.

Breathtaking scoring drives, heroic plays, and star power were in evidence for both Alabama and Auburn as they battled on November 30 before a crowd of 75,808 at Legion Field and a national television audience on ABC.

"It was one of the greatest games I've ever been associated with," Alabama Coach Ray Perkins said after the wild finishing sequence. "All year long, I've said this group of men has been special to work with. I'm just honored to be a part of this team and this game."

The Crimson Tide rushed out to a 13–0 lead early in the second quarter as Tiffin booted a pair of field goals and fullback Craig Turner scored on a one-yard plunge. Auburn bounced back behind the running of Bo Jackson, who scored from seven yards out in the second quarter. The Tigers got a dramatic field goal of their own to end the first half, as Chris Johnson connected from 49 yards away to trim Alabama's lead to 16–10 at intermission.

Jackson, who amassed 142 yards and two scores on 31 carries, gave Auburn its first lead at 17–16 with a one-yard scoring plunge at the 7:03 mark of the fourth quarter after a scoreless third period.

Alabama responded quickly, as Gene Jelks rambled 74 yards for a score at the 5:57 mark. He was the game's leading rusher with 192 yards on 18 attempts.

The Crimson Tide led 22–17 at that point, but its two-point conversion pass failed, helping set the stage for the nail-biting finish.

Auburn used the next five minutes for a methodical march punctuated by fullback Reggie Ware's one-yard scoring run with 57 seconds remaining. Quarterback Pat Washington and Jackson fueled the clock-draining drive. However, the Tigers' two-point conversion pass also failed, leaving the Tide an opening.

Current Alabama Coach Mike Shula, who hit 14 of 28 passes for 195 yards that day, calmly guided the Tide downfield for the winning score. The sequence included a 20-yard reverse by Al Bell on a fourth-and-4 and Shula passes of 16 yards to Jelks and 19 yards to Greg Richardson. The 45-yard drive culminated with the scramble to get the Tide's field-goal team on the field and Tiffin punching through the winning kick off Larry Abney's hold—a moment forever frozen in time in the memories of Tide fans.

Bennett Blasts Beuerlein
October 4, 1986

Against another opponent, the play might have been meaningless. But when one of the best defensive players in Alabama's history, future Hall of Famer Cornelius Bennett, leveled Notre Dame quarterback Steve Beuerlein on October 4, 1986, the play achieved legendary status.

Beuerlein, a 17-year NFL quarterback, visited the Alabama campus in the fall of 2005 on a scouting trip as part of his duties as a color analyst for CBS Sports. During his visit, Beuerlein asked Alabama sports information director Larry White why that play continued to hold such a fascination for Crimson Tide fans. White took the ex-quarterback to the Bryant Museum to show

Auburn's Bo Jackson goes up and over the Alabama line in the Iron Bowl. One of the greatest athletes of all time, Jackson was a superstar in both baseball and football, but he was outgained in the 1985 Iron Bowl thanks to the inspired running of Gene Jelks.

him memorabilia, including a picture of Bennett's high-impact sack during that 28–10 Alabama win over the Irish at Legion Field in Birmingham.

As an answer to Beuerlein's query, the 'Bama love affair with that play probably hinges on the fact it came in Alabama's only win ever against Notre Dame.

Derrick Thomas Dominates
Alabama vs. Penn State
October 22, 1988

Alabama's winning 8–3 margin over Penn State was one of the strangest scores in school history but strikingly appropriate given the stalwart defensive performances of these national powers. Derrick Thomas put his personal stamp on the proceedings with a showing that is still raved about inside the Alabama program.

CBS had the telecast that day, and play-by-play man Brent Musburger described Thomas' game as "the most dominating performance I've ever seen by a college player."

The final stats—Thomas was credited with eight tackles and three sacks—tell only part of the story. No. 55 was also credited with nine quarterback hurries, as the Nittany Lions struggled to get Thomas in check all game.

Alabama led 6–3 in the fourth quarter when Thomas sacked Tony Sacca for a safety with 10:43 remaining. Penn State's final offensive play was one in which Thomas again pestered Sacca, forcing an errant throw that was intercepted by Lee Ozmint.

Thomas, who would win the Butkus Award in 1988, also had a five-sack game against Texas A&M on his way to 27 sacks that season, but he cemented his legend on that sunny day at Legion Field. He would be named college defensive player of the week by *Sports Illustrated*, the *Sporting News*, *College & Pro Weekly*

Siran Stacy and Gary Hollingsworth
Alabama vs. Tennessee
October 21, 1989

Two of the nation's traditional defensive powers, who were both unbeaten and untied, wilted in the face of an onslaught that featured 935 total yards and 10 touchdowns on a cool afternoon at Birmingham's Legion Field. Alabama running back Siran Stacy and quarterback Gary Hollingsworth were at the center of the offensive explosion that ended with Alabama on top 47–30.

Stacy simply ran all over the Volunteers in compiling a school-record 317 all-purpose yards and scoring four touchdowns. Stacy's big day consisted of 125 rushing yards, 158 receiving yards, and 34 yards on kickoff returns. He joined Gene Jelks as only the second player in Crimson Tide history to account for 100 rushing yards and 100 receiving yards in the same game. Stacy caught a 75-yard touchdown pass in the second quarter and scored on runs of five, six, and 15 yards in the Tide's 28-point second half.

Hollingsworth connected on 32 of 46 passes for 379 yards and three touchdowns in the win. The 379 yards still rank as the third-highest single-game total in school history.

"If you would have told me before the game Tennessee would score 30 points, I wouldn't have believed it," then-Alabama coach Bill Curry said. "But if you would have, I would have told you this team of ours would find a way to score more than 30."

Stacy would go on to become a consensus All-SEC choice and a second-team All-American that season with 141 all-purpose yards per game. Hollingsworth passed for 2,379 yards in 1989, an Alabama single-season record that stood until 2005.

Alabama 9, Tennessee 6
at Knoxville, October 20, 1990

Tennessee was a heavy favorite in this renewal of the Third Saturday in October series against the Crimson Tide. The Volunteers were unbeaten, ranked No. 3, and scoring at a clip of 42.2 points per game, third-best in the nation. Alabama, in its first season under Gene Stallings, had opened 0–3 but rallied to win two straight heading into Knoxville.

Neither offense found its rhythm in this field-goal fest, as Alabama accounted for 222 total yards and Tennessee just 175. Tennessee kicker Greg Burke made field goals of 20 and 51 yards, while Alabama's Philip Doyle countered with boots of 30 and 26 yards to forge a 6–6 tie in the fourth quarter. A punt return by Dale Carter set the Vols up at the Alabama 35-yard line late in the game, but Efrum Thomas sniffed out a third-down screen pass from Andy Kelly to Vince Moore for a two-yard loss, setting up Burke's 50-yard field-goal try.

Stacy Harrison broke through the line to snuff the kick, which squirted backward and was recovered at the Tennessee 37. Doyle came on four plays later and drilled the game winner from 47 yards out with four seconds remaining. "The scenario can't get any better for a kicker," Doyle said.

"This has to rank right up there with the biggest wins I've ever had in my career," Stallings said. "We had terrible field position throughout the game, but we got tremendous effort from the defense."

Doyle became the SEC's fifth-leading all-time scorer with 310 points after his nine-point game against Tennessee.

The Inaugural SEC Championship Game
Alabama 28, Florida 21
Birmingham, Alabama, December 5, 1992

The nation's top-rated defense allowed a season-high three touchdowns but capped the inaugural SEC Championship Game with a score of its own as Alabama improved to 12–0 and set up a national championship showdown against No. 1 Miami.

Cornerback Antonio Langham was the late hero, jumping a pass route to pick off Shane Matthews and race 27 yards for a touchdown with 3:16 remaining to break a 21–21 impasse. Langham, who had also clinched Alabama's win over Auburn in the Iron Bowl the previous week with an interception return for a touchdown, was named the MVP of the championship game.

The Crimson Tide, which had won the inaugural SEC championship 60 years earlier, also laid claim to the first SEC title game, played in chilly conditions before a crowd of 83,091 at Legion Field in Birmingham.

"Lose it and you're just another team," offensive guard George Wilson had said earlier in the week. "Win it, and you've got a chance at the national championship. The magnitude of this game is just tremendous."

David Palmer had a career-high 101 receiving yards and posted 122 all-purpose yards for the Crimson Tide. Derrick Lassic compiled 121 rushing yards and two touchdowns for Alabama, offsetting a two-TD performance from Florida back Errict Rhett.

Tide quarterback Jay Barker improved his record as a starter to 15–0 as Alabama ran its winning streak to 22 consecutive games, second in the nation to Miami. Of course, the Crimson Tide had some magic up its sleeve one month later when it shocked the Hurricanes 34–13 to win the Sugar Bowl and the national championship.

Shaun Alexander Runs Wild
Alabama at LSU, November 8, 1996

Shaun Alexander was a third-team redshirt freshman running back one month into the 1996 season. He was a household name nationally after blistering LSU for a school-record 291 rushing yards and four touchdowns on a cool, breezy evening at Tiger Stadium on November 8.

Alabama had not lost in Baton Rouge since 1969, and Alexander would make certain that long streak would continue. Starting tailback Curtis Alexander had broken a wrist a few weeks earlier, and his replacement, Dennis Riddle, had run for 478 yards in the previous three games as No. 10 Alabama rolled into Tiger territory to face No. 12 LSU.

While Riddle had 15 carries for 84 yards, this night belonged to the media-friendly freshman who would go on to break the school's all-time rushing record.

Alexander broke a scoreless tie with his 17-yard romp around end with 10:42 left in the second quarter. After LSU failed on a fake field-goal attempt at the Tide 27 in the third quarter, Alexander took a handoff on the next play and raced 73 yards for another touchdown.

Before it was over, Alexander had rushed for two more scores, from 72 and 12 yards, to complete the scoring. He had also eclipsed Bobby Humphrey's single-game Alabama rushing record by seven yards. Though Alexander would not become the undisputed starter at tailback until his junior season, he racked up honors as national player of the week following his scintillating performance near the banks of the Mississippi River.

Stunner in the Swamp
Alabama 40, Florida 39 (OT)
October 2, 1999

Florida was unbeaten, ranked No. 3, and riding a 30-game winning streak at the Swamp when a 3–1 Alabama team came calling on October 2, 1999. The teams, who later that season would meet in the SEC Championship Game for the fifth time in the eight-year history of the game, combined for 896 total yards in a shootout of epic proportions.

Andrew Zow picked the Gator defense apart with a short and mid range passing attack that accounted for 336 yards and two touchdowns. Florida's Doug Johnson countered with 309 yards and four scores on 22-of-31 passing. Florida was more explosive, but Alabama was more resolute in dominating the time of possession 41:22 to 18:38.

Shaun Alexander, who rushed 28 times for 106 yards and three touchdowns, countered a one-play, 73-yard Darrell Jackson scoring strike with his one-yard touchdown run as Alabama led 13–7 at intermission.

The scoring heated up in the second half, with the Tide and Gators exchanging the lead five times. Alexander and Jackson scored two more times apiece in regulation, Florida's Bennie Alexander returned an interception 42 yards for a touchdown, and Alabama's Antonio Carter grabbed a 14-yard touchdown from Zow in the furious second half.

Florida might have salted the game away when Alabama punted with a 33–26 deficit but the Gators fumbled at their own 21-yard line. Alexander cashed in a 13-yard scoring run with 1:25 left to forge a tie at 33–33, and Alabama held on for Florida's last possession.

Johnson hit Reche Caldwell with a six-yard touch-down pass in overtime, but Jeff Chandler's extra-point attempt went awry. The Tide needed only one play in

The Greatest Moments

It wasn't the prettiest kick of all time, but Jamie Christensen's 45-yard effort beat Texas Tech. The plucky sophomore, nicknamed "Money," became one of the most legendary kickers in school history thanks to the 2006 Cotton Bowl winner.

overtime—Alexander's 25-yard sprint on a seldom-used counter—but two shots at the extra point to win.

Chris Kemp missed his first try at the PAT, but because Florida jumped offside, he got another chance. This time Kemp delivered, and Alabama scored one of the greatest road wins in its history.

The 2005 Season

Alabama's 10–2 record in 2005 signaled that the Crimson Tide was back in the New Year's Day bowl business after a couple of down years due to major NCAA sanctions. The Crimson Tide's rebound was in part a product of a talented and focused senior class coupled with a stable coaching staff. Kicker Jamie Christensen also gave Alabama a boost in its bounce-back campaign.

Christensen opened the year on the sideline, courtesy of a one-game suspension for an unspecified violation of team rules. But the sophomore joined the starting lineup the following week and proved mostly reliable heading into a week six visit to Ole Miss following an Alabama open date.

The Crimson Tide found itself in a 10–10 defensive slugfest before driving 62 yards to the Ole Miss 14, leading to Christensen's 31-yard field goal as time expired. Christensen also starred the following week, drilling a 34-yarder with 13 seconds left as Alabama edged archrival Tennessee 6–3.

Christensen saved his pluckiest moment—but certainly not his prettiest—for the final play of Alabama's season. Tied 10–10 with Texas Tech in the Cotton Bowl, Christensen struck a sidewinding, hooking line drive just inside the left upright and over the cross-bar for a 45-yard field goal as time expired to propel the Crimson Tide to a thrilling victory over the Red Raiders.

Thanks, Acknowledgments, and Sources

Thank you to my family for your love, support, and patience. The same goes for my extended family around the country and world. You all know who you are, and how important you are to me (even when I ignore your emails, phone calls, and instant messages while doing things like writing books).

Thank you Tom Bast, Mitch Rogatz, Don Gulbrandsen, and everyone at Triumph Books who worked on this project.

Thank you fans. Without you, this project never would have happened.

The sources for this book are essentially too numerous to list, but most of the accumulated information simply came from years of being a sportswriter, along with the numerous official team sources. That means more media guides, Internet sites, press conferences, interviews, transcripts, and press releases than you could imagine—and numerous bowls, conferences, services, and teams. Some additional sources deserve special mention:

University of Alabama 2004–08 media guides

University of Alabama 1993 media guide

2008 University of Alabama supplemental media guide

rolltide.com

ESPN.com

100 Things Crimson Tide Fans Should Know and Do Before They Die, by Christopher Walsh, 2008

The Official 2008 Division I and Division I-AA Football Records Book

The College Football Hall of Fame website

The Pro Football Hall of Fame website

ESPN College Football Encyclopedia: The Complete History of the Game, by Michael MacCambridge, 2005

2008 SEC Football Media Guide

Where Football is King: A History of the SEC, by Christopher Walsh, 2006.

Crimson Storm Surge: Alabama Football, Then and Now, by Christopher Walsh, 2005.

The Paul W. Bryant Museum website, http://bryantmuseum.ua.edu

NCAA.com

NFL.com

Sugar Bowl Classic: A History, by Marty Mule, 2008.

About the Author

Christopher Walsh has been an award-winning sportswriter since 1990, and currently covers the University of Alabama football program for the *Tuscaloosa News*. He's been twice nominated for a Pulitzer Prize, won three Football Writers Association of America awards, and received the 2006 Herby Kirby Memorial Award, the Alabama Sports Writers Association's highest honor. Originally from Minnesota and a graduate of the University of New Hampshire, he currently resides in Tuscaloosa.

His previous books include:

100 Things Crimson Tide Fans Need to Know & Do Before They Die, 2008.

Who's No. 1? 100-Plus Years of Controversial Champions in College Football, 2007.

Where Football is King: A History of the SEC, 2006.

No Time Outs: What It's Really Like to be a Sportswriter Today, 2006.

Crimson Storm Surge: Alabama Football, Then and Now, 2005.

Return to Glory: The Story of Alabama's 2008 Season, 2009 (contributing writer).

The "Huddle Up" series will remain a work in progress. To make comments, suggestions or share an idea with the author, go to http://whosno1.blogspot.com/. Check out other 2009 editions: Texas, Michigan, Notre Dame, Ohio State, Oklahoma, Tennessee, and the New York Giants.

Dedication

For Megan

Triumph Books and colophon are registered trademarks of Random House, Inc.

This book is available in quantity at special discounts for your group or organization. For further information, contact:

Triumph Books
542 South Dearborn Street
Suite 750
Chicago, Illinois 60605
(312) 939-3330
Fax (312) 663-3557

Printed in U.S.A.
ISBN: 978-1-60078-183-4

Design by Mojo Media Inc.

Photos courtesy of AP Images except where otherwise noted.